The Indiana Territory, 1800–2000
A Bicentennial Perspective

Contributors

M. Teresa Baer, editor, Indiana Historical Society,
  Indianapolis

Darrel E. Bigham, professor of history,
  University of Southern Indiana, Evansville

Andrew R. L. Cayton, professor of history,
  Miami University, Miami, Ohio

Douglas E. Clanin, editor, Indiana Historical Society,
  Indianapolis

James J. Divita, professor of history,
  Marian College, Indianapolis

George W. Geib, professor of history,
  Butler University, Indianapolis

James H. Madison, professor of history,
  Indiana University, Bloomington

Nancy L. Rhoden, professor of history,
  University of Southern Indiana, Evansville

The Indiana Territory, 1800–2000

A Bicentennial Perspective

———

Edited by Darrel E. Bigham

INDIANA HISTORICAL SOCIETY
INDIANAPOLIS 2001

Ind
977.2
I39ite

This book is a publication of the
Indiana Historical Society
450 West Ohio Street
Indianapolis, Indiana 46202-3269 USA
www.indianahistory.org
Telephone orders   1-800-447-1830
Fax orders   317-234-0562
Shop on-line   shop.indianahistory.org

The paper in this publication meets the minimum requirements of American National Standard for Information Sciences—Permanence of Paper for Printed Library Materials, ANSI Z39.48–1984. ∞

Library of Congress Cataloging-in-Publication Data

The Indiana territory, 1800-2000 : a bicentennial perspective / edited by Darrel E. Bigham.
   p. cm.
   Papers delivered at the Indiana Territory Bicentennial Symposium, held in Vincennes, Ind., June 28, 2000.
   Includes index.
   ISBN 0-87195-155-X
   1. Indiana—History—Congresses. I. Bigham, Darrel E. II. Indiana Territory Bicentennial Symposium (2000 : Vincennes, Ind.)

F526.5 .I54 2001
977.2'03—dc21

                                                              2001039311

Contents

Robert M. Taylor, Jr.: A Life Remembered   vii
Raymond L. Shoemaker

Introduction   1
Darrel E. Bigham

Commemorating the Past: The Indiana Territory,
1800–2000   29
James H. Madison

Race, Democracy, and the Multiple Meanings
of the Indiana Frontier   47
Andrew R. L. Cayton

Religion on the Indiana Frontier, 1679–1816   71
James J. Divita

Jefferson, Harrison, and the West:
An Essay on Territorial Slavery   99
George W. Geib

Great Britain and America at 1800:
Perspectives on the Frontier   125
Nancy L. Rhoden

Adventures in Historical Editing:
The William Henry Harrison Papers Project   149
Douglas E. Clanin

William Henry Harrison and the
Indian Treaty Land Cessions   167
M. Teresa Baer

Index   187

Robert M. Taylor, Jr., 1941–1999

Robert M. Taylor, Jr.:

A Life Remembered

by

RAYMOND L. SHOEMAKER

CAN REMEMBER EXACTLY WHERE I WAS WHEN I HEARD THE NEWS ABOUT several important events in my life. I was walking through Central Area at West Point in 1963 when I heard the news over the public-address system about President John F. Kennedy being shot. I remember hearing about Robert Kennedy's assassination while on the way to my office at Ford Ord, California, in 1968, shortly after returning from Viet Nam. I also will remember where I was when an ashen Tom Krasean found me the morning of 14 October 1999 to tell me the stunning news that Bob Taylor had died a few hours earlier. It took a few seconds for me to comprehend what he was telling me and several more to recover from the shock. I could not begin to tell you what I did the rest of that day, but those few moments remain clear to me.

On the other hand, there have been many other world-shaking events during my life that I have no idea where I was when I heard about them. I suppose that the reason that I can recall the exact moment for certain events is their importance to me personally. Bob Taylor was not only an invaluable employee of the Indiana Historical Society and a vital asset to the field of history, he was a good friend. My first rational thought was, I am ashamed to say, "What are we going to do now?" Bob had initiated many important programs that only he could bring to fruition. In fact, I had just spoken to him the previous evening about the plans for an upcoming conference that would be unlike any of the others that we had conducted. Bob was very excited about it and hoped that it would be a success. He had high hopes for his Education Division—by far the most complex part of the institution—and the way in which it would serve the public through programs in our new building and around the state. He had assembled an enthusiastic, professional, and committed staff to create and present programs that would fulfill the Society's commitment to public service. They ranged from an imaginative exhibitions program in our gallery to workshops and discussions in parts of the state that we had not had much of a presence in heretofore—such as a Lyceum in the Calumet Region—and finding volunteers to assist with those functions. His scope also included local history services, talking books, the Indiana Junior Historical Society, which, although not new programs, were upgraded significantly.

Bob and I had sort of grown together while at the Society. We both had held several positions and had to remain flexible as the organization changed around us. Bob began his career at the Society as assistant director of the Indiana Guide Project and moved through several positions before being named the director of the Education Division.

Bob graduated from high school in 1959 and spent the next twenty years working his way through college and graduate school. He received his bachelor's degree from Franklin College in Franklin, Indiana, in 1963, where he was president of the Blue Key Men's Honorary Society, president of his senior class, and selected a top ten senior. He then entered the Andover-Newton Theological Seminary in Newton Center, Massachusetts, where he graduated first in his class and received a Turner Fellowship and a cash award to be used for study at a university of his choice. He also served as a pastoral assistant in the First Baptist Church of Springfield and Weston. He then went to the University of Iowa, where he received his master's in history in 1970. In Iowa he directed the local Upward Bound program, which is a federal antipoverty program, a task that he continued when he attended

Kent State University in pursuit of his doctorate. He received his Ph.D. in history from Kent State in 1979, after spending a year between his M.A. and Ph.D. teaching at Indiana University–Purdue University at Fort Wayne.

Bob joined the Indiana Historical Society, shortly after completing his doctorate, as the assistant director of the Indiana Guide Project. The project's purpose was to produce a study of Indiana that would replace the old Indiana Guide book prepared under the auspices of the Works Projects Administration in 1941. The book was organized into circular tours that could be completed by car in one day, each tour beginning and ending at a major location. Five years into the project the director left, and Bob was appointed in his place. Bob was able to put his own stamp on the project, which still needed a great deal of work and considerable reorganization, including writing an introductory essay on the history of Indiana. *Indiana: A New Historical Guide* was published in 1989 and has received excellent reviews from professional journals and has become an indispensable tool for travelers touring the state.

During his time as director of the Guide project, Bob was asked by John Windle, a knowledgeable amateur architectural historian and Society board member, to take on the task of producing an essay on the historical background to complement Windle's *The Early Architecture of Madison, Indiana*. Bob did this in less than two years, the result of which was a beautifully illustrated and significant study of architecture in this charming, nineteenth-century Indiana town located on the Ohio River.

Following the completion of the Madison architectural project, Bob was made "section coordinator" for the Society. That was a rather convoluted title to give him the unenviable job of working with the Society's special interest groups—medical history, military history, black history, and, of course, genealogy—as a liaison between these groups and the Society. The sections had strong and creative, if not cooperative, leadership that Bob had to corral in order for their activities to fit within the Society's mission and budget. This was not an easy task, and Bob had many frustrating experiences trying to keep the sections within the mainstream of

Society activity. Somehow he was able to accomplish this and become a trusted and respected adviser to the sections' leadership. The military and medical sections were phased out in 1985 and 1991, and their quarterly journals were absorbed by the Society's new popular history magazine, *Traces of Indiana and Midwestern History*. Bob continued to manage the genealogy section (renamed family history section) as he finished work on the *Guide.*

In 1989, as the *Guide* was being printed, Bob was instrumental in the decision to begin a massive study of ethnic groups in Indiana. The Society's ethnic history project dispelled the popular conception that Indiana was a homogeneous state with little diversity, revealing that over thirty distinct ethnic groups live in Indiana. As director of the ethnic history project Bob had to identify each ethnic group that warranted a separate study and contract with authors for each of those groups. Those who have been involved with edited works understand the difficulty of getting every author to produce a worthy work and to produce it on time. This project was no exception. He had to encourage and cajole the authors continually—even replacing one or two—to obtain good, publishable essays. The result was a 1992 conference, "Ethnic Indiana, Past and Present" and an invaluable work about ethnicity in Indiana titled *Peopling Indiana: The Ethnic Experience* published in 1996.

While he was still in the midst of preparing *Peopling Indiana*, Bob was appointed director of the Research Projects and Grants Division in 1990. This new division had the responsibility for a variety of research projects and grant requests, including the ethnic history project, that had been scattered throughout the organization. It was during this time that the Clio Grant Program was established. From yet another reorganization in 1992 came the Education Division, which not only encompassed the grants program, but now included exhibitions, talking books, local history services, and the Indiana Junior Historical Society (which had moved from the Indiana Historical Bureau to the Society in 1991). Not surprisingly, Bob Taylor was asked to head this conglomeration of disparate activities. Once again, he rose to the task. All of these programs were greatly expanded under Bob's leadership. The departments of Educational and Public Programming and

Volunteer Services were added to the Education Division in 1998 in anticipation of the Society's move into the new building and its expanded public outreach mission.

Not one merely to observe, Bob threw himself into the activities of his division with great glee. He especially enjoyed participating in programs and activities that drew children into the building. One of the last pictures of Bob was one of him lying on the floor at the Society engaged in animated conversation with several young children who were working on an educational project. Although he was profoundly interested in everything going on in his division, he was not one to micromanage. His job, as he saw it, was to hire good people, give them the support they needed, and then let them do their jobs. As one of his more irreverent staff put it, "Bob's job was to protect our backs."

Bob never forgot that he was a historian. Over the years he taught several courses in the history department at Indiana University–Purdue University at Indianapolis. He presented numerous papers and chaired sessions at scholarly conferences. However, he was not much interested in national conferences. The majority of his work was at the local level—befitting a family historian. He has dozens of publications, including five books that he wrote or edited. Two of those books previously mentioned—*Indiana: A New Historical Guide* and *Peopling Indiana: The Ethnic Experience*—were huge projects requiring years of work on Bob's part.

Most of all, Bob never forgot that he was human—warts and all. He never took himself too seriously and continually gave credit to others for work that he produced. He was especially proud and supportive of the Education Division staff and always bragged about their creativity. He did take credit for recognizing his staff's talents and letting them "push the envelope" with their ideas and programs. He was a good friend to all, giving sage advice and saying exactly what he meant. Each of us knew that we did not have to worry about our backs when Bob was around; he spoke his mind to our faces. We all miss him greatly, and his absence has left a void.

Raymond L. Shoemaker, Administrative Director
Indiana Historical Society

Introduction:

The Indiana Territory Bicentennial Symposium

by

DARREL E. BIGHAM

Overview

THIS VOLUME COMPRISES THE FIVE PAPERS DELIVERED AT THE Indiana Territory Bicentennial Symposium, held in Vincennes, Indiana, on 28 June 2000. Historic Southern Indiana (HSI), a heritage-based regional development program of the University of Southern Indiana (USI) in Evansville, sponsored the event. This book also includes two related papers that were presented 29 June at a public meeting that the Indiana Historical Society sponsored in Vincennes.

The symposium papers and the two additional essays are inter-related, although they were originally unconnected. HSI had for several years advocated a suitable observance of this landmark event. The name Indiana formally came into being on 4 July 1800 when Congress separated the eastern portion of the Northwest Territory that would eventually become the state of Ohio from the remainder, named the Indiana Territory. The small Franco-American settlement of Vincennes, settled in 1732, became the capital of an extensive territory that for the most part included the present states of Illinois, Indiana, Michigan, and Wisconsin and the eastern part of Minnesota. (When Ohio became a state three years later, the eastern part of Michigan and a sliver of southwestern Ohio were added to the Indiana Territory.)

In the early spring of 1999, I was surprised to discover that no statewide private or public agency was planning to observe this event, though a local committee in Vincennes had been recently organized to arrange a celebration. (As the paper by James H. Madison reveals, Indiana apparently took only the sesquicentennial of the Indiana Territory seriously, for the most part glossing over the centennial in 1900.) With the help of members of the staff of the George Rogers Clark National Historical Park and the Vincennes State Historic Sites, the HSI office assembled a daylong conference designed to provide scholarly perspective on this event that would appeal to a broad audience. By the late spring a solid team of presenters had been assembled, and the Vincennes committee decided to use the HSI event on 28 June to launch its week-long observance culminating on 4 July.

When officials of the Indiana Historical Bureau and the Indiana Historical Society learned that this event was being planned, they offered various forms of support. The Bureau promoted the event and provided copies of relevant reading materials for registration packets. The Society, under the leadership of its Education Division director, Robert M. Taylor, Jr., helped publicize the event. Taylor also raised the question whether publication of the papers was practicable. Because of publishing costs, HSI initially had planned to make the conference papers available to the public only through its web site.

Taylor died suddenly in October 1999, leaving those of us who knew this omnitalented man deeply saddened and eager to find ways to remember him appropriately. As a consequence of conversations I had with then executive director Peter T. Harstad, the Society chose to complement the HSI symposium with a program on William Henry Harrison the following evening and to publish the proceedings in Taylor's memory. Hence the two major sections of this volume were created. This book also contains Raymond L. Shoemaker's tribute to Taylor.

The Bicentennial Symposium was held on the campus of Vincennes University. While the HSI office secured speakers and arranged funding and publicity, the local committee handled logistics and secured in-kind support to facilitate the event. Of special note in this regard were the efforts of Dale Phillips, superintendent of the George Rogers Clark National Historical Park; William Menke, curator of the Vincennes State Historic Sites; and Ellen Harper, executive director of the Vincennes–Knox County Convention and Visitors Bureau. Jane Reynolds, administrative assistant for HSI, and Kathy Funke, director of USI's news and information services, were especially helpful in coordinating the efforts of the Evansville and Vincennes committees. One hundred people attended the symposium.

This volume, it is hoped, will be useful not only for adult scholars of Indiana and midwestern history but also for students of Indiana history at both the high school and the collegiate levels. It will supplement Hubert H. Hawkins's *Indiana's Road to Statehood: A Documentary Record* (Indianapolis: Indiana Historical Bureau, 1969). Teachers and students will benefit enormously from the March 1999 issue of *The Indiana Historian: A Magazine Exploring Indiana History*. This issue, titled "The Indiana Territory," contains highly useful maps, timelines, and primary documents.[1]

A Brief History of the Indiana Territory

The formation and development of the Indiana Territory reflected arguably the most important achievements of the Confederation government that was superseded by the one created in the Constitution of 1787: the Ordinance of 1785 and the Northwest Ordinance of 1787. The former established the basis of American land policy until passage of the Homestead Act in 1862. It required that before publicly held land could be sold the government had to purchase Indian claims and to survey the land according to the system described in the ordinance. In brief, it created a rectilinear survey in the Old Northwest based on a series of meridians and baselines, beginning in what is now southeastern Ohio. As compared with the metes-and-bounds system used in the South, the rectilinear method provided an orderly and reliable device that minimized conflicts over land claims. Every six miles a north-south line intersected the baseline, creating a range. Within this framework, congressional townships were formed measuring six miles by

The Northwest Territory

six miles. These townships were divided into thirty-six sections, each one mile square or 640 acres. In subsequent legislation, Congress permitted sale of smaller units—half, quarter, half-quarter, and quarter-quarter sections. For a time, from 1800 to 1820, land could be purchased on the installment plan over five years. Significantly, section sixteen was reserved for the support of common or public schools.[2]

Equally important was the Northwest Ordinance, created 13 July 1787, which governed the approximately 265,000 square miles north of the Ohio River and west of Pennsylvania and New York. The third most important document in American history, after the Declaration of Independence and the Constitution, it created six articles of compact between the original states and the territory—

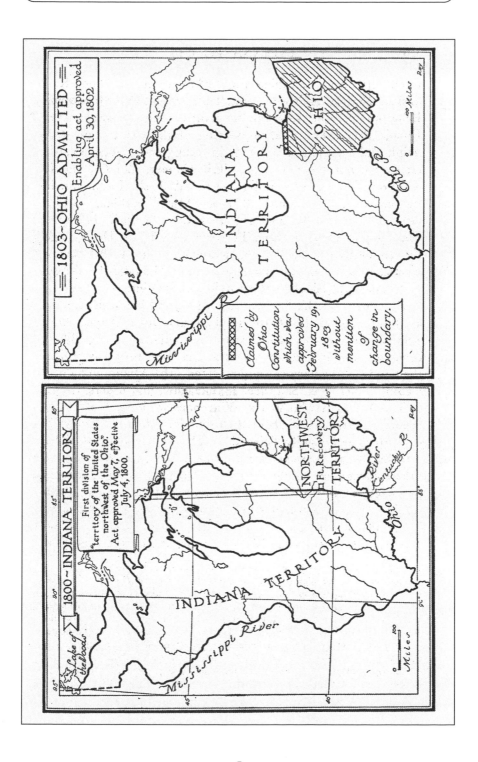

1803~OHIO ADMITTED
Enabling act approved
April 30, 1802

INDIANA TERRITORY

OHIO

Ohio R.

Mississippi

Ray

100 Miles
0

Claimed by Ohio Constitution which was approved February 19, 1803 without mention of change in boundary.

1800~INDIANA TERRITORY

First division of "Territory of the United States northwest of the Ohio". Act approved May 7, 1800, effective July 4, 1800.

Lake of the Woods

INDIANA TERRITORY

NORTHWEST (Ft. Recovery) TERRITORY

Kentucky R.

Ohio R.

Mississippi River

100 Miles
0

Ray

5

the nation's first bill of rights. Significantly, slavery and involuntary servitude were prohibited. Under the ordinance thirty-one states ultimately entered the Union. It created a three-stage process for territorial settlement, growth, and government. When a territory had five thousand adult white males—the basis of the electorate in those days—it was eligible for admission to the second stage. At sixty thousand residents it qualified for statehood. Three to five states were to be formed from this area, moreover, as states on equal footing with the original states. In the first stage, presidentially appointed territorial governors, secretaries, and judges were quite powerful. In the second, the people secured some power to vote for limited representation in their government. Only in the third, with statehood, could the people govern themselves.

Government of the Northwest Territory began in Marietta in present-day Ohio on 15 July 1788. Arthur St. Clair was the first governor. Formation of county governments followed. Knox County, named after Henry Knox, Continental Army general and later the first secretary of war, was soon formed, and it comprised what is now the entire state of Indiana and then some. Vincennes, established by François-Marie Bissot, Sieur de Vincennes, in 1732, became its county seat. A major challenge to St. Clair was relations with the Indian tribes, who routed his army in 1791. The Indians suffered a major defeat at the Battle of Fallen Timbers (near present-day Toledo) on 20 August 1794, and the resulting Treaty of Greenville, signed 3 August 1795, ceded about two-thirds of the future state of Ohio and a small portion of future southeastern Indiana, as well as sixteen small tracts at the portages between rivers and along river routes. In Indiana these included the Wabash-Maumee portage, Clark's Grant (opposite present-day Louisville), and the Vincennes Tract. Tribes were promised $20,000 in goods and annuities worth $9,500, split into $500 or $1,000 portions for each tribe.

The second stage of territorial government was reached on 29 October 1798. Twenty-five-year-old William Henry Harrison, son of a Virginia delegate to the Continental Congress, was elected the first delegate to Congress from the territory. The most animated political debates occurred over the financial burdens of government and the civil rights of residents in the western portions of the territory. On 7 May 1800, with Harrison's help, Congress split the Northwest Territory into two sections, effective on 4 July. The Indiana Territory included almost all of the land west of the western border of present-day Ohio. The "gore"—a sliver of land in southeastern Indiana—and the eastern portion of what is now Michigan remained in the Northwest Territory. These two sections were transferred to the Indiana Territory when the eastern territory was admitted to the Union as the state of Ohio on 19 February 1803. Vincennes, the oldest settlement in the territory, became the first territorial capital.[3]

Effective 4 July 1800, therefore, Indiana was back on stage one for territorial government. President John Adams had named Harrison governor on 13 May, but the Virginian did not arrive in Vincennes until 10 January 1801. John Gibson, who Adams had designated territorial secretary, was by virtue of his office acting governor before Harrison's arrival.[4] The president also appointed William Clark, John Griffin, and Henry Vanderburgh as territorial judges. The governor in turn appointed all local and territorial officials.

The first territorial capital had a population of 714 in 1800; another 819 whites and 15 slaves resided near the town. The territory comprised 5,641 residents. Within three years of arriving, the governor had built a splendid Tidewater mansion, Grouseland, on the northern side of the town. Well preserved, it remains a vivid reminder of Harrison's vision for the American West and of the transmission of aristocratic Virginia values to the rude Indiana frontier. During its early days, it doubled as the territorial land office as well as the governor's residence.[5]

As governor, Harrison focused on negotiation with Indian tribes for title to their lands, which could then be surveyed, sold, and legally settled under terms of the Ordinance of 1785. Most of the land that is now Indiana was in Indian hands when Harrison was appointed. From 1803 to 1809 he concluded eight treaties, bringing millions of acres under American control. Harrison signed five of these treaties in Vincennes and two in Fort Wayne. The other— forged with the Sauk and Fox in St. Louis on 3 November 1804—he signed in his capacity as governor of the new District of Louisiana. At the end, he had opened what is now southern Indiana and most of present-day Illinois and parts of present-day Wisconsin to white settlement. These treaties, conducted in public, guaranteed that Indians would be paid money and goods in public and that bills would be submitted promptly to the War Department. By standards of his age, Harrison was generally considerate, and for Indians around Vincennes he often provided support at his own expense.[6]

During Harrison's tenure, moreover, the same pressures that had led to the division of the Northwest Territory in 1800 prompted two additional territorial partitions. When Indiana reached the second stage of territorial government in 1804, residents of the far northern and western portions of Indiana petitioned Congress for relief. On 11 January 1805 Congress created the Michigan Territory. The Indiana Territory consequently included the present states of Indiana, Illinois, Wisconsin, and eastern Minnesota until 3 February 1809, when the Illinois Territory was organized. The boundaries of what was left included for the most part those in place when the state of Indiana was admitted to the Union, except for some alteration of the Michigan-Indiana border. Vincennes was no longer geographically central, and the more populous southeastern region of Indiana lobbied for a change in the location of the capital. The territorial assembly moved the capital to Corydon in Harrison County effective 1 May 1813.[7]

Indiana's transition from territory to statehood took sixteen years. In the first stage the governor and the judges made the laws, and residents had no representative government. The federal government paid about $5,500 yearly for salaries and expenses of government. Total expenditure was about $200 more. Only those white males aged twenty-one and over who owned fifty or more acres of land could vote. For its time this was a relatively liberal version of suffrage.

On 5 December 1804 Governor Harrison issued a proclamation announcing the territory's advancement to the second stage of government. Congressional legislation permitted the governor to do so whenever he had evidence a majority of landowners desired the change. The president continued to appoint the governor, the secretary, and the judges. On 3 January 1805 voters elected the first territorial House of Representatives. The governor selected five

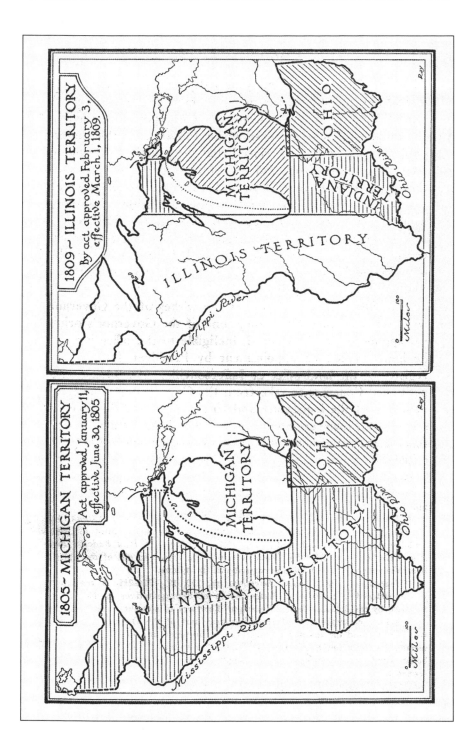

1809 ~ ILLINOIS TERRITORY
By act approved February 3, effective March 1, 1809.

ILLINOIS TERRITORY

MICHIGAN TERRITORY

OHIO

INDIANA TERRITORY

Ohio River

Mississippi River

0 100 Miles

Ray

1805 ~ MICHIGAN TERRITORY
Act approved January 11, effective June 30, 1805.

INDIANA TERRITORY

MICHIGAN TERRITORY

OHIO

Ohio River

Mississippi River

0 100 Miles

Ray

9

persons from a list of ten nominated by the House to serve on the Legislative Council (upper house). The two legislative bodies in turn selected Benjamin Parke as the first territorial delegate to the United States Congress. The first Indiana General Assembly met 29 July through 26 August 1805. The governor, though, retained his powers to appoint local and territorial officials, to convene or dissolve the general assembly, and to veto any legislative measure. Territorial expenditures averaged $10,000 annually, with the federal government continuing to pay the approximate $6,700 for salaries of top-appointed officials.[8]

In 1809 Congress passed legislation permitting qualified voters in the Indiana Territory to elect directly the territorial delegate to the Congress as well as members of the Legislative Council. Two years later it revised the Suffrage Act of 1808 and extended voting rights to all free white males aged twenty-one or more who paid county or territorial taxes and had resided in the territory one year. The federal census of 1810 disclosed that the territory's population was 24,520.

In modern terms the amount of money needed to pay for territorial government was miniscule. This reflected the simplicity of the economy and the society that government served. The cost of providing more representative government contributed heavily to the development of the Northwest Territory. As it evolved to the second stage, more expenses, and thus more taxes, were required. Those most distant from the seat of government complained of oppressive taxes for services that did not benefit them. This was a major reason that residents in the western portions of the Northwest Territory requested partition in 1800, as did persons living in the north and west of the Indiana Territory in 1805 and 1809.

In the first stage the federal government paid for the governor ($2,000), the secretary ($750), the three judges ($800 each), and a contingent fund ($350). The territory had to pay for a treasurer and an attorney general, for printing costs, for salary and expenses of a legislative clerk, for postage, and for other miscellaneous charges. At the second stage federal salaries were increased and the contingent fund continued. The territory paid for a treasurer, an auditor, an attorney general, legislators, and a chancellor. It was also required to pay for public printing (upwards of $1,000 a year), for tax collectors, for elections, and for supplies and other items.

The first legislative act of the governor and the judges on 12 January 1801 was to require a listing of taxable property. Two years later they passed the first comprehensive tax law. The first session of the general assembly modified the act for levying and collecting taxes on land, and subsequently higher taxes were levied to support government costs. Such expenses were minimal, though, because government did very little. Education, charities, internal improvements, corrections, and regulatory activities were a thing of the future.[9]

On 11 December 1811, shortly after the Battle of Tippecanoe, the Indiana House of Representatives petitioned Congress for permission to form a state constitution in preparation for admission to the Union. Indiana's financial problems and the nation's distractions due to imminent war with Great Britain delayed statehood. All told, the territorial legislature met in four sites during Vincennes's tenure as capital. Exactly where it met is uncertain. Probably it convened in the home of Francis Vigo, in the house of Antoine Marchal, and in the tavern of Mark Barnett. The fourth location, where it met between 22 November and 19 December 1811, has been preserved as one of the properties of the Vincennes State Historic Sites. By virtue of an act of the general assembly on 11 March 1813 the capital was moved approximately one hundred miles to the east, to Corydon.[10]

On 11 December 1815, after the end of the War of 1812, the Indiana General Assembly again petitioned Congress for statehood. On 19 April 1816 Congress approved and President James Madison signed an enabling act that permitted voters in Indiana to elect delegates to a June meeting to determine Indiana statehood. Election of delegates occurred on 13 May, and between 10 and 29 June, forty-three of them met at Corydon. After overwhelmingly adopting a resolution seeking statehood, the delegates composed the state's first constitution. Jonathan Jennings of Charlestown, who had been a delegate to Congress and leader of the anti-Harrison, antislavery, and prodemocracy element in the territory, was elected governor on 5 August. The first legislative session under the new constitution was convened on 4 November. William Hendricks, a Jennings ally, was elected to a term in the United States Congress. (Ironically, on 2 December Harrison commenced a brief span as an Ohio delegate to Congress. In 1819 he was elected to the Ohio Senate, where he served two terms. He was elected to the United States Senate in January 1825.) On 11 December 1816 Congress adopted and President Madison signed a resolution admitting Indiana as the nineteenth state.[11]

During its territorial period, Indiana experienced often rocky relations with the Indians, attempted and then repealed efforts to introduce slavery, and acquired the trappings of civilization on the frontier. Governor Harrison was charged with the acquisition of Indian lands and the protection of whites who settled them. As indicated earlier, between 1803 and 1809 he arranged a number of treaties, but in a message to the territorial general assembly in 1806 he acknowledged the unsatisfactory condition of the Indians.

[The Indians] will never have recourse to arms, I speak of those in our immediate neighborhood, unless driven to it by a series of injustice and oppression. Of this they already begin to complain; and I am sorry to say that their complaints are far from being groundless. It is true that the general government has passed laws for fulfilling, . . . the stipulation contained in our treaty, . . . The laws of the territory provide, also the same punishment for offenses committed against Indians as against white men. Experience, however, shows that there is a wide difference in the execution of those laws. The Indian always suffers, and the white man never.[12]

After Harrison negotiated the Fort Wayne Treaty of 1809, the Shawnee warrior Tecumseh and his brother, the religious leader known as the Prophet, encouraged unrest among the Indians. Like Pontiac before him, Tecumseh believed that only an Indian confederacy could successfully resist the American government. Turmoil had been present since at least 1805, when in August Harrison held a council at his home in Vincennes. Over the next year, he became increasingly aware of the two brothers' growing hostility to whites, and in 1807 he demanded that the Prophet and his followers move away from Greenville, Ohio. In 1808 the Indians shifted to a new residence, Prophetstown, near present-day Battle Ground, in Tippecanoe County, Indiana. Angry over the Fort Wayne treaty, which ceded 2.5 million acres to the national government, Tecumseh met Harrison on the grounds of Grouseland in August 1810. There the Shawnee leader warned he would tolerate no more cessions without consent of all the tribes. In July of the following year the two met again, and Tecumseh asked Harrison not to disturb the existing state of affairs.[13]

By that time Harrison had erected Fort Knox II north of the town, and Capt. Zachary Taylor was placed in command. On 25 September Harrison and one thousand men departed north to march on Prophetstown. On 1 October the troops began to build Fort Harrison, near present-day Terre Haute, and four weeks later they continued their march northward. In Tecumseh's absence, Harrison fought the Prophet and his men at the Battle of Tippecanoe on 7 November 1811. Having ended for a time Tecumseh's confederacy, Harrison returned to Vincennes on 18 November.

During the ensuing War of 1812, many tribes were aligned with the British against the Americans. Harrison received full command of northwestern troops in September 1812 and took Detroit from the British. (On 28 December he resigned as territorial governor.) His army defeated British Maj. Gen. Henry Procter at the Battle of the Thames near present-day London, Ontario. Tecumseh was killed in that battle, which effectively destroyed Indian resistance and British power in the Old Northwest. On 11 May 1814 Harrison resigned from the army and retired to his home in North Bend, Ohio. On 22 July he negotiated a treaty with Indian tribes at Greenville. In August 1815 he settled his last treaty, the Treaty of Spring Wells (near Detroit), which was signed on 8 September.[14]

Another vital issue for territorial Indiana was slavery, and that question was tied to the expansion of white suffrage and the legislature's desire for greater power. Many of Harrison's allies in and around Vincennes chafed at Article 6 of the Northwest Ordinance, which prohibited slavery and involuntary servitude. For one thing, they interpreted that to mean that slaves in the territory prior to 13 July 1787 would remain slaves. Many proslavery citizens petitioned

Congress asking for relief from this article. Congress did not redress their grievances, but territorial officials evaded Article 6 with indenture laws. The most significant of these was the 1805 Indenture Act, which stipulated that slaves brought into the territory, who were over age fifteen, could be indentured for a term set by their masters. Males under that age had to serve to age thirty-five and females to age thirty-two. Children born of these "indentured" servants had to serve until ages thirty if male and twenty-eight if female. This explains why, in a region deemed free by the Northwest Ordinance, 237 slaves were enumerated in the 1810 territorial census.[15]

Antislavery, antiaristocracy citizens gained a majority in the House of Representatives after the formation of the Illinois Territory in 1809, as the eastern part of the region was populated largely by migrants from eastern states and by persons from southern states who had opposed slavery there. One result was Congress's liberalizing the suffrage. Another was the election of Jonathan Jennings to Congress. And in December 1810 the general assembly repealed the slave laws. It did not end existing indentures, though, and some abuse of the Northwest Ordinance continued. Not until the 1830s did the Indiana Supreme Court formally free those blacks who had fallen between the cracks of the system after 1810.[16]

Territorial status also evidenced the emergence of rudimentary social, economic, and cultural structures. The first "college" in the territory, Jefferson Academy, was established in Vincennes in 1801; Vincennes University succeeded it in 1806. A grammar school appeared five years later, and the first circulating library was established in Vincennes in 1806. The first historical organization, the Vincennes Historical and Antiquarian Society, appeared in 1808. A year later the Vincennes Society for the Encouragement of Agriculture and the Useful Arts was founded. Itinerant printer Elihu Stout established the first newspaper, the *Indiana Gazette*, in Vincennes in 1804; after 1807 it was known as the *Western Sun*. Although St. Francis Xavier parish in Vincennes traced its roots to 1749, it was not until the territory was organized that church formation quickened. Predictably, the earliest churches throughout the territory were Baptist, Methodist, and Presbyterian; the latter claimed to have sent the first pastor to the region in 1808. The

Shakers organized a community north of Vincennes on Busseron Creek in 1805, and in 1814 a much larger and longer lived community of Harmonists, followers of the premillenialist and anti-Lutheran pastor George Rapp, formed a settlement at Harmonie on the lower Wabash in Posey County.[17]

Economic activity, while primitive, also quickened. By 1810 the territory boasted one cotton mill, 1,350 spinning wheels, and 1,256 looms. These created thousands of yards annually of cotton, woolen, flaxen, and mixed goods such as linsey-woolsey. Eighteen tanneries produced leather valued at $93,000, and twenty-eight distilleries generated 35,950 gallons of whiskey annually. One nail factory wrought $4,000 worth of nails. The 1810 census listed thirty-three gristmills and three horse mills grinding 40,900 bushels of wheat and fourteen sawmills cutting 390,000 feet of lumber. The first steamboat, the *New Orleans,* navigated the Ohio in 1811, and proprietor Nicholas Roosevelt subsequently purchased land in and around Troy to supply wood and supplies for river craft.[18]

The territory's first post office was established at Vincennes in 1800, and about twenty existed by the time Indiana achieved statehood. Post riders carried the mail between post offices in their saddlebags. In 1800 Vincennes received mail only once every four weeks, but after it became the capital weekly mail service began between the Falls of the Ohio and that town. It took about eight weeks for Governor Harrison to send a letter to Washington and to receive a reply. Regular stagecoach service was established, with the route between the Falls and the territorial capital generally but not always following the ancient Buffalo Trace. The conditions of the roadway were primitive, and the journey took about three days each way.[19]

Most immigrants to the Indiana Territory arrived from the South; many had entered Kentucky and the Bluegrass region through the Cumberland Gap and then traveled across the Ohio into the Old Northwest. Southerners came mostly overland, bringing their few household belongings by packhorse or wagon. Others who came from the East traveled by horseback or wagon to towns on the upper Ohio, chiefly Pittsburgh and Wheeling, and descended the Ohio by flatboat or in rare cases keelboat. Steamboats were generally an insignificant means of travel in territorial days.[20]

One should note, finally, that the criminal justice system in the territory was simple if not primitive. Horse theft was a common offense, and felons were given fifty to two hundred stripes on their bare backs and committed to the county jail until the value of the horses was repaid. Theft of a hog brought twenty-five to thirty-nine stripes and a fine of $50 to $100. The use of whipping indicated that money to pay fines or to build and maintain jails was scarce.[21]

Beginning with the enabling act signed by President Madison on 19 April 1816, the Indiana Territory's days were numbered, and they came to an end with statehood eight months later. The Constitution of 1816, which governed the state until 1851, reflected much of the culture and society of the Indiana Territory. Of the forty-three delegates to the constitutional convention, for instance, twenty-seven had lived in Kentucky prior to coming to Indiana. Half were in their forties, and another sixteen were in their thirties. Slightly more than half had had some legal training.[22]

The constitution, largely borrowed from Kentucky and Ohio, was relatively democratic.

> The constitution opened with a preamble and bill of rights, stating such enlightenment and revolutionary-era concepts as "all men are born equally free and independent," and "all power is inherent in the people." Hoosiers were promised freedom of worship, of the press, and of speech and the right to bear arms and to assemble peaceably. The convention adopted the American system of checks and balances and divided the powers of government among legislative, executive, and judicial branches. Reflecting their recent struggles to expand representative power, the delegates made the legislature the dominant branch, able to override the governor's veto by a simple majority vote. They set the governor's term at only three years and prohibited him from holding office longer than six years in any nine-year period.[23]

Members of the House of Representatives—who had to be twenty-one years old and to have resided in the state for a year—were to be elected annually. Senators, who had to be twenty-five years old, served three-year terms. They, too, had a one-year residency requirement. All males over age twenty-one who had resided in the state for one year could vote. Slavery and involuntary servitude were prohibited. The constitution ambitiously promised a free and general system of education from township schools to a state university. And it provided a penal code based on the principle of reformation, not vindictiveness, as well as asylums for the aged, infirm, and unfortunate. All of these noble sentiments regarding education, criminal justice, and social welfare, though, were to be enacted as soon as circumstances permitted.[24]

This was clear proof of the value of the Ordinance of 1785 and the Northwest Ordinance of 1787. Both had provided a framework for orderly development on the frontier. Though the form varied according to place and time, entrepreneurs and most citizens in the new territories of the trans-Appalachian West desired that sort of stability. Congress in the 1780s had "provided territorial organization sufficient to accommodate settlement on the trans-Appalachian frontier until 1850. Government now came to the frontier before people, and it helped to prepare for and to accelerate the arrival of settlers."[25] Not surprisingly, the growth and development of the new state of Indiana after 11 December 1816 would be phenomenal.

Symposium Essays

The Indiana Territorial Bicentennial Symposium was organized around six broad themes: the rationale for observing a bicentennial of the Indiana Territory; the character of the town of Vincennes when it became the territorial capital; the nature of relations between whites and Indians in the Indiana Territory; the status of religious institutions and values in early Indiana; the Indiana Territory within the broader framework of the Jefferson administration and westward expansion; and the way in which Indiana and the West figured in international relations, especially those of

America and Britain. The following is a summary of each presentation at the symposium. (For health reasons, Richard Day was unable to complete a printed version for inclusion in this publication.) After this is a brief review of the papers of Douglas E. Clanin and M. Teresa Baer on the Harrison papers given on the following day.

In "Commemorating the Past: The Indiana Territory, 1800–2000," James H. Madison reflects on the state's early heritage and how our sense of the past is revealed in our manner of commemoration. Historical remembrances, he notes, tend to have common characteristics: they are upbeat and straightforward, seek to create community, and focus on beginnings as a means of reassuring participants that their present is solid and enduring and has come a long way from its origins. Commemorations "are more often about the present than the past."[26] Focusing on the sesquicentennial of the Indiana Territory in 1950, he helps us reflect more broadly on "what Hoosiers have remembered over the decades and also what they have not remembered." He concludes by noting that "all of these stories and historic places were selected by earlier generations. Their choices and their silences shape our memory and our sense of the past." We cannot be "neutral receptors of their particular version of the past," though, for each generation must decide what the George Rogers Clark Memorial or the commemoration of milestones in the state's history mean. "Commemoration is always an ongoing dialogue between past and present."

Richard Day seeks to take us back to Vincennes as it was in the spring and summer of 1800, when the coming of territorial government accelerated changes in the dynamics of the relationships among Anglo-Americans, Franco-Americans, and Native Americans. An isolated place, a three-days' journey from the Falls of the Ohio and a three-months' round-trip from New Orleans, it was relatively small and compact. Most homes were situated on the first three streets paralleling the Wabash River. Present-day Willow Street was on the south end of the town, and Grouseland—Harrison's Tidewater mansion—lay outside the northern edge. Place-names, architecture, lot sizes, and folkways greatly reflected rural French culture, though the increasing number of tall, rangy upper southern whites was beginning to effect substantial change—for instance, in the removal of the nearby Piankashaws and the securing of title to most of the land in Knox County. To the French, this was a village in the rural French sense, compact and cohesive. Anglo-Americans tended to reside on the perimeter, even situating their churches there. They brought a number of changes—frame dwellings and business structures, the first brick home in Indiana, and the first newspaper and academy. About fifty African Americans resided near Busseron Creek and another one hundred near Maria Creek. Most of the French homes were poorly constructed in the typical vertical-post style, and stockades surrounded most houses to keep the hogs out. Visitors often remarked about the beauty of the town's site and the ugliness of the village. After Harrison, probably the leading figure in the settlement was Francis Vigo, a Genoan who had aided George Rogers Clark and subsequently made a fortune in trade and real estate development. Also notable were Nathaniel Ewing, agent at the federal land office, and John Badollet, a Huguenot merchant. The community boasted a number of artisans, including gunsmiths, silversmiths, and furniture makers.

Clearly, as this discussion suggests, the dynamics of race and democracy created multiple meanings of the Indiana frontier. Andrew R. L. Cayton's essay, "Race, Democracy, and the Multiple Meanings of the Indiana Frontier," encourages analysis of the Indiana borderlands as contested history. Residents two hundred years ago, like those of the present, sought to explain "the single most important development in the history of the continent"—the conquest of trans-Appalachian North America by citizens of the United States. This development "remains controversial because we cannot agree on its larger significance." Essential to this dialogue is the complex relationship between democracy and race—between inclusiveness and exclusiveness, between the dignity of all and the limits of American idealism.

Though many now lament the inability of residents of the Wabash and Ohio river valleys to devise some means of accommodating one another in a time of dramatic physical and social change, we should consider "the degree to which the problem of what we now call multiculturalism was on the minds of prominent inhabitants of the Indiana frontier. Indeed, their failure to create a world that promoted rather than discouraged diversity was a failure of execution rather than of imagination." Their chief problem was, like ours, "how to balance respect for others with respect for the integrity of one's own culture." We tend not to take seriously the way in which some Americans and some Indians sought to develop understanding and empathy. That reflects our knowledge of what happened to the Indians, the French, and the African Americans, but it also echoes the way in which Enlightenment curiosity about diversity and the possibility of universal understanding was "giving way to Romantic ideas of a strong link between particular kinds of people in particular kinds of places with particular kinds of behavior and beliefs."

The most significant example of the Enlightenment vision was President Thomas Jefferson's summary of "our policy respecting the Indians" in an 1803 letter to Governor Harrison, the intentions of which have been greatly misinterpreted. The romantic racism that superseded this among whites is mirrored, Cayton declares, by Tenskwatawa and Tecumseh: a vision of segregation, not integration, "of tolerance at a distance, not acceptance of diversity. . . . The Indian version of the history of the Indiana frontier was defeated at Tippecanoe. But it did not die with Tecumseh." Their words reflect historians' tendency to use Indians "as narrative foils to praise or condemn white Americans and their governments." Meanwhile, historians "seem utterly baffled by the ostensible hero of the story: the Virginia-born William Henry Harrison."

Ultimately Hoosier storytellers, in seeking to define Indiana, built on the romantic conception of Indiana and in creating Indiana as a community—whether good or bad, triumph or tragedy—betrayed the visions of Jefferson and Harrison. "The story was theirs[,] and the legacy of conquest was their right to tell the story as they wished."

James J. Divita's paper, "Religion on the Indiana Frontier, 1679–1816," also deals with multicultural relations and religious diversity. He notes that new white populations arrived and that the migrating Indians had contact with them and their descendants. The arrival of Catholicism offered a major challenge to the natives' religion. In turn, Anglo-Americans came to outnumber earlier residents, to settle native land, and to increase religious diversity as they introduced Protestantism. In the larger context of Indiana's religious history, the period from the coming of the French explorer René-Robert Cavelier, Sieur de La Salle, in 1679 to the end of the territorial period in 1816 marks a distinctive state of flux in the lands along the Wabash River.

This era marks chronologically as well as historically the foundation time for Indiana religion. Divita tells us that the Indian and European population of eighteenth-century Indiana "appeared here almost simultaneously." Catholic beliefs and ways influenced Indian beliefs and practices. "Evangelization of the Indians also activated Protestants," bringing Moravian and Baptist missions. Religious tolerance initially "characterized this state of flux." Political and economic factors prompted Catholic out-migration from Vincennes to New Madrid, reducing potential tensions with Protestants in the territorial era, which included the Second Great Awakening. "Indiana was big enough—and sparsely populated—so that both great faiths could coexist. No major confrontations occurred before the arrival of Irish and Germans in the 1830s and 1840s."

In the Indiana Territory, Anglo-American settlement sharpened religious controversy. Today's Indiana religion "is majority Protestant but strongly diversified, a characteristic already evident during the territorial period." And the Indiana Territory was able to accommodate diversity, although outbreaks of religious intolerance were the natural price paid for "a religiously cosmopolitan Indiana."

George W. Geib's essay, "Jefferson, Harrison, and the West: An Essay on Territorial Slavery," links Jefferson's famous "fire-bell in the night" observation on the Missouri admission debate of 1820 to the fall of 1804, when Governor Harrison and the judges of the Indiana Territory "helped to create the situation that roused Jefferson from his retirement sixteen short years later." This was due to the fact that briefly Indiana and Missouri shared territorial government officials, whose decisions in Vincennes "would be felt far out into the trans-Mississippi West."

In creating the concept of an "empire of liberty" and the ordinances of 1785 and 1787, Geib argues, American leaders deliberately rejected the metropolitan model, the weaknesses of which were vividly revealed in the insurrection of slaves in the breakaway

21

colony of Haiti. Shortly after the Louisiana Purchase (a direct result of Napoléon's failure to quell that rebellion), the new District of Louisiana, though legally distinct, was placed under the administrative authority of the Indiana Territory, which at the time adjoined the Mississippi River and Louisiana. For nine months, beginning 1 October 1804, Louisiana was governed from Vincennes. Governor Harrison, who never supported Article 6 of the Northwest Ordinance, was at the time enmeshed in devices to legitimize virtually permanent indentured servitude for African Americans. Two of the territorial judges, and the third—Henry Vanderburgh—introduced Harrison to the concept of the "'custom of the country,' by which local practices were continued and respected in the face of proposed change." As slavery was a "custom" around Vincennes, the "alliance he forged with Vanderburgh on the issue would prove of importance in the 1804 Missouri laws."

For good or ill, Harrison was for less than a year President Jefferson's representative to create the institutional form of the "empire of liberty" in what later became Missouri and Arkansas. On a fateful day in Vincennes in October 1804, he and his three judges wrote fifteen fundamental laws for Louisiana. (A sixteenth was added in April 1805.) Thirteen were based on Northwest Territory and/or Indiana Territory laws. The laws reflected their backgrounds and the high proportions of upland southern settlers in Indiana and Louisiana, as well as the remoteness of the frontier and the lack of trained attorneys. The act of Congress permitting Jefferson to take possession of Louisiana stipulated that common local custom as well as civil law that had long prevailed under Spanish rule were to be respected. Slavery was a "custom of the country" there. With little fanfare, Jefferson's representatives thus extended slavery legally into the West by adopting a law based on Virginia's slavery statute. When Harrison arrived in St. Louis in October 1804, moreover, he was well known "as an aggressive and opportunistic Indian negotiator." He would spend a great deal of time hammering out an agreement with the Sauks that was a typical Harrison arrangement. "The temptation to compare Harrison's energy on this issue with his quick treatment of the slavery issue is great."

Geib concludes his piece by discussing the Turner thesis and its subsequent critics. He suggests that John D. Barnhart's "valley of democracy" thesis would not, though, appeal to African Americans. The paradox—that a substantial part of the inland river valleys became home to coercion, and not liberty—involves the Indiana Territory, where the first American laws on slavery in Louisiana were written. In short, "if 1820 required a fire-bell, 1804 clearly kindled the coals of that conflagration."

The final symposium paper, "Great Britain and America at 1800: Perspectives on the Frontier," offered by Nancy L. Rhoden, looks at the larger international context of the Indiana frontier. Westward expansion owed much to larger political and diplomatic action as well as to a web of individual and family decisions. The United States and Britain, during much of the time that the Indiana Territory existed, held vastly different perspectives on the frontier's future. "Revolutionary questions of self-determination and sovereignty . . . , which had been essential in the Anglo-American conflict that began in the 1760s, did not disappear at [the Revolutionary] war's end," Rhoden notes, "but rather persisted on the frontier." Americans saw the trans-Appalachian West "as a suitable area for land speculation and future agricultural development [while] the British government favored its usefulness to the fur trade and its links to Canada."

On the western frontier, competing claims of sovereignty characterized the era of 1783 to 1800. Migrants flooded into the area north of the Ohio River, fed by Congress's decision to replenish its empty treasury through the sale of Indian lands, particularly after states ceded their claims to the region. In the 1780s and 1790s, though, the Indians of the Old Northwest and the British believed they could defeat small groups of American settlers and a weak national army. That situation had changed dramatically by 1812, however, when more than 250,000 Americans lived in the Old Northwest. Even then, "British officials in London, unaware of the exact dimensions of this migratory force, still discussed the creation of a buffer state north of the Ohio." British policy regarding American relations between 1783 and 1815 comprised two somewhat contradictory trends: accommodation with the former colonists, especially regarding trade, and restriction of America's boundaries, even possibly America's demise.

The Jay and Pinckney Treaties and the Treaty of Greenville "answered many of the Anglo-American arguments concerning frontier sovereignty which had raged since the Revolutionary War." At the creation of the Indiana Territory in 1800 concerns about the future of the Republic continued. The frontier was far from stable. And the British threat on the frontier persisted. After 1800 British officials "began to revert to previous frontier policies, and the British presence would reassert itself most vigorously by 1812." When the Indiana Territory was formed, though, Americans "may have felt increasingly confident, or at least optimistic, that their claims of sovereignty in the West could be recognized internationally."

In his paper, "Adventures in Historical Editing: The William Henry Harrison Papers Project," Douglas E. Clanin has four purposes, three of them stated. He offers background on the provenance of the Harrison papers, provides an administrative history of a project that began in the late 1970s and was completed in 1999, and concludes with some of his impressions of Harrison's life and career. He also presents an intimate account of his involvement in the project and the subject himself, William Henry Harrison.

Harrison, a speaker at the second meeting of the Indiana Historical Society in December 1830, made known less than three years later his intentions to contribute the bulk of his papers to the Society. It was not until a century later, however, that the Society's collection of Harrison papers commenced, and approximately one thousand manuscripts, along with broadsides, pamphlets, and books on Old Tippecanoe were purchased. The microfilm publication issued in 1999 had its roots in efforts of the late Gayle Thornbrough and the late Dorothy Riker, "remarkable documentary editors," to revise Logan Esarey's collection of Harrison's papers published in 1922 that was, although seriously flawed, "by 1922 standards . . . probably as good as one could expect." Beginning in 1981 it was clear to Clanin, who was hired the year before following Riker's retirement, that many more than two volumes would be required for a revised letterpress edition. A detailed and often personal account of the project follows, including an explanation for the decision to publish in microfilm format. The ten-reel publication comprises copies of nearly 3,600 documents garnered not only from the Society's collection, but also from public repositories, private collections, and printed sources.

Clanin acknowledges that, like Washington, the real Harrison is only partially revealed in his writings. He concludes his paper with a survey of Harrison's life in the years covered in the papers. Among other things, he encourages future scholars of Harrison and his times to be aware of those circumstances that made Harrison a cautious military leader.

M. Teresa Baer, an editor at the Society, was full-time editorial assistant on the Harrison Papers Project from 1998 to 1999. Her paper, "William Henry Harrison and the Indian Treaty Land Cessions," which focuses on Harrison's securing of Indian land treaty cessions, inquires whether Harrison was a hero or a villain for these treaties. Her view—"the answer depends on one's interpretation of history"—offers a contrast to Cayton's paper. Harrison's papers reveal, she concludes, a person who thought himself to be a competent leader, a friend to whites and Indians, and "a hero and a villain too."

Conclusion

Growing up in Pennsylvania, I, like so many of my peers, assumed that the nation's history evolved from east to west. Hence I assumed that the name Indiana, given to a western Pennsylvania county and its seat, also traveled east to west. The opposite is the case. Indiana County, Pennsylvania, was formed a few years after the Indiana Territory and named in its honor. The Borough of Indiana was chartered in 1816, the same year as the admission of the state of Indiana to the Union.

Like so many other easterners, I also assumed that the name "land of Indians" signified the presence of many Native Americans in this western state. Nothing could be more erroneous. That is perhaps the supreme irony, one which Cayton's essay so eloquently addresses. The formation and development of the Indiana Territory, as a microcosm of westward expansion of Anglo-American civilization, represents a major element in the vast drama of American history. As Madison also reminds us, as we seek to understand both the history of this region and the means by which we celebrate its milestones, each generation is going to have to decide upon the meanings of the physical remains of that past, whether a national park or a collection of Harrison papers.

Notes

1. *The Indiana Historian: A Magazine Exploring Indiana History* (Mar. 1999).
2. Ibid., 3–4.
3. Ibid., 5, 7–8.
4. When Harrison left in June 1812 at the onset of the War of 1812 to command American forces in the northwest, Gibson became acting governor, a position he held until May 1813, when Thomas Posey, who had been appointed territorial governor on 3 March, arrived in the territorial capital. Posey served until 7 November 1816 and was the last governor of the Indiana Territory.
5. *Indiana Historian*, 7–8.
6. Ibid., 8; John D. Barnhart and Dorothy L. Riker, *Indiana to 1816: The Colonial Period*, The History of Indiana, vol. 1 (Indianapolis: Indiana Historical Bureau and Indiana Historical Society, 1971), 325–42.
7. *Indiana Historian*, 9.
8. Ibid., 6.
9. Ibid., 11.
10. Ibid., 6, 8; Barnhart and Riker, *Indiana to 1816*, p. 347.
11. *Indiana Historian*, 6, 11–12. During its sixteen years as a territory, Indiana grew to include fifteen counties. Out of Knox, the first, sprang Clark, Dearborn, and Harrison, all in the eastern portion of the territory, by 1810. Franklin, Jefferson, and Wayne, also in the east, were created in 1811. The western counties of Gibson and Warrick were organized in 1813, and those of Orange, Perry, and Posey were established in 1814. Jackson and Washington, in the center, and Switzerland, in the east, were organized in 1815 and 1816. Town governments were established in Charlestown in 1807, Brookville in 1808, and Madison in 1810. See Barnhart and Riker, *Indiana to 1816*, pp. 331–32, 360–64, 420–22.
12. Quoted in *Indiana Historian*, 10. Three issues in the same publication (Sept., Oct., and Nov. 1992) provide more detail on Native Americans. See also Barnhart and Riker, *Indiana to 1816*, pp. 324–31, 378–87, 397–411; R. David Edmunds, *Tecumseh and the Quest for Indian Leadership* (Boston: Little, Brown and Co., 1984), 159; and Logan Esarey, *Messages and Letters of William Henry Harrison*, vol. 1, 1800–1811 (Indianapolis: Indiana Historical Commission, 1922), 1:199.
13. *Indiana Historian*, 9–10.
14. Ibid., 10–12; Barnhart and Riker, *Indiana to 1816*, pp. 370–80; Edmunds, *Tecumseh and the Quest for Indian Leadership*, 132–33. When Indiana became a state, about two-thirds of its territory remained in Indian hands. The New Purchase Treaty (or Treaty of St. Marys) of 1818 opened most of the central and north-central regions to white settlement.
15. *Indiana Historian*, 12; Barnhart and Riker, *Indiana to 1816*, pp. 347–48; Louis B. Ewbank and Dorothy L. Riker, eds., *The Laws of Indiana Territory, 1809–1816* (Indianapolis: Indiana Historical Bureau, 1934), 138–39; Emma Lou Thornbrough, *The*

Negro in Indiana before 1900: A Study of a Minority (Bloomington and Indianapolis: Indiana University Press and Indiana Historical Bureau, 1993), 6–7, 13, 16, 17; and William Wesley Woollen, Daniel Wait Howe, and Jacob Piatt Dunn, eds., *Executive Journal of Indiana Territory, 1800–1816*, Indiana Historical Society Publications, vol. 3, no. 3 (Indianapolis: Indiana Historical Society, 1900), 83–85.

    16. *Indiana Historian*, 12; Barnhart and Riker, *Indiana to 1816*, p. 360; Thornbrough, *Negro in Indiana before 1900*, p. 9.

    17. Barnhart and Riker, *Indiana to 1816*, pp. 366–67, 435–36, 437–38; Ewbank and Riker, eds., *Laws of Indiana Territory*, 138–39.

    18. Barnhart and Riker, *Indiana to 1816*, p. 365; *Indiana Historian*, 14.

    19. *Indiana Historian*, 14; Barnhart and Riker, *Indiana to 1816*, pp. 436–47.

    20. *Indiana Historian*, 14.

    21. "Territorial Days of Indiana, 1800–1816," *Indiana History Bulletin* 27 (May 1950): 91–120, 106.

    22. Barnhart and Riker, *Indiana to 1816*, pp. 441–44.

    23. James H. Madison, *The Indiana Way: A State History* (Bloomington and Indianapolis: Indiana University Press and Indiana Historical Society, 1986), 51, 53.

    24. Ibid., 53; Barnhart and Riker, *Indiana to 1816*, pp. 451–59.

    25. Malcolm J. Rohrbough, *The Trans-Appalachian Frontier: People, Societies, and Institutions, 1775–1850* (Belmont, Calif.: Wadsworth Publishing Co., 1990), 89–90.

    26. He cites in this respect John R. Gillis, ed., *Commemorations: The Politics of National Identity* (Princeton, N.J.: Princeton University Press, 1994).

Suggested Further Reading

Barnhart, John D. *Valley of Democracy: The Frontier versus the Plantation in the Ohio Valley, 1775–1818*. Bloomington: Indiana University Press, 1953.

Barnhart, John D., and Dorothy L. Riker. *Indiana to 1816: The Colonial Period*. The History of Indiana, vol. 1. Indianapolis: Indiana Historical Bureau and Indiana Historical Society, 1971.

Bigham, Darrel E. *Towns and Villages of the Lower Ohio*. Lexington: University Press of Kentucky, 1998.

Buley, R. Carlyle. *The Old Northwest: Pioneer Period, 1815–1840*. 2 vols. Indianapolis: Indiana Historical Society, 1950.

Carmony, Donald F. *Indiana, 1816–1850: The Pioneer Era*. The History of Indiana, vol. 2. Indianapolis: Indiana Historical Bureau and Indiana Historical Society, 1998.

————. "Indiana Territorial Expenditures, 1800–1816." *Indiana Magazine of History* 39 (Sept. 1943): 237–62.

Carter, Clarence Edwin, comp. and ed. *The Territorial Papers of the United States*. Vol. 7, *The Territory of Indiana, 1800–1810*. Washington, D.C.: U.S. Government Printing Office, 1939.

Cayton, Andrew R. L. *Frontier Indiana*. Bloomington: Indiana University Press, 1996.

Clanin, Douglas E., et al., eds. *The Papers of William Henry Harrison: 1800–1815*. 10 reels of microfilm. Indianapolis: Indiana Historical Society, 1993–99. This microfilm set and printed guide contain more than 3,600 documents relating to Harrison's service as governor of the Indiana Territory (1800–1812), governor of the District of Louisiana

(1804–5), and commander of the United States Northwest Army, War of 1812 (1812–14).

Dunn, Jacob Piatt. *Slavery Petitions and Papers.* Indianapolis: Bowen-Merrill Co., 1894.

Edmunds, R. David. *Tecumseh and the Quest for Indian Leadership.* Boston: Little, Brown and Co., 1984.

Esarey, Logan. *Messages and Letters of William Henry Harrison.* Vol. 1, *1800–1811.* Indianapolis: Indiana Historical Commission, 1922.

Ewbank, Louis B., and Dorothy L. Riker, eds. *The Laws of Indiana Territory, 1809–1816.* Indianapolis: Indiana Historical Bureau, 1934.

Kappler, Charles J., comp. and ed. *Indian Affairs: Laws and Treaties.* Vol. 2, *Treaties.* Washington, D.C.: U.S. Government Printing Office, 1903.

Kettleborough, Charles, ed. *Constitution Making in Indiana.* Indiana Historical Collections, vol. 5. Indianapolis: Indiana Historical Bureau, 1916. The text of the Constitution of 1816 is found on pages 83–125.

Lindley, Harlow, ed. *Indiana as Seen by Early Travelers: A Collection of Reprints from Books of Travel, Letters, and Diaries Prior to 1830.* Indiana Historical Collections, vol. 3. Indianapolis: Indiana Historical Commission, 1916.

McCord, Shirley S., comp. *Travel Accounts of Indiana, 1679–1961: A Collection of Observations by Wayfaring Foreigners, Itinerants, and Peripatetic Hoosiers.* Indianapolis: Indiana Historical Bureau, 1970.

Middleton, Stephen. *The Black Laws in the Old Northwest: A Documentary History.* Westport, Conn.: Greenwood Press, 1993.

Pence, George, and Nellie C. Armstrong. *Indiana Boundaries: Territory, State, and County.* Indiana Historical Collections, vol. 19. Indianapolis: Indiana Historical Bureau, 1933.

Philbrick, Francis S., ed. *The Laws of Indiana Territory, 1801–1809.* Illinois State Historical Library Collections, vol. 21. Springfield: Illinois State Historical Library, 1930.

Rohrbough, Malcolm J. *The Trans-Appalachian Frontier: People, Societies, and Institutions, 1775–1850.* Belmont, Calif.: Wadsworth Publishing Co., 1990.

Smelser, Marshall. "Tecumseh, Harrison, and the War of 1812." *Indiana Magazine of History* 65 (Mar. 1969): 25–44.

Sugden, John. *Tecumseh: A Life.* New York: Henry Holt and Co., 1998.

Taylor, Robert M., Jr., ed. *The Northwest Ordinance, 1787: A Bicentennial Handbook.* Indianapolis: Indiana Historical Society, 1987.

"Territorial Days of Indiana, 1800–1816." *Indiana History Bulletin* 27 (May 1950): 91–120. This was also issued as a separate publication by the Indiana Territory Sesquicentennial Commission.

Thornbrough, Emma Lou. *The Negro in Indiana before 1900: A Study of a Minority.* Bloomington and Indianapolis: Indiana University Press and Indiana Historical Bureau, 1993.

Woollen, William Wesley, Daniel Wait Howe, and Jacob Piatt Dunn, eds. *Executive Journal of Indiana Territory, 1800–1816.* Indiana Historical Society Publications, vol. 3, no. 3. Indianapolis: Indiana Historical Society, 1900.

Commemorating the Past:

The Indiana Territory, 1800–2000

by

JAMES H. MADISON

T HE TWO HUNDREDTH ANNIVERSARY OF THE INDIANA TERRITORY is a time to reflect not only on the state's early heritage but also on our sense of the past as revealed in our manner of commemoration. How do we decide which events of our past to remember and to celebrate? Who decides? What form do these commemorations take? What messages do celebrations convey about the past and about the present?

Historical commemorations tend to have several characteristics. They are usually upbeat, featuring the very best side of the event commemorated. They are straightforward rather than ambiguous. They send a simple rather than complex message. Commemorations attempt to create community—that is, to draw a circle of inclusion for those individuals or groups connected to the event commemorated. Commemorations often focus on beginnings, on the laying of foundations for the future. Remembering such beginnings not only reassures latter-day participants that their present is built on a solid and enduring base but also allows for celebration of how far their civilization has progressed since those old times. Historical commemorations, in fact, are often more about the present than the past.[1]

Indiana State Archives, Indiana Commission on Public Records

The Hoosier Heritage Caravan, ready to roll, 1950.

All these features are found in one of Indiana's most interesting commemorations, the sesquicentennial celebration of the Indiana Territory in 1950. A look first at this particular celebration provides an introduction to a broader consideration of what Hoosiers have remembered about the Indiana Territory over the decades and also what they have not remembered.

The Indiana Sesquicentennial of 1950

The general assembly in 1949 authorized creation of the Indiana Territory Sesquicentennial Commission. Gov. Henry F. Schricker appointed twenty-two citizens to the commission, representing business, government, and historical and civic organizations. The chairman was Curtis G. Shake of Vincennes, an Indiana Supreme Court judge who earlier had been active in creating the George Rogers Clark Memorial. Judge Shake had only recently returned from service at the war crimes trials in Germany. Howard Peckham, head of both the Indiana Historical

Bureau and the Indiana Historical Society, served as ex officio secretary. Peckham's energy and imagination were central to the commission's activities. Important also was Governor Schricker's involvement. He attended several of the meetings and stayed in contact with Peckham, Shake, and others. The commission's first meeting was in the governor's office on 9 December 1949. At the next meeting, on 6 January 1950, the group formed into several working subcommittees. The members focused on publicity efforts, on encouraging local community celebrations, and on raising money to support their work. Emerging eventually as their primary sesquicentennial project was the Hoosier Heritage Caravan.[2]

The Sesquicentennial Commission designed the Hoosier Heritage Caravan to take Indiana history to the people. The caravan's scale and sophistication were impressive, testimony largely to Peckham's abilities. After investigating use of a railroad car or a bus as means of conveyance, Peckham, with support from the Indiana Motor Truck Association, settled on a truck. Then there was the fund-raising. The legislature appropriated not a single dollar for any of the sesquicentennial projects, forcing Peckham to spend much effort raising funds from the private sector. He convinced the Fruehauf Trailer Company to provide a brand-new moving van and International Harvester to donate the tractor to pull it. The governor agreed to assign a state police officer to drive the truck and provide security. Shell Oil donated gasoline and oil; the Hoosier Casualty Company provided insurance. Local chapters of the Indiana Junior Chamber of Commerce took responsibility for advertising and sponsoring the truck in each community. With endorsement from the Indiana Manufacturers Association, Peckham wrote to 135 corporations in Indiana seeking money. Fifteen responded with gifts totaling $2,000, which paid for fitting the truck with electrical wiring, lights, display cases, and fans.[3]

Into the modified moving van the commission placed dozens of original historical documents and artifacts. Among the highlights were the Indiana Constitution of 1816, the journal of the territorial assembly for 1808, and Gen. Anthony Wayne's flag used at the signing of the Treaty of Greenville in 1795. On the truck walls were twelve panels with documents, posters, and illustrations focusing on the themes of: first inhabitants, moving frontier, protection of our land, government of the people, free expression, freedom of religion, free education, free labor, getting places, finding fun, public health, and, finally, the "composite Hoosier." In the center was a large case displaying pioneer tools and modern industrial products. The caravan's first stop was Vincennes on 2 July. For the next four months the truck traveled the state, stopping in every county and covering 3,700 miles. Except for four days in Vincennes and a week at the state fair, the caravan moved to a new town every day. Approximately 135,000 people toured the exhibit.[4]

The other major celebration in 1950 was state day at Vincennes, 1–4 July. The Sesquicentennial Commission and local groups cooperated to put on a grand show. It included several parades, an Indiana Territory queen and court, a pageant each night with a cast of four hundred depicting the story of the Indiana Territory, a new three-cent postage stamp, national broadcast of a religious service on Sunday, 2 July, beard-growing

Indiana governor Henry F. Schricker and Illinois governor Adlai E. Stevenson, Vincennes Sesquicentennial Parade, 4 July 1950.

Byron R. Lewis Historical Library, Vincennes University

Byron R. Lewis Historical Library, Vincennes University

The Vincennes Teachers Association float reenacts the meeting of Tecumseh and William Henry Harrison in the Vincennes Sesquicentennial Parade, 4 July 1950.

contests, fireworks, and speeches by Governor Schricker and Illinois governor Adlai Stevenson. One dignitary who did not attend was President Harry Truman. Peckham and others on the commission badgered Schricker to invite the president, but the governor stalled. Peckham finally wrote Shake that the governor "is obviously irritated by the President's policy on the coal strike and even wondering out loud how popular he would be in Indiana by next summer."[5]

There were other sesquicentennial events in 1950: school programs; a commemorative plate (which raised $267.20); a pamphlet (*Territorial Days of Indiana, 1800–1816*, prepared by the Indiana Historical Bureau with nearly ten thousand copies distributed); Ross F. Lockridge, Sr.'s Hoosier Historical Institutes emphasizing sesquicentennial themes; a radio address by Governor Schricker; special programs at the Indiana Society of Chicago and the Indiana Society of Washington, D.C.; articles in several national magazines; and an exhibition at the Library of Congress. The Indiana Historical Society published R. Carlyle Buley's Pulitzer Prize–winning *The Old Northwest: Pioneer Period,*

1815–1840 as its contribution, and the Indiana Historical Bureau published the *Journals of the General Assembly of Indiana Territory, 1805–1815.*[6]

Such wide and disparate celebrations of the origins of the Indiana Territory surely included many themes and messages. But the celebratory tone dominated in general and the celebration of freedom in particular. The brochure handed to each of the tens of thousands of Hoosiers who entered the caravan exhibition claimed that "the builders of Indiana made it great by exercising the freedoms they had fought for in the American Revolution: freedom to govern themselves, freedom to speak and publish and worship as they pleased, freedom to acquire property through initiative and to bequeath it to all their family." The word "freedom" appeared nine times in the brochure's first paragraph and was sprinkled throughout the full document. In the Indiana Territory there were "no ceilings on rewards for incentive, no limits on what business a man might legally pursue." Speakers and writers readily picked up on the freedom theme. Governor Schricker praised the caravan in a *Chicago Tribune* interview as showing us "the freedoms that we take for granted today." Peckham encouraged corporate contributions by promising the sesquicentennial would make people aware of "the importance of the freedoms that were guaranteed us."[7]

The cold war was well along in 1950, a time when many Americans believed that their freedom needed to be protected from Communist aggression abroad and subversion at home. Although sesquicentennial publicity never pointed explicitly to Communist dangers to freedom, that message was implicit throughout. The *Indianapolis Star* was more direct. In an article praising the Hoosier Heritage Caravan's "original and priceless" exhibitions, the *Star* promised visitors that "you a Hoosier, will receive an ideological impact a Communist wouldn't understand." Indiana Bell's employee magazine in August 1950 featured the sesquicentennial and labeled Vincennes as the "Fortress of Freedom." The company magazine advised readers that they were "engaged in a war against an extended threat to the same freedoms as those won in the American Revolution," adding that the sesquicentennial was also "an opportunity to give thanks for the Christian principles" of freedom.[8]

Another feature of the sesquicentennial reflected Indiana of 1950. This was a time of backlash against the New Deal of President Franklin Roosevelt and Gov. Paul McNutt. Hoosiers took pride in low taxes and low expenditures, in small government that maximized individual freedom and allowed business minimal restraint. Democrats as well as Republicans sang the praise of small government and local and individual responsibility. Schricker was a Democrat but of the old style rather than the New Deal. Speaking about the sesquicentennial to the Indiana Society of Chicago, the governor celebrated Indiana territorial history as "a continual struggle for greater self-government and local responsibility." Consequently, the state was "not planning a lavish and costly celebration which will light up the sky for a few days and then burn out. Rather it is stimulating local organizations in every county to promote community observance of this important anniversary." In a radio address Schricker proclaimed that the people of the Indiana Territory were "possessed of courage and enterprise and self-reliance." The pamphlet given visitors to the caravan claimed that Indiana pioneers "planned for themselves, they did for themselves." Praise of inexpensive and small government extended to the celebration's conclusion. At the Sesquicentennial Commission's last meeting in December 1950, Peckham announced that the American Association for State and Local History had just honored the commission with its Award of Merit. Governor Schricker was doubtless proud of the award, but he seemed more eager to add, according to the minutes, "his thanks to the members for having served without compensation, for having raised their own funds, and for having ended an eventful program without a deficit." That was the Indiana way, celebrated in 1950, as the Sesquicentennial Commission adjourned *sine die*.[9]

The sesquicentennial of the Indiana Territory was, as historical commemorations go, an unusually impressive one, a combination of serious historical scholarship, of opportunities for citizens to see and think about their past, and of entertaining and even silly nonsense. And like all commemorations it was about the present as much as the past, about 1950 as much as 1800. It was also a commemoration that tended to celebrate rather than analyze, to simplify rather than confuse with ambiguity, to minimize the conflicts of the past in favor of a happy consensus. Indiana's ethnic and racial tensions, for example, were dismissed in 1950 with the claim that the state was "a melting pot" so that various immigrant and racial groups "today are all Indianians, . . . and the **composite hoosier** has emerged as a typical and thorough American."[10]

The particular focus and limited scope of the 1950 celebrations are indeed specific to time and place in reflecting their cold war setting and anti–New Deal government parsimony. But in other ways the 1950 commemoration was part of the long-standing and traditional presentation of early Indiana history. Looking more broadly at that history, there are four issues that have commonly gotten lost or twisted in our celebrations, our books, our memories—issues of central importance that were swept under the carpet and ignored or treated as inconsequential in 1950 and earlier.

The Savage Indian

The first and most familiar of these issues is the portrayal of Native Americans. In traditional presentations of Indiana's past Indians sometimes were simply ignored. A historical marker in Jennings County, for example, commemorates the Grouseland Treaty Line of 1805 by stating simply that the land was "opened . . . for settlement." This common phrase, "opened for settlement," is one of the more incomplete, misleading, and frequent historical statements. A booklet prepared for the 1950 territorial sesquicentennial asserted that the territory north and west of the Ohio River "was then inhabited by a few Frenchmen and British garrisons." The writer, who was probably Dorothy Riker, surely knew that others had lived there before the French and British and still did in 1800. Native Americans often got lost in the hurry to get Hoosier pioneers onto the land.[11]

When Native Americans were acknowledged as actors in the historical drama they often were presented as objects standing in the way of inevitable progress, barriers of resistance to be removed. The Hoosier Heritage Caravan brochure asserted simply that "with the surge of incoming settlers, land had to be taken from the Indians by forced treaties."[12] Such bald statements of inevitability served to close off discussion. So did simple portrayals of Indians as savages.

A key event in the taking of land was George Rogers Clark's winning of Fort Sackville in 1779. No event is more celebrated in Indiana history than this "Conquest of the West," formalized in stone and bronze in the Clark Memorial dedicated in 1936. One fascinating piece of that campaign got lost in most celebrations, however. When the British lieutenant-colonel Henry Hamilton refused to surrender, Clark's men brought four captured Indians before the fort. On Clark's order his men brutally tomahawked the Indian prisoners, scalped them, and flung their bodies into the Wabash River. For several days blood stained the plaza in front of the fort. Traditional accounts, such as Hubbard Madison Smith's *Historical Sketches of Old Vincennes: Founded in 1732*, published in 1903, tell this story only from Clark's point of view, not Hamilton's and certainly not the Indian warriors, who Smith dismissed simply as "murderers." There was no acknowledgment that tomahawking bound prisoners might itself be considered murder. Clark was, in fact, an Indian hater, a warrior himself uninterested in seeking compromise with Indians, incapable of understanding the possibility of a middle ground between different peoples, mixed and intermingled. It was them or us, inevitably, unthinkingly. The irony, as historians Bernard W. Sheehan and Richard White have pointed out, is that Clark himself could often be the savage, as cruel and fearless as any, giving the war whoop and bloodying his hands as well as the best of Indian warriors. The other player at Fort Sackville was Hamilton, the "hair buyer general." Traditional accounts are dualistic in giving Clark heroic qualities and ascribing to this British officer the same ignoble qualities as the savages. Vincennes historian John Law in his 1839 account, *The Colonial History of Vincennes:*

Under the French, British and American Governments, painted Hamilton as "a cruel, heartless and savage monster."[13]

Law's 1839 history of Vincennes points to another common theme in traditional accounts of Native Americans. Progress was preordained because "the weak yielded to the strong." Indian tomahawks, Law wrote, have been "converted into plough-shares, and in a few years more the race will be extinct. Such is the inevitable destiny of the red man on this continent." Law, interestingly, added a sentiment less common in his day: "Truly, as a nation, we shall have sad reckoning in the court of Heaven for the injustice done to the red man."[14]

The Lazy French

More complicated than Native Americans are the French. Indeed, the French remain the great unknown peoples of Indiana's early history. If traditional accounts dismissed the Indians as savages, the French were worse. They were lazy. They did not understand democracy. They mixed with Indians. In his address to the Vincennes Historical Society in 1839 Law asserted

French House, Vincennes.

that the French at Vincennes "were devoid of public spirit, enterprize, or ingenuity; were indolent and uninformed." But "the race is nearly extinct; they have become amalgamated with another people," and "the laws of civilization, as sure as the laws of nature, will force them to yield to the manners, habits, customs, dress and language, of their more powerful neighbors."[15] A later Vincennes historian elaborated on these negative character traits. According to Henry S. Cauthorn, writing in 1901, "labor was distasteful" to the French for they had no "desire to accumulate worldly goods and possessions." Instead they had a love of "ease and pleasure." Horse racing, cockfighting, and dancing were their pleasures. Cauthorn, like many historians, focused on dancing, the sounds of which were "more frequently heard than that of the loom or the anvil." Such became the standard view of the French, captured in the 1950s in Lockridge's popular junior high school Indiana history textbook: the French "in their happy-go-lucky, easy going ways . . . took little more thought of the morrow than their savage associates."[16]

Historians know a bit more about the French now. White shows us how generally successful the French were in creating a common ground, a middle ground, for living relatively peacefully with Native Americans, for engaging in mutually beneficial exchanges of fur, sex, and protection, for living with permeable boundaries, for living, we might say today, as a pluralistic or multicultural society. It was this middle ground that disintegrated when Clark and the Americans came with their notions of individual landownership, liquor trade, and propensity for violence. There was little middle ground to be found in Vincennes by the 1780s.[17]

Carl J. Ekberg's recent book, *French Roots in the Illinois Country: The Mississippi Frontier in Colonial Times*, shows that these "lazy" folks actually produced enough agricultural goods not only to feed themselves but also to ship large quantities, especially of flour, to New Orleans. And they produced this surplus with a land system radically different from the American system. Their open field agricultural practices actually worked well not only as an economic system of production but as community anchor, part of creating what Ekberg concludes was a "remarkable degree of local autonomy" in the villages of the Illinois Country. The new Americans had little understanding and no interest in this European-style cooperative and communal system. In 1807 Jonathan Jennings wrote disparagingly from Vincennes of "the French, who cultivate in Common. Their Customs are often very ridiculous and grating to the feelings of an American." What Jennings did not see was the social cohesion that came from the village and open-field system and that helped make, for example, for a very law-abiding people who were most adverse to physical violence. This was not so for the Americans. With their coming, violent crimes of murder and rape increased greatly. So too did dueling. No wonder the French viewed the Americans as ruffians, prone to drunkenness and fighting, finding particularly revolting the American penchant for eye gouging. This French system of open fields and common pastureland quickly gave way in Vincennes and other French communities of the Illinois Country to the American system of individual landownership and dispersed settlement and to American notions that connected individual property ownership with self-reliance and individual freedom.[18]

Commemorators of Indiana's early history seldom acknowledged the existence of this European way of life. Even less frequently did they assess its possible merits in comparison to the familiar and easily celebrated American way, to even consider that the French enthusiasm to dance on a summer evening along the Wabash might suggest a community with some merit. Perhaps the French at Vincennes offer a case to compare the ongoing American tension between individual and community. Even as gifted a historian as John D. Barnhart, who in his 1953 book *Valley of Democracy: The Frontier versus the Plantation in the Ohio Valley, 1775–1818*, presented many of the separate pieces of Ekberg's more recent book, could not get inside the French village culture to compare it clearly with that of the American conquerors. Seeking instead the origins of American democracy in the Indiana Territory, Barnhart, like earlier writers, quickly disposed of the French by emphasizing how undemocratic they were. He never explained just why the frontier environment that so efficiently transformed Americans into democrats did not do the same for the poor French. Barnhart's was the standard brush-off of the French. These innocent and childish people came under American rule, according to Law, "without a murmur and without a thought of the future." The French habitant simply "shrugged his shoulders, and gave an additional whiff from his pipe," as he said, "'*Tout le meme chose.*'"[19]

The Silent Slave

A third problem was slavery. Slavery was particularly troublesome in historical commemorations devoted to freedom and democracy because all around, past and present, were issues of race. Race never withered away like the French or Indians. There was no denying the fact that there were slaves in the Indiana Territory, even that William Henry Harrison himself was a slaveholder—as were such notables as Luke Decker and Thomas Posey. Jacob Piatt Dunn, Jr.'s superb book published in 1888 carefully built a case that in the Indiana Territory slavery was "the great central matter of controversy to which all other questions were subordinate." Dunn's scholarship got only limited play in territorial commemorations, however, which commonly soft-pedaled the fact and meaning of slavery. A Vincennes Chamber of Commerce account published for the Clark Memorial dedication in 1936 celebrated the "gentility" of Harrison's Grouseland, where "through the windows stately music often mingled with the crooning songs of negro slaves." Traditional portrayals offered a brief acknowledgment that there were black servants, sometimes even called slaves, but then jumped quickly to democracy and progress and the victory of the Jonathan Jennings faction in territorial politicking. That victory is, of course, most significant, since among the Jennings group's goals was eradication of slavery from the territory. Building on the Northwest Ordinance of 1787, the men around Jennings did indeed drive a nail into that coffin.[20]

But traditional celebrations of the victory of antislavery democrats over proslavery aristocrats seldom examined white assumptions regarding African Americans. The Indiana Territory was most certainly a government of, by, and for white men. It was and still is appropriate to celebrate the fact that this government came to include all white men, not just those men of property. But celebrations of this great achievement left little space to examine the place of women and none to examine the place of African Americans. Dunn's detailed and sophisticated analysis of the politics of slavery seldom hinted at the life of slaves themselves and at one point even asserted that "they were all treated kindly." There was no place for African-American Hoosiers in the various commemorations of the Indiana Territory. The only acknowledgment of race in the Hoosier Heritage Caravan of 1950 was a statement that "Negroes found sanctuary here," in Indiana, an assertion contradicted by long-term commitments of white Hoosiers in the territory and state to keep blacks, whether slave or free, out of Indiana.[21]

The Democratic Pioneer

Native Americans, French, and free and enslaved African Americans were integral parts of the Indiana Territory but were seldom acknowledged in the various commemorations. The spotlight was always on the heroic white pioneers. These central actors, the early Hoosiers who built farms and homes and pushed for more democratic government, surely deserved a place in the spotlight. But here too there were critical issues that stayed in the dark. In particular, the self-interest, even greed, that wound through so much of Indiana's territorial history was often ignored. Celebrations commemorated freedom-loving pioneers without examining the causes and consequences of their drive to get ahead as landowners and speculators, merchants, and officeholders. There were few hints that the allure of the market for land and goods, an allure these early Hoosiers so eagerly felt, could be cruel and costly not only to Indians, French, and African Americans, but even to white pioneers. Motives thought more noble than market capitalism were featured instead, cast in terms of freedom and democracy. The possible costs of pioneer-style capitalism raised issues too ambiguous and too contested. Historical commemorations assuredly did not lead citizens to think hard about economic inequalities, power-seeking elites, male-female relationships, or degradation of the natural environment. Rather, the simple associations of individual freedom and democracy were far more pleasing, perhaps especially to the political and economic leaders in charge of historical commemorations. The corporate support deemed necessary to the 1950 sesquicentennial not only suggests the anti-Communist and anti–New Deal tendencies but also the lessened likelihood of raising questions about negative consequences that might have followed in the wake of land-hungry pioneers.[22]

Our historical commemorations of the Indiana Territory tended to be limited in perspective, particularly in perspectives other than those of the claimants to victory, the white pioneers.[23] They highlighted a simple and uncontested past in bold outline, with none of the ambiguity and subtlety that is the real stuff of history and of life. Others, the losers, were ignored or presented as cardboard figures. Issues central to our lives today, above all pluralism, were seldom imagined. The story is one of straight-line progress, celebrating pioneer victories and demonstrating how indebted we are to those first Hoosiers and how far we have come since those beginnings.

The Hoosier Heritage Caravan of 1950 told important stories, stories still worth telling. The same is true of the George Rogers Clark Memorial, the territorial capitol, Grouseland, the *Western Sun* print shop, and other forms of remembering our past in Vincennes and across Indiana. We must remember, however, that all of these stories and historic places were selected by earlier generations. Their choices and their silences shape our memory and our sense of the past. We must not be neutral receptors of their particular version of the past even if they carved it in stone or cast it in bronze. Each generation must decide what the Clark Memorial or the bicentennial of the Indiana Territory mean. Commemoration is always an ongoing dialogue between past and present.

Notes

1. For an introduction to scholarship on commemoration, see John R. Gillis, ed., *Commemorations: The Politics of National Identity* (Princeton, N.J.: Princeton University Press, 1994).

2. Curtis G. Shake, *The First Capitol of Indiana Territory (1800–1813) and of the District of Louisiana (1804–1805)* (Vincennes, Ind.: The Territorial Hall Committee, Vincennes Fortnightly Club, 1934) and "Final Report of the Indiana Territory Sesquicentennial Commission," n.d., Indiana Territory Sesquicentennial Commission, 1949–1951, Indiana Historical Bureau General Files, box 3a, Indiana State Archives, Commission on Public Records, Indianapolis (hereafter cited as ITSCP); Minutes of the Indiana Territory Sesquicentennial Commission, 9 Dec. 1949, box 3a, ITSCP.

3. Howard Peckham, letter to Rome Osburn, 27 Apr. 1950, box 3a, ITSCP; Minutes of the Indiana Territory Sesquicentennial Commission, 17 Feb., 28 June 1950, ibid.; Shake, "Final Report of the Indiana Territory Sesquicentennial Commission."

4. The Hoosier Heritage Caravan, brochure, photographs, and itinerary, box 3a, ITSCP; *Chicago Tribune*, 9 July 1950; *Indianapolis Star Magazine*, 20 Aug. 1950.

5. Vincennes Program, 1–4 July 1950, box 3b, ITSCP; Peckham, letter to Curtis G. Shake, 28 Feb. 1950, box 3a, ibid.

6. Shake, "Final Report of the Indiana Territory Sesquicentennial Commission"; *Territorial Days of Indiana, 1800–1816* (Indianapolis: Indiana Territory Sesquicentennial Commission, 1950); Hoosier Historical Institutes, 1950, brochure, box 3a, ITSCP; Henry Schricker speech, "Theater Guild on the Air," radio program, Gary, 7 May 1950 and Indiana Society of Chicago, press release, 3 Feb. 1950, drawer 163, box B, Henry Schricker Papers, Indiana State Archives; Indiana Society of Washington, D.C., program, 19 Feb. 1950, box 3b, ITSCP; R. Carlyle Buley, *The Old Northwest: Pioneer Period, 1815–1840*, 2 vols. (Indianapolis: Indiana Historical Society, 1950); Gayle Thornbrough and Dorothy Riker, eds., *Journals of the General Assembly of Indiana Territory, 1805–1815*, Indiana Historical Collections, vol. 32 (Indianapolis: Indiana Historical Bureau, 1950).

7. Hoosier Heritage Caravan brochure; *Chicago Tribune*, 9 July 1950; Peckham to Osburn. There were some regulations on business in the Indiana Territory, including a very high tax on billiard tables. See John D. Barnhart and Dorothy L. Riker, *Indiana to 1816: The Colonial Period*, The History of Indiana, vol. 1 (Indianapolis: Indiana Historical Bureau and Indiana Historical Society, 1971), 413, 416.

8. *Indianapolis Star Magazine*, 20 Aug. 1950, p. 5; *Indiana Telephone News* 40 (Aug. 1950): 2. In planning Indiana's celebration, Peckham drew on the experience of the American Freedom Train, which toured the country from 1947 to 1949 and included a stop in Vincennes in July 1948, and the New York Freedom Train. Joseph J. Stahl, letter to Peckham, 6 Apr. 1950, box 3a, ITSCP; *Official Document Book, New York State Freedom Train* (Albany, N.Y.: Distributed by the New York State Library, 1950); Richard Day, *Vincennes: A Pictorial History* (St. Louis: G. Bradley Publishing, 1988), 175; Stuart J. Little, "The Freedom Train: Citizenship and Postwar Political Culture, 1946–1949," *American Studies* 34, no. 1 (spring 1993): 35–67; Michael Kammen, *Mystic Chords of Memory: The Transformation of Tradition in American Culture* (New York: Alfred A. Knopf, 1991), 572–81.

9. Henry Schricker, speech to the Indiana Society of Chicago, 11 Feb. 1950, box 3a, ITSCP; Schricker speech, "Theater Guild on the Air"; Hoosier Heritage Caravan brochure; Minutes of the Indiana Territory Sesquicentennial Commission, 8 Dec. 1950, ITSCP.

10. Hoosier Heritage Caravan brochure. For evidence that Wisconsin, in its sesquicentennial celebration of statehood in 1948, devoted considerably more attention to ethnic diversity, see John Bodnar, *Remaking America: Public Memory, Commemoration, and Patriotism in the Twentieth Century* (Princeton, N.J.: Princeton University Press, 1992), 139–49.

11. Historical Marker information and list. See Indiana Historical Bureau web site, http://www.statelib.lib.in.us/www/ihb/ihb.html; *Territorial Days of Indiana*, 1.

12. Hoosier Heritage Caravan brochure.

13. Bodnar, *Remaking America*, 123–25; Bernard W. Sheehan, "'The Famous Hair Buyer General': Henry Hamilton, George Rogers Clark, and the American Indian," *Indiana Magazine of History* 79 (Mar. 1983): 22–23; Richard White, *The Middle Ground: Indians, Empires, and Republics in the Great Lakes Region, 1650–1815* (New York: Cambridge University Press, 1991), 375–76; Hubbard Madison Smith, *Historical Sketches of Old Vincennes: Founded in 1732* (Indianapolis: Press of Wm. B. Burford, 1902), 51; Judge [John] Law, *The Colonial History of Vincennes: Under the French, British and American Governments* (Vincennes: Harvey, Mason and Co., 1858), 67. For an overview of scholarship on Clark, see James Fisher, "A Forgotten Hero Remembered, Revered, and Revised: The Legacy and Ordeal of George Rogers Clark," *Indiana Magazine of History* 92 (June 1996): 109–32.

14. Law, *Colonial History of Vincennes*, 92, 93.

15. Ibid., 17, 18.

16. Henry S. Cauthorn, *A History of the City of Vincennes, Indiana from 1702 to 1901* (Terre Haute, Ind.: Moore and Langen Printing Co., 1902), 41; Ross F. Lockridge, *The Story of Indiana* (Oklahoma City: Harlow Publishing Corp., 1951), 38–39. For a more subtle, invidious comparison between Americans and French, see *Territorial Days in Indiana*, 3. Jacob Piatt Dunn, Jr., found the French living "contented, careless lives," but Dunn devoted more serious attention to their culture than most early writers. Jacob Piatt Dunn, Jr., *Indiana: A Redemption from Slavery* (1888; reprint, Boston: Houghton Mifflin Co., 1905), 102. See also Andrew R. L. Cayton, *Frontier Indiana* (Bloomington and Indianapolis: Indiana University Press, 1996), 45–60.

17. White, *Middle Ground*, especially, 421–33.

18. Carl J. Ekberg, *French Roots in the Illinois Country: The Mississippi Frontier in Colonial Times* (Urbana: University of Illinois Press, 1998), 82–88, 211–12, 239–63 (quotation on p. 240, Jennings quote on p. 256). See also Ronald L. Baker, *French Folklife in Old Vincennes* (Terre Haute: Indiana Council of Teachers of English and Hoosier Folklore Society, 1989).

19. John D. Barnhart, *Valley of Democracy: The Frontier versus the Plantation in the Ohio Valley, 1775–1818* (Bloomington: Indiana University Press, 1953), 161–63. Barnhart's strong Turnerian commitments contributed to his pull toward the conquering pioneers. Law, *Colonial History of Vincennes*, 128, 129.

20. Merrily Pierce, "Luke Decker and Slavery: His Cases with Bob and Anthony, 1812–1822," *Indiana Magazine of History* 85 (Mar. 1989): 31–49; *Historical Vincennes* (Vincennes, Ind.: Vincennes Chamber of Commerce, 1936), 21; Dunn, *Indiana*, 442.

21. Dunn, *Indiana*, 431; Hoosier Heritage Caravan brochure; Emma Lou Thornbrough, *The Negro in Indiana before 1900: A Study of a Minority* (Bloomington and Indianapolis: Indiana University Press, 1993), 1–30. Eric Hinderaker, *Elusive Empires: Constructing Colonialism in the Ohio Valley, 1673–1800* (Cambridge: Cambridge University Press, 1997), 268–70.

22. See Cayton, *Frontier Indiana*; Nicole Etcheson, *The Emerging Midwest: Upland Southerners and the Political Culture of the Old Northwest, 1787–1861* (Bloomington: Indiana

University Press, 1996); Andrew R. L. Cayton and Peter S. Onuf, *The Midwest and the Nation: Rethinking the History of an American Region* (Bloomington: Indiana University Press, 1990); John Lauritz Larson, "Pigs in Space, or, What Shapes America's Regional Culture?," in Andrew R. L. Cayton and Susan E. Gray, eds., *The American Midwest Essays on Regional History* (Bloomington: Indiana University Press, 2001).

23. For an exception, see Elmer Holmes Davis, *Old Indiana and the New World: Address at the Opening of the Library of Congress Exhibition Commemorating the Territory of Indiana, November 30, 1950* (Washington, D.C.: Library of Congress, 1951). Davis's address is an interesting and unusual analysis of change in Indiana and of ambiguity, suggesting that the territorial pioneer foundations have little relevance for the present. The catalog for the Library of Congress exhibition is more traditional. See *Indiana: The Sesquicentennial of the Establishment of the Territorial Government* (Washington, D.C.: Government Printing Office, 1950).

Race, Democracy, and the Multiple Meanings of the Indiana Frontier

by

ANDREW R. L. CAYTON

THE HISTORY OF THE INDIANA FRONTIER HAS ALWAYS BEEN CONTESTED. As the people who lived in the Wabash valley in the late eighteenth and early nineteenth centuries struggled to turn their collective experiences into self-serving explanatory stories, so have historians labored to analyze and revise those stories to reflect the concerns of their own times. The conquest of trans-Appalachian North America by citizens of the United States—the single most important development in the history of the continent—remains controversial because we cannot agree on its larger significance. In conversation, in print, in museums, in movies, in song, and on occasions such as the bicentennial anniversary of the Indiana Territory, we invest the history of American frontiers with a variety of meanings that are often contradictory. No issues are more central to these discussions than the complex relationship between democracy, broadly understood as popular participation in government, and race, or identity rooted in perceived physical differences. Together they embody the best and worst of the American experience: Democracy reflects our desire to respect the dignity of all human beings, while race usually demarcates the limits of American idealism. Democracy is as theoretically inclusive as race is exclusive.

However our frontier histories diverge, most ultimately return to questions about the ways in which human beings organize and understand themselves and to a plot that considers both the benefits and costs of the rapid replacement of one kind of world with another. Common to every history of the Indiana frontier is the indisputable fact that life in the state in 1820 was vastly different from what it had been in the territory only thirty years earlier. Rarely in human history have so many people transformed a physical and human landscape so thoroughly and so quickly as white Americans transformed the Wabash valley between the 1790s and the 1820s. And yet different people have told the story in different ways and have invested it with multiple meanings. If we agree on most of the facts of the transformation, we have not always agreed on how or why it happened, and we have agreed even less on its legacy.

Two hundred years after the creation of the Indiana Territory, many Americans lament the fact that the residents of the Wabash and Ohio valleys were unable to devise some means of accommodating each other. Recoiling from their brutality and intolerance, we regret their inability to create some kind of common ground, to sustain some degree of mutual respect. The fact that the transformation of diverse frontiers into American states involved the elimination of Indians, the subjugation of African Americans, and the marginalization of the French and the Spanish appalls us. But that tragedy should not prevent us from considering the degree to which the problem of what we call multiculturalism was on the minds of prominent inhabitants of the Indiana frontier. Indeed, their failure to create a world that promoted rather than discouraged diversity was a failure of execution rather than of imagination.

Many people on all sides were interested in finding some kind of accommodation. The main difficulty was an eternal one: how to balance respect for others with respect for the integrity of one's own culture, how to take different religions, customs, and beliefs seriously without advocating a cultural relativism in which all ways of living were acceptable. Convinced of the moral superiority of their ways of life, some Americans and some Indians nonetheless sought to understand each other, to develop empathy, to find a way to live both in their own ways and with each other.

48

By and large we do not take such efforts seriously. Our reluctance to do so rests on more than our knowledge of what happened to Indians, the French, and African Americans. It also reflects a larger transformation in thinking about diversity in the early Republic. In that period an enlightened curiosity about other peoples and the possibility of universal understanding was giving way to romantic ideas of a strong link between particular kinds of people in particular kinds of places with particular kinds of behavior and beliefs. More specifically, a fumbling toward a world in which educated people could imagine multiple perspectives receded before a growing exaltation of the glories of specific races, nations, and states. In the nineteenth century, historians and other interpreters of the past reduced the moral complexities of the Indiana frontier into a straightforward narrative of the triumph of white male Americans over supposedly inferior peoples.

The Significance of Sympathy

The immediate origins of the Indiana Territory lay in the pressing challenges posed by the great distances and exploding population of the eastern section of the Northwest Territory, which in its entirety stretched from the Ohio River north to the Great Lakes and west to the Mississippi River, covering the present-day states of Ohio, Indiana, Illinois, Michigan, Wisconsin, and a part of Minnesota. Since the 1780s and especially since the Treaty of Greenville in 1795 established a border with the Indians more than one hundred miles north of the Ohio River, the number of Americans living in the river valleys of what is now southern Ohio had increased dramatically. Some of these settlers, particularly those from Virginia, were eager to form an autonomous state and escape from what they saw as the corrupt and unrepresentative territorial government headed by Arthur St. Clair. Governor St. Clair and his allies, on the other hand, wanted to maintain federal control of the region north of the Ohio River for as long as possible and were, therefore, opposed to immediate statehood. Both groups supported the division of the Northwest Territory into smaller units.

Where territorial residents differed was over how many new ter-ritories should be created out of the existing one. Governor St. Clair called for at least three, on the premise that none would soon have enough people to qualify for statehood. His critics wanted two ter-ritories so that the growing number of residents of the eastern one could immediately apply for admission to the United States. They carried the day. On 7 May 1800 the United States Congress passed legislation dividing the Northwest Territory and forming the Indiana Territory. The act proclaimed, "That from and after the fourth day of July next, all that part of the Territory of the United States Northwest of the Ohio river which lies to the westward of a line beginning at the Ohio, opposite to the mouth of Kentucky river, and running thence to Fort Recovery, and thence north until it shall intersect the territorial line between the United States and Canada, shall, for the purposes of temporary government, consti-tute a separate territory, and be called Indiana Territory."[1] On 13 May President John Adams appointed twenty-seven-year-old William Henry Harrison as governor of the new territory. And within three years Ohio became the seventeenth member of the United States.[2]

By drawing borders for the new territory and giving the space within those borders a name, the U.S. government was defining a place with fewer than five thousand American residents. The cre-ation of the Indiana Territory was an act of imperial hubris on a grand scale. The American claim to the region rested on the 1783 Treaty of Paris, which, by ending the American War for Independence, had established a border between the United States and British Canada; on the 1794 Jay Treaty between Great Britain and the United States, which confirmed those borders; and on Virginia's and Connecticut's cessions of their claims to land in the Northwest Territory. But the creation of the territory blithely ignored the wishes of the Indian, French, and African peoples who had lived along the Wabash River since the middle of the eigh-teenth century. Congress had not even consulted with American set-tlers in the Ohio valley. The United States arbitrarily organized a landscape called the Indiana Territory, which would in 1816, shorn of its western half (Illinois), morph into the state of Indiana.

Acting with an enlightened confidence in their ability to bring order out of chaos and civilization out of savagery, American leaders could not envision a world any better than one founded on the principles enunciated in the Northwest Ordinance of 1787. The Northwest Ordinance lauded the supremacy of the United States, the legitimacy of republican government, and the idea that people eventually would be able to form states that would take their place in the American Union on an equal basis with the original thirteen. It also stressed commitment to the material and moral development of the region, achieved through the establishment of institutions such as schools, churches, courts, and the like and through a general spirit of improvement that would soon create a world of commerce and industry, towns and cities, all linked into the vital economic and political networks of the early Republic.

The most famous (or notorious, depending on one's perspective) expression of this vision was President Thomas Jefferson's summary of "our policy respecting the Indians" in an 1803 letter to Governor Harrison. Jefferson proclaimed, "Our system is to live in perpetual peace with the Indians, to cultivate an affectionate attachment from them, by everything just and liberal which we can do for them within the bounds of reason, and by giving them effectual protection against wrongs from our own people." At the same time, however, Jefferson noted that the United States wished "to draw them to agriculture, to spinning and weaving. . . . When they withdraw themselves to the culture of a small piece of land, they will perceive how useless to them are their extensive forests." The Native Americans, Jefferson suggested, would then sell their lands "from time to time in exchange for necessaries for their farms and families." The idea was for the government to sell goods to Indians at the lowest possible price, thus driving away private traders and eventually putting Indians so far in debt that they would have to part with their lands as payment. "In this way our settlements will gradually circumscribe and approach the Indians, and they will in time either incorporate with us as citizens of the United States, or remove beyond the Mississippi. The former is certainly the termination of their history most happy for themselves; but, in the whole course of this, it is essential to cultivate their love." Surely, Jefferson argued, the Indians now knew that "we have only to shut our hand to crush them."[3]

The popular brief translation of Jefferson's letter is that Indians were welcome within the United States to the extent that they became like Americans. If they traded hunting for farming, if they accepted the legitimacy of American governments and American institutions, they could, in theory, live in peace. Scholars doubt the sincerity of Jefferson's promises. Despite his appeal for affection, he resorted to force when necessary. In the words of the anthropologist Anthony F. C. Wallace, Jefferson's "was a geopolitical vision not so much of an empire that embraced a diversity of nations, races, and cultures as of an ethnic homeland, European in origin and spirit, agrarian in economy, governed by republican institutions derived from old Anglo-Saxon and even pre-imperial Roman model."[4]

Wallace is right about the consequences of Jefferson's rhetoric but not about his intentions. The attitudes of men such as Jefferson and Harrison were rooted in an eighteenth-century Anglo-American world that emphasized emotion as much as reason. They, like many of their contemporaries, prided themselves on their politeness, on their ability to deal with other human beings in a respectful fashion. A cult of politeness had developed in Great Britain in the early eighteenth century, in no small part as a response to urban life and to the brutalities of the seventeenth century. "The aim of politeness," writes the historian John Brewer, "was to reach an accommodation with the complexities of modern life and to replace zeal and religious bigotry with mutual tolerance and understanding."[5] The means to this end were reading, talking, and thinking with other men. Gentlemen practiced self-control and learned good taste through the rituals of public life. Earning the respect of other people was a matter of performing well in their presence. Polite behavior without an audience was like a child without a parent to offer rewards or punishments.

As Brewer indicates, a central concern of this rise in what some have termed gentility was learning to sympathize with other human beings, even those with whom one disagreed. One of the great themes of Anglo-American history in the seventeenth and eighteenth centuries is the growing regularity of contact with "others," people who were visibly different.[6] By the 1700s some people were endeavoring to overcome their natural repulsion from difference, to find a way to deal with others politely. But overcoming hostility toward, or fear of, difference was not easy; it required hard work. The payoff was not just tolerance but an improved world. Richard Steele, one of the editors of the newspaper *The Spectator*, described his call for contributors from all walks of life as an effort to "give a lively Image of the Chain of mutual Dependence of Humane Society, [to] take off impertinent Prejudices, enlarge the Minds of those, whose Views are confined to their own Circumstances."[7]

While these ideas originated in western Europe, they quickly influenced Europeans in North America who aspired to the status of gentlemen in no small part by trying to do what writers in newspapers and journals such as *The Spectator* told them to do. French settlers in the Wabash and Mississippi valleys in the eighteenth century imported books from Paris and other European cities and had their own version of polite, salon culture in the villages of Kaskaskia, Vincennes, and Kekionga.[8] After the American Revolution, leading citizens of the United States wrote often about the necessity of emotional connections with other people. In 1796, while praising letters "as substitutes for conversation" among neighbors, the Connecticut physician-poet Elihu Hubbard Smith denounced selfishness. "We are not made for ourselves alone," he wrote in his diary, "but for each other; for all. For the benefit of all, therefore, should our lives, our thoughts, our energies, be employed; and each act much be pronounced good or bad; only in proportion as it promotes the welfare of all."[9]

This need for emotional connection, this need to emphathize with other peoples, was integral to an enlightened citizen's identity as a polite person, worthy of the respect and deference of others. Of course gentlemen and women were primarily interested in other gentry; people they saw as "savage" were not accorded the same degree of respect or interest. Still, out of a feeling of necessity, enlightened Anglo-Americans extended genteel behavior to people who were not their peers. Dealing with others was not simply a pose (although it was that); it was also a moral and social imperative.

"While we are in the world," urged a writer in the *Kentucky Gazette* in 1790, "we must converse with the world." The writer advised that "all mankind, indeed, are our brethren, and we are interested, in their pleasures and pains, their sufferings, or their deliverances throughout the world. Accounts of these should produce in us suitable emotions which would tend to the exercise of different virtues, and the improvement of our tempers. We should accustom ourselves hereby to rejoice with those who rejoice, and mourn with those who mourn."[10]

This was the intellectual and emotional context in which Jefferson wrote his letter to Harrison. He was not lying; he was not creating a rhetorical smoke screen to obscure the use of brutal power. Jefferson and Harrison had persuaded themselves that they were operating with the purest of intentions. They wanted affection to dominate the relationship between Americans and Indians; they wanted trade to flow smoothly, carrying not just goods but ideas. Above all, they wanted the Indians to enjoy the blessings of civilization, which they saw as a harmonious brotherhood of men united in the cause of peace and prosperity and the general improvement of mankind. Jefferson, like many leading Americans, was trying to feel for and understand the plight of the Indians. His sympathy was as genuine as it was ethnocentric and paternalistic.

In some ways we hold Jefferson and company to incredibly high standards. We expect them to do what almost no other human beings have been able to do consistently; that is, to concede that the basic principles around which they are organizing their society were false and to accept the perspective and the values of peoples whom they were defeating in battle. Their sin in our eyes is their commitment to their vision of the world, the fact that they believed in themselves, for better or worse. If their failure lay in their inability to imagine a world of multiple perspectives, they were hardly unique in the history of this planet.

But fail they did. We know that the history of the conquest (and that is indeed what it was) of Indiana was brutal, that it involved deception and viciousness, and that American frontiersmen and women were often downright nasty.[11] So where is the benefit in emphasizing the efforts, and largely rhetorical ones at that, of

American leaders to destroy Indian cultures politely, to empathize with those whose lands they were taking and whose people they were killing? First, it lies in the fact that as people tried (and mostly failed but tried nonetheless) to rise above brutality, they helped create the moral language with which we criticize them today.[12] And second is that, try as they might, European Americans at all levels simply could not overcome their fear, and thus their hostility, to people of color. It was hard enough to reach an accommodation with other Europeans whose languages and religions were exotic. But to overcome color was almost impossible.

In fact, in the early Republic, at precisely the time of the conquest of the Indiana Territory, Americans began to transform the rhetoric of enlightened sentimentality into romantic racism. Emotion remained at the core of their conception of the relationships among people. But for a variety of reasons, ranging from the French Revolution to African Americans' assertiveness during and after the American Revolution to the need to justify the removal and near extermination of American Indians, the ideal of a universal community of human beings, structured around polite exchanges and mutual respect, disintegrated. In the early nineteenth century the world seemed darker and less tameable. It produced Frankensteins and Napoleons. And people were better off not only in sticking with their own kind but in celebrating their differences. Uniqueness, not universality, became the goal. Americans—like Germans, Scots, and others—celebrated themselves. As the age of Jefferson gave way to the age of Jackson, fear triumphed over affection, and Indians simply had to go.

Developing a Plot

Nineteenth-century Americans developed what amounted to an official history of the Indiana Territory, complete with a plot, characters, and themes that underscored the inevitability of the transformation of a few scattered, ragged villages of Indians, French, and Virginians into an organized state of towns, farms, businesses, and institutions. In the sixteen years that elapsed between the creation of the territory and the creation of the state, thousands of white

Americans moved to the land north of the Ohio River, west of the Ohio line, and east of the Wabash River. They defeated Indians, displaced French settlers, established towns, roughed out farms, cut down forests, laid out roads, decided to uphold the Northwest Ordinance's prohibition on slavery, and secured a democratic form of government for themselves and their posterity. Like the histories of most American territories, it is a tale remarkable in the speed and thoroughness with which Americans both revised the world and made that revision seem inevitable. How could it possibly have happened differently? More than military, demographic, or economic, the American conquest of the Wabash valley was not complete until it seemed perfectly legitimate, until large numbers of people accepted it as the only logical and natural explanation of what was happening. It was all to the good; whatever the costs, Indiana was a better place in 1816 than it had been in 1790.

The conquest of Indiana required a story that justified its outcome. Integral to the persuasiveness of this tale was the dismissal of alternative narratives. Acquiring legitimacy did not mean an erasure of competing stories, but it did require their appropriation within the official story. Most obviously, these counternarratives came from Indians. In telling the story of frontier Indiana, historians and novelists have been surprisingly fair in their inclusion of nonwhites. Indeed, Indiana storytellers have given the Shawnee Tecumseh and his brother Tenskwatawa a disproportionate share of time on the stage of Indiana frontier history. As we know from records kept by American officials, Indians saw the story of the Indiana Territory very differently. They did not doubt that things were changing. Indeed, the creation of the Indiana Territory was another nail in their coffin, nothing less than the end of the world as they knew it. The story unfolding along the Wabash was a tragedy, not a triumph, involving the loss of land and influence. The Indian history of the region was no less fictional than that of the Americans. The Indians claimed, on occasion, to have lived there from "time immemorial, without molestation or dispute," which was hardly the case. Most Indians had been in Indiana for less than a century and had fought with one another, not to mention the French and the British, for decades. Still, when the Miami leader

Little Turtle claimed at the Greenville negotiations in 1795 that "the print of my ancestors' houses are every where to be seen in this portion," he was speaking the truth.[13]

By 1800 Little Turtle had become a leader among Indians seeking some sort of accommodation with the Americans. Others were not so pliable as he, however. Most prominent in opposing the American meaning of the Indiana Territory were the Shawnee brothers Tenskwatawa and Tecumseh. The former, known as the Prophet because of his leadership of a religiously based resistance movement, saw the history of the region as conquest, not progress. He urged Indians to return to supposedly traditional ways, not to wear European clothes or eat European food or live like Europeans. According to Tenskwatawa, the Master of Life denied ever giving life to the Americans. The British, French, and Spanish might be all right. But the Americans were "the children of the Evil Spirit," who had sprung "from the scum of the great Water when it was troubled by the Evil Spirit. . . . They are numerous, but I hate them. They are unjust. They have taken away your lands, which were not made for them."[14] The Prophet was more accommodating when he met with Governor Harrison in Vincennes in August 1808. In fact, he enunciated what may sound like a multicultural version of Indiana's future. Harrison heard him argue that "we ought to live agreeable to our several customs, the red people after their mode and the white people after theirs."[15]

Tenskwatawa was calling for tolerance at a distance, not acceptance of diversity. His was a vision of segregation, not integration. Indeed, the intense nativism among the Shawnee and Delaware in the early nineteenth century paralleled the growth of romantic racism among European Americans. The Prophet was breaking with the eighteenth-century model of contact points such as Kekionga and Vincennes where Indians and Europeans mingled and misunderstood each other. The Wabash valley had been multicultural in the 1700s. No longer. Now, not only whites but Indians saw themselves as unique and were unwilling to sacrifice the core beliefs of their society. This Indian nativism, according to historian James Wilson, whose recent book *The Earth Shall Weep: The History of Native America* is dedicated to retelling the history of North America from

Indian perspectives, amounted to "a new *racial* consciousness: nativists identified themselves as members not merely of specific tribes but of a 'red race' which was in fundamental opposition to the invading 'white race.' "[16]

In August 1810 Tecumseh defied Harrison at a meeting on the lawn of Grouseland, Harrison's home in Vincennes. With the governor's family watching from the house and surrounded by dozens of armed men, the Shawnee recited his version of the history of the Indiana Territory. The French had behaved well, treating Indians like their children and giving them presents. The British were less admirable. But the Americans were the worst of all. They cheated and deceived Indians on a regular basis. Americans were unworthy of friendship or respect. "[Y]ou have taken our lands from us and I do not see how we can remain at peace with you if you continue to do so." Responsibility for the troubles along the Wabash lay with the Americans. They had "force[d] the red people to do some injury. It is you," Tecumseh told Harrison, "that is pushing them on to do mischief. . . . You are continually driving the red people when at last you will drive them in the great lake where they can't either stand or work." Tecumseh was not afraid to use the whites' own history to defy them. Warning that the Americans would create "great troubles among us" if they tried to settle Indian land, he asked how the Indians could "have confidence in the white people." After all, "when Jesus Christ came upon the earth you kill'd and nail'd him on a cross, you thought he was dead but you were mistaken."[17]

The Significance of Characters

This Indian version of Indiana frontier history was defeated at Tippecanoe. But it did not die there. To the contrary, it has had remarkable staying power and informs much recent scholarship on the history of the region. If Tecumseh and Tenskwatawa lost the war of weapons, they remain important figures in the war of words. We quote and requote them. Scholars, novelists, and playwrights honor their perspective all the time. Almost no one thinks of talking about Indiana in the early 1800s without talking about Tecumseh. Does this triumph of perspective eliminate the pain and suffering experienced by native peoples? Does it give them back their land? No, of course not. Ironically, however, it is evidence that they have not been erased from the history of the region. Indians, romanticized and given motives they would never recognize, nonetheless are at the core of an important counternarrative that seems particularly popular with those Americans who perceive the federal government as intrusive in their own lives. As large numbers of citizens at the turn of the twenty-first century increasingly question the fundamental conception of their government as the embodiment of the people, they identify ever more intensely with past victims of federal imperialism whose defense of home and land was overrun by an unrelenting federal government. Tecumseh functions less as a real historical figure (do even his most ardent admirers wish that he had won?) than as the symbol of resistance to the efforts of unlimited authority to rob people of their way of life.

In fact the tendency of frontier history is not to ignore Indians but to use them as narrative foils to praise or condemn white Americans and their governments. Perhaps this inclusiveness results from the fact that the Wabash valley was literally at the center of European and Indian conflicts in eastern North America from the middle of the eighteenth to the early nineteenth century. Perhaps it is a product of the inherent drama of the meetings between the larger-than-life figures such as Tecumseh and Harrison. Whatever the reason, scholars of the Indiana frontier cannot be accused of ignoring the importance of Indians.

In the early twentieth century Indiana University professor Logan Esarey made Indians key players in his monumental two-volume work *A History of Indiana from Its Exploration to 1850.* Readers cannot accuse Esarey of erasing the history of the Miami, Shawnee, Delaware, or Potawatomi. But they can accuse him of condescension and of using the Indians to inflate the achievements of white settlers. The Indians who appear throughout his narrative are "primitive" peoples incapable of reason or organization. Above all, they are dangerous foes. Certain that "more humane treatment would have subdued their haughty pride and converted the whole tribe [of Miami] into valuable citizens," Esarey was mostly interested in persuading his readers that Indians in 1800 "were a savage folk who massacred women and children, drank the blood of their victims, and made merry as they burned their captives at the stake. More white men have been tortured at old Kekionga than at any other place in the State."[18]

Like a host of historians before him, Esarey invested the defeated with formidable qualities because triumph over a tenacious and talented enemy is more glorious than victory over a scattered and demoralized one. As Shakespeare justified the reign of Henry VII and the Tudors by writing about their flawed but formidable predecessors, so Indiana's historians made the American triumph more spectacular by emphasizing what they had overcome to achieve it. There is nothing mysterious about this process; the producer of every action movie knows that the villain must be at least as interesting as the hero.

Since the 1960s a new generation of historians has reversed this story. These historians tell the same tale of American victory, but they do so from the perspective of the Miami, the Delaware, the Shawnee, and others. Indians in these stories are complex figures who are celebrated in sophisticated ways for their resistance to American efforts to destroy them. But they, like the Americans, are divided and confused in their attempts to explain what was happening. Why were they unable to stop the Americans? In the 1960s historian Reginald Horsman offered detailed studies of Indian relationships with the British government in the late eighteenth and early nineteenth centuries, showing that Indians were not pawns but active participants in their own lives.[19] In the 1980s R. David Edmunds led an effort among historians to retell the story of the Indiana frontier from the perspective of Indians in his biographies of Tenskwatawa and Tecumseh.[20] Harvey Lewis Carter followed with a careful biography of the Miami chief Little Turtle.[21] Most recently, John Sugden has given us a detailed biography of Tecumseh.[22] For all the work of historians, no one has done more to emphasize the importance of Indians than the novelist Allan Eckert.[23] These books all honored the Indians by taking them seriously. The Shawnee Prophet in particular has been rehabilitated as a figure of intellectual and emotional power who was able to offer some Indians for a period of time an alternative vision of their future. And Little Turtle has emerged as one of the central players in the history of the Northwest Territory. Whether in fact or fiction, or in the middle ground between the two genres, Indians are no longer pawns but sophisticated human beings who, contrary to Esarey, made intelligent choices about what to do and how to do it.

In the 1990s Richard White and Gregory Evans Dowd went even further. They wrote books suffused with a sense of loss and tragedy, detailing Indian efforts to sustain their world in the face of massive demographic and military incursions. Some Indian nativists, Dowd demonstrated, blamed their demise on their own people, on their failure to observe the proper rituals of power, on their eagerness to accept American goods and American promises.[24] In Dowd's story of internal anguish and division, Indians are ambiguous, perplexed, often frightened people trying to hold on to some scrap of meaning as their world disintegrates around them. How else could one survive the human whirlwind that swept through the Wabash valley between the 1790s and the 1810s? It was a nightmare that was over almost as soon as it began.

In by far the most sophisticated and moving of the new histories, White described the Great Lakes region in the eighteenth century as a world of multiple misunderstandings, of the intersection of different peoples in a kind of middle ground of misperception that allowed Indians and French to function in close contact with each other. This world fell apart in the second half of the eighteenth century, disrupted and destroyed by commercial capitalism and the vast hordes of encroaching Americans. The region became violent, nasty, and brutal. In White's book the Americans are definitely the villains. Backcountry settlers are labeled "Indian haters." White recognizes a fundamental truth of cultural collision on the frontier, which is that Americans at all levels wanted to create borders where the Indians and French had blurred them. It was critical to murder and mutilate, to dismiss any possibility of accommodation or agreement, to insist that a line be drawn between civilized Europeans and the savage "others."[25] More than anything else, Indians were people for white Americans to define themselves against. They wanted no part of a middle ground. "The progress of events," concludes the historian Eric Hinderaker, "increasingly polarized the residents of the [Ohio] valley into two distinct groups, defined by race and driven to violence in the defense of their interests."[26]

The Americans' propensity for defining themselves against Indians only intensified in the twentieth century. Historians and audiences wanted to admire Indians who seemed like whites. Edmunds and White have noted that Tecumseh has become the most well-known symbol of Indian resistance because he was constructed as something close to a white man.[27] He was a bold, defiant, intelligent, and dignified foe whose character affirmed the moral truth of the ultimate American victory.[28] Tecumseh plays in the Indian wars of trans-Appalachian North America the same role as Rommel in World War II, Lee and Jackson in the Civil War, and Hannibal in the Carthaginian Wars. Here, we might say, is a great man whose defeat could have come only at the hands of a great people. Or here, we do say, is a man whose nobility lingers in our imaginations precisely because he did not win. If Tecumseh had managed the impossible, that is, to turn away the Americans and keep Indiana for Indians, one wonders whether he would be quite so popular with audiences today.

Meanwhile, historians seem utterly baffled by the ostensible hero of the story: the Virginia-born William Henry Harrison. What to make of this competent, intelligent young man who rode his fame as an Indian fighter to Congress and the White House? Harrison is the ultimate success story of the early Republic. Unlike most territorial officials, he survived his term as an appointed governor without compromising his higher political ambitions. This was no mean achievement, and we should acknowledge Harrison's considerable personal skills, especially his ability to remain ambiguous even in the most delicate of situations. How many appointees of John Adams managed to keep their office when Thomas Jefferson assumed the presidency in 1801? Still, it is precisely Harrison's lack of commitment and absence of passion, both of which were crucial to his rise in American government, that makes his historical reputation minor compared to that of the defeated Tecumseh. We admire people who are willing to risk everything for what they believe in as long as they are no longer any threat to us. Poor Harrison, however. He comes across as a bland and minor federal functionary in the work of the new Indian historians. For White, the villain is the flamboyant George Rogers Clark, who never lacked for strong opinions and outrageous behavior. But Harrison, no. Not only did he seem like a trimmer, when he did declare himself on an issue, he came down on what many think of as the wrong side twice, once with the Indians and once with African Americans.

For those who have presented the history of the Indiana Territory as part of a larger American progress toward democracy, Harrison's lack of enthusiasm for popular government and his support for de facto slavery have made him a decidedly problematic character. Esarey thought him "one of the best territorial governors ever sent out by the United States."[29] Jacob Piatt Dunn, Jr., was more ambivalent, suggesting that he was an "honest" but not a "great" man, one whose "influence, aside from this matter of slavery, was for the good of the commonwealth."[30] John D. Barnhart, perhaps the most eloquent advocate of the democratic significance of the Indiana Territory, refrained from directly criticizing Harrison the proslavery aristocrat. While Barnhart disliked Harrison's politics, he wrote of him that he "remained quite popular, perhaps in part because he was public spirited and above much of the petty politics which accompanied the larger struggle" for democratic government.[31] Ironically, however, Harrison's lack of "greatness"—the characterization of him as a decent, honest man doing his job as well as he could in juxtaposition with the extraordinary figure of Tecumseh—reinforces the larger moral of American triumph. For that victory was not the work of one extraordinary man, of a Caesar or a Cromwell, but of the essential justice of the American cause. It was inevitable, and no one person was decisive one way or another in the progress of a free people.

Slavery and Hoosier Democracy

Like Indians, African Americans have figured in histories of the Indiana Territory to the extent that they tell us good or bad things about whites. Even as they complicate the theme of inevitable progress, they affirm its major moral that things turned out for the best. Indeed, some Hoosier historians have suggested that the white citizens of the state benefited from the challenges raised by the presence of African Americans as well as Indians. This pattern is most obvious in their treatment of slavery.

Whites had enslaved blacks in the Wabash valley since the middle of the eighteenth century. Many American settlers, including Governor Harrison, were interested in continuing the practice. Article 6 of the Northwest Ordinance of 1787, however, forbade the introduction of slavery or indentured servitude north of the Ohio River. Nonetheless, in 1802 citizens convened at Vincennes to petition Congress for permission to own slaves. They did not succeed. But their portrayal of the antislavery clause as a restriction on their freedom as Americans "to enjoy their property" where and how they saw fit was only the opening salvo in a campaign to keep slavery in Indiana.[32] In 1805 the territorial legislature argued that toleration of the "evil" and "repugnant" institution of slavery would benefit the region economically and would diffuse slaves throughout the nation rather than concentrate them dangerously in one region. Meanwhile, the territorial government authorized what amounted to slavery; an 1803 "Law concerning Servants" required all "negroes and mulattoes" who arrived in the territory as contractually bound servants to fulfill their contracts or face punishments ranging from physical beatings to an extension of service. Other people were explicitly forbidden from interfering with these contracts.[33] Masters had to take care of their servants. They could not sell their contracts without permission, and courts were required to hear complaints of poor conditions. By treating all blacks as indentured servants, the Indiana Territory was merely upholding contracts arranged in other states. The legislature further solidified de facto slavery in 1804 by giving white masters sixty days to arrange for indentures; blacks who refused them would be returned to their original state. Finally in 1806 legislators adopted a slave code replete with severe restrictions on the movement and actions of black servants. In short, as Paul Finkelman concludes, the territorial government "gave legal recognition to slavery in the territory and provided the mechanisms to control the institution."[34]

Within a few years, however, a "popular party" repudiated and defeated the proslavery faction. Pressing for statehood, members of the party attacked the slave-owning pretensions of the governor and his allies. Their victory ensured the 1816 Indiana Constitution's permanent ban on slavery as something that "can only originate in usurpation and tyranny."[35] In 1820 the state supreme court ruled that the constitution freed all enslaved African Americans living in Indiana and in 1821 declared that adult blacks could not be held as indentured servants without their permission. By 1830 there were only three slaves left in the territory.[36]

More than a century ago, while detailing these developments, Dunn argued in *Indiana: A Redemption from Slavery* that "the slavery of Indiana, small as was its actual extent, was the chief agency in the moulding of our infant growth. . . . It was the tap-root of our political growth,—the great central matter of controversy to which all other questions were subordinate." Dunn's prodigious research demonstrated conclusively that there was strong support for slavery among leading residents of the Indiana Territory. But this was not a story about hypocrisy, nor one told from the perspective of blacks. The moral of Dunn's account was the triumph of men who had learned from their flirtation with sin. When Indiana became a state, he wrote, its citizens were "more strongly opposed to the institution of slavery than they ever could have been without it." Writing in the shadow of the Civil War, Dunn wanted Americans to do "justice . . . to an almost forgotten generation of Indiana men" who had "saved Indiana from slavery."[37] In other words, Dunn's story of race commended the moral fiber of noble white men. African Americans figure only as pawns in this tale, not as active people who made their own history.

More recently, Finkelman has used the same evidence to indict territorial leaders as proslavery hypocrites who sought to evade the Northwest Ordinance of 1787 in order to forward their own personal agendas. Where Dunn would have us see the triumph of the popular party as a progressive moment, Finkelman wants us to recognize the limits of democracy. Indiana became an autonomous state and a white man's paradise. Attacks on aristocracy and on blacks went hand in hand. Indeed, racial prejudice lay behind much of the antipathy to slavery. Whites did not want blacks in Indiana; their racial solidarity inhibited the growth of ethnic and class tensions in the state.

In an 1808 report to the territorial assembly, General Washington Johnston revealed the extent to which he and his peers were less worried about the impact of the institution on blacks than they were about its effect on whites. Johnston was anxious about how the presence of slaves would undermine white society. Slavery, he warned, would impede the development of industry and equality. In a free state men would honor labor because it would not be associated with degraded blacks. As important, "the man of an independent spirit" would find that "no proud nabob can cast on him a look of contempt." "How long," he wondered, can "the Political Institutions of a People admitting slavery . . . be expected to remain uninjured, how propper a school for the acquirement of Republican Virtues, is a state of things wherein usurpation is sanctioned by law, wherein the commands of Justice are trampled under feet . . . the habit of unlimited domination in the slave holder will beget in him a spirit of haughtyness and pride productive of a proportionabl habit of servility and dispondence in those who possess no negroes . . . the Lord of three or four hundred negroes will not easily forgive and the mechanic and labouring man will seldom venture a vote contrary to the will of such an influential being."[38]

Dunn's contention that the successful struggle against the introduction of slavery served to make Indiana a better place for white democracy merely echoed Johnston's remarks. In the end, slavery was prohibited in Indiana less because it was a moral wrong than because of its baleful effect on white Americans. No wonder that the achievement of democratic statehood in Ohio, Indiana, and Illinois was quickly followed by black codes, which severely restricted the movement of African Americans north of the Ohio River.[39] No wonder those who did migrate to "free" states tended to congregate in relatively isolated rural settlements or near sympathetic whites such as Quakers.[40] Or that the 1851 Indiana Constitution went so far as to forbid blacks from living in Indiana. One delegate to the constitutional convention linked Indians and blacks with an extreme proposal; he thought "in all sincerity, and without any hard feelings toward them—that it would be better to kill them off at once, if there is no other way to get rid of them. We have not come to that point yet with the blacks, but we know how the Puritans did with the

Indians, who were infinitely more magnanimous and less impudent than this colored race."[41] The lives of blacks had become little more than evidence in an ongoing debate about the nature of democracy. Like Indians, their primary function was to temper the American character and draw the borders of American democracy.

The comment of the delegate brings this story of the Indiana frontier full circle. As with Indians, so with blacks. Indiana's citizens, like many Americans, transformed the Enlightenment's ideal of universal liberty into a romantic notion that explicitly tied democracy to race. By the 1850s many Hoosiers suspected that it was the absence of both Indians and African Americans that made Indiana, like the other states of the Old Northwest, distinctive. By the 1860s they were certain of it. What better way to explain the morality of their conquest of the slaveholding, aristocratic, decadent South? The Hoosier soldiers who followed Ulysses Grant and William Tecumseh Sherman through Tennessee, Mississippi, Georgia, and the Carolinas during the Civil War did so confident that democracy flourished in particular places and among particular kinds of people. They fought for the Union, for the United States, for Indiana. The Jeffersonian ideal of universal brotherhood based on affection and empathy was long gone.

At the end of the day, Hoosier storytellers were not interested in asking universal questions or talking about the need for affection and understanding across cultural divides. They were in the business of creating borders, not erasing them. They were defining Indiana. They wanted to construct a local tale, one that struck an emotional chord with the residents of Indiana and not the world, one that allowed Hoosiers to stroll the banks of the Wabash River or look at a monument in an Indiana town or contemplate the terrain of Tippecanoe and see the peculiar origins of the unique world in which they lived. Constitutions and congressional acts legally created the state of Indiana. But Indiana did not become a community until its citizens developed a romantic conception of it, until they began to believe that what had happened in that special place had made them who they thought they were. Never mind whether it was good or bad, whether it was triumph or tragedy. Never mind if it betrayed the vision of Jefferson as well as Tecumseh. The story was theirs, and the legacy of conquest was their right to tell the story as they wished.

Notes

1. Charles Kettleborough, *Constitution Making in Indiana: A Source Book of Constitutional Documents with Historical Introduction and Critical Notes,* Indiana Historical Collections, vol. 1 (1916; reprint, Indianapolis: Indiana Historical Bureau, 1971), 41–42.

2. Quoted in John D. Barnhart and Dorothy L. Riker, *Indiana to 1816: The Colonial Period,* The History of Indiana, vol. 1 (Indianapolis: Indiana Historical Bureau and Indiana Historical Society, 1971), 311–12. See also Andrew R. L. Cayton, *Frontier Indiana* (Bloomington: Indiana University Press, 1996), 167–96 and *The Frontier Republic: Ideology and Politics in the Ohio Country, 1780–1825* (Kent, Ohio: Kent State University Press, 1986); Donald J. Ratcliffe, *Party Spirit in a Frontier Republic: Democratic Politics in Ohio, 1793–1821* (Columbus: Ohio State University Press, 1998).

3. Thomas Jefferson to William Henry Harrison, 27 Feb. 1803, *Thomas Jefferson: Writings,* ed. Merrill D. Peterson (New York: Library of America, 1984), 1117, 1118. The classic study of Jeffersonian benevolence is Bernard Sheehan, *Seeds of Extinction: Jeffersonian Philanthropy and the American Indian* (Chapel Hill: University of North Carolina Press, 1973).

4. Anthony F. C. Wallace, "'The Obtaining Lands': Thomas Jefferson and the Native Americans," in *Thomas Jefferson and the Changing West: From Conquest to Conservation,* ed. James P. Rhoda (Albuquerque: University of New Mexico Press, 1997), 38.

5. John Brewer, *The Pleasures of the Imagination: English Culture in the Eighteenth Century* (New York: Farrar, Straus and Giroux, 1997), 102.

6. Andrew R. L. Cayton and Fredrika J. Teute, "On the Connection of Frontiers," in *Contact Points: American Frontiers from the Mohawk Valley to the Mississippi, 1750–1830,* eds. Andrew R. L. Cayton and Fredrika J. Teute (Chapel Hill: University of North Carolina Press, 1998), 1–15.

7. Quoted in Brewer, *Pleasures of the Imagination,* 104.

8. John Francis McDermott, "The Enlightenment on the Mississippi Frontier, 1763–1804," *Studies on Voltaire and the Eighteenth Century* 26 (1963): 1129–44 and "French Settlers and Settlements in the Illinois Country in the Eighteenth Century," in *The French, the Indians, and George Rogers Clark in the Illinois Country: Proceedings of an Indiana American Revolution Bicentennial Symposium* (Indianapolis: Indiana Historical Society, 1977), 3–33.

9. Elihu Hubbard Smith, *The Diary of Elihu Hubbard Smith,* quoted in David S. Shields, *Civil Tongues and Polite Letters in British America* (Chapel Hill: University of North Carolina Press, 1997), 318. See also Richard L. Bushman, *The Refinement of America: Persons, Houses, Cities* (New York: Alfred A. Knopf, 1992), and Steven C. Bullock, *Revolutionary Brotherhood: Freemasonry and the Transformation of the American Social Order, 1730–1840* (Chapel Hill: University of North Carolina Press, 1996).

10. Quoted in David Waldstreicher, *In the Midst of Perpetual Fetes: The Making of American Nationalism, 1776–1820* (Chapel Hill: University of North Carolina Press, 1997), 110.

11. James H. Merrell, *Into the American Woods: Negotiators on the Pennsylvania Frontier* (New York: W. W. Norton, 1999).

12. I elaborate on this point in "'Noble Actors' upon 'the Theatre of Honour': Power and Civility in the Treaty of Greenville," in Cayton and Teute, eds., *Contact Points*, 235–69 and "The Meanings of the Wars for the Great Lakes," in *The Sixty Years' War for the Great Lakes, 1754–1814*, eds. David Curtis Skaggs and Larry Nelson (East Lansing: Michigan State University Press, 2001), 373–90.

13. Little Turtle, 22 July 1795, *American State Papers: Indian Affairs*, 1:571.

14. Quoted in Cayton, *Frontier Indiana*, 207.

15. Ibid., 213–14.

16. James Wilson, *The Earth Shall Weep: The History of Native America* (New York: Atlantic Monthly Press, 1998), 149.

17. Quoted in Cayton, *Frontier Indiana*, 218, 219.

18. Logan Esarey, *A History of Indiana from Its Exploration to 1850*, 2 vols. (Indianapolis: B. F. Bowen and Co., 1918), 1:78, 80, 86–87.

19. See, among several titles, Reginald Horsman, *Matthew Elliott, British Indian Agent* (Detroit: Wayne State University Press, 1964).

20. R. David Edmunds, *The Shawnee Prophet* (Lincoln: University of Nebraska Press, 1983) and *Tecumseh and the Quest for Indian Leadership* (Boston: Little, Brown, 1984).

21. Harvey Lewis Carter, *The Life and Times of Little Turtle: First Sagamore of the Wabash* (Urbana: University of Illinois Press, 1987).

22. John Sugden, *Tecumseh: A Life* (New York: Henry Holt, 1998).

23. Allan W. Eckert, *The Frontiersmen: A Narrative* (Boston: Little, Brown, 1967) and *A Sorrow in Our Heart: The Life of Tecumseh* (New York: Bantam, 1992).

24. Gregory Evans Dowd, *A Spirited Resistance: The North American Indian Struggle for Unity, 1745–1815* (Baltimore: Johns Hopkins University Press, 1992).

25. Richard White, *The Middle Ground: Indians, Empires, and Republics in the Great Lakes Region, 1650–1815* (Cambridge: Cambridge University Press, 1991), especially 383–96.

26. Eric Hinderaker, *Elusive Empires: Constructing Colonialism in the Ohio Valley, 1673–1800* (Cambridge: Cambridge University Press, 1997), 189.

27. Edmunds, *Shawnee Prophet*, 189–90; White, *Middle Ground*, 518–19.

28. Esarey, *History of Indiana from Its Exploration to 1850*, vol. 1:209.

29. Ibid., 1:183.

30. Jacob Piatt Dunn, Jr., *Indiana: A Redemption from Slavery* (Boston: Houghton Mifflin, 1888), 414, 412.

31. John D. Barnhart, *Valley of Democracy: The Frontier versus the Plantation in the Ohio Valley, 1775–1818* (Bloomington: Indiana University Press, 1953), 173.

32. Dunn, *Indiana*, 305.

33. Paul Finkelman, "Evading the Ordinance: The Persistence of Bondage in Indiana and Illinois," *Journal of the Early Republic* 9 (spring 1989): 35.

34. Ibid., 38–39.

35. Indiana Constitution (1816), art. 8, sec. 1.

36. *State v Lassalle*, 1 Ind 60 (1820); *Mary Clark, a woman of Color*, 1 Ind 122 (1821).

37. Dunn, *Indiana*, 442, 443.

38. Quoted in Cayton, *Frontier Indiana*, 247.

39. Stephen Middleton, *The Black Laws in the Old Northwest: A Documentary History* (Westport, Conn.: Greenwood Press, 1993).

40. Stephen A. Vincent, *Southern Seed, Northern Soil: African-American Farm Communities in the Midwest, 1765–1900* (Bloomington: Indiana University Press, 1999), 62–66; Joan E. Cashin, "Black Families in the Old Northwest," *Journal of the Early Republic* 15 (fall 1995): 449–75.

41. Quoted in Emma Lou Thornbrough, *The Negro in Indiana before 1900: A Study of a Minority* (Bloomington: Indiana University Press, 1993), 66–67.

Religion on the Indiana Frontier, 1679–1816:

From the Catholic Reformation to the Second Great Awakening

by

JAMES J. DIVITA

F ROM THE LATE SEVENTEENTH TO THE EARLY NINETEENTH CENTURIES, multicultural relations and religious diversity characterized present-day Indiana. New populations arrived, migrating Indian peoples had contact with European immigrants and their descendants, and the appearance of Catholicism challenged the dominance of traditional native religion. Then Anglo-Americans outnumbered the earlier residents, began to settle native land, and increased religious diversity with the introduction of Protestantism. Indiana's history shows that the state has experienced several transitional periods, but in the almost 150 years between the coming of the French explorer René-Robert Cavelier, Sieur de La Salle, in 1679 and the end of the territorial period in 1816, the lands along the Wabash experienced their first state of flux.

Because of its geographic location, Indiana became a cultural and religious crossroads. While the Spanish dominated present-day southwestern United States and the English established thirteen colonies along the Atlantic seaboard, the vast interior of the North American continent became the special reserve of the government in Versailles. La Salle made the St. Lawrence and Mississippi Rivers the backbone of the French empire, and Montreal and New Orleans became the two foci of economic and political power. The

Maumee and Wabash Rivers, linking the Great Lakes and the Mississippi, were the shortest route between these two cities. Britain successfully challenged French control of this and other river routes; subsequently, the Americans recognized the value of these river routes and demanded that the British cede all lands up to the east bank of the Mississippi.

Religion was an ordinary part of both Indian and European lives. So changes in political and military presence caused innovation in Indiana religion during this period, for these changes resulted in an interplay of various religious beliefs and practices— and thus multicultural relations. At first traditional Indian religion coexisted with the French spirit of the Catholic Reformation, but the British conquest of New France (French America) helped weaken Catholicism. After the local population chose the Americans over the British in the American Revolution and present-day Indiana passed under American control, the area was introduced to the diversity and vitality of British and German Protestantism. The beginning stages of the Second Great Awakening accompanied Indian fear of American encroachment, a fear that led to a political and military backlash with religious overtones just before the War of 1812.

Except for archaeological evidence, we know little about the Mound Builders and other Indians who resided, hunted, and traded here before the coming of the Europeans. We do know that the important Indian tribes that the French and English met south of the Great Lakes were recent arrivals. The Miami moved from present-day Wisconsin into lands southeast of Lake Michigan about the same time La Salle portaged between the St. Joseph and Kankakee Rivers at present-day South Bend. The Potawatomi replaced the Miami along the St. Joseph River and north of the Eel River by 1695, and the Miami relocated along the Maumee and upper Wabash Rivers. Farther south we find the Wea, Piankashaw, Shawnee, and Lenni Lenape. The first two tribes were Miami clans who lived on the central and lower Wabash, while the Shawnee ranged widely throughout the Ohio River valley. The English name for the Lenni Lenape, Delaware, betrayed their Atlantic Coast origin. They were the last arrivals in Indiana, settling along the White River with Miami permission after 1760.[1]

Like good hunters, fishermen, and agriculturists, these Indians believed that they should be in tune with the environment to survive; the world, however, was full of both good and evil spirits. The most feared and respected was Manitou, a spirit who could be both helpful and hurtful.[2] A shaman had to be employed to use his herbs and incantations to encourage good spirits to control the disease and sickness spread by evil spirits. To explain the past and future, many Indians related creation stories to the missionaries and believed in the existence of the Great Spirit and the Happy Hunting Ground.

The enthusiasm of the missionaries and their willingness to face personal discomfort and danger for a higher spiritual good flowed from the spirit of the Catholic Reformation. The rise of Protestantism in the sixteenth century was one of the greatest challenges that Catholicism experienced in its long history. Out of this challenge came spiritual revival and reform legislation that resulted in a morally sound and educated clergy and a greater emphasis on lay spirituality. When the great explorers of the day presented them with an opportunity for evangelization, and with a renewed Church behind them, missionaries felt called to preach the Christian message in the newly known lands beyond Europe.

The Jesuits were responsible for much of the evangelization activity in Asia, Africa, and the Americas during the Catholic Reformation. Ignatius of Loyola, a Spanish soldier who turned to religion during a time of recuperation from battle wounds, founded the Jesuits (officially called the Society of Jesus) in 1534. Members of this new Catholic religious order were known for intellectual prowess, linguistic and preaching abilities, and physical and spiritual discipline. Not only were they formidable foes of what they viewed as Protestant heresies, but they also undertook to "spread the Good News" of the redemption of Christ to all humankind. Their successes, even temporary, in lands from India, Japan, and China to Paraguay and Arizona attest to their historical place in worldwide religion.

Jesuits arrived in New France in 1625. From the time of Christopher Columbus, efforts to increase geographic knowledge, broaden commercial contacts, or extend political power also included a religious motive; explorers ordinarily included priests in their party. The Jesuit Jacques Marquette accompanied Louis Jolliet into the Illinois Country in 1673 and canoed the Indiana shore of Lake Michigan in 1675. When the Jesuit-educated La Salle sought to locate trade opportunities in the Illinois Country in 1679, he invited Franciscan Recollects to accompany him because they were more tolerant of liquor trade with the Indians than the Jesuits were. But the sons of Loyola were not far behind. In the 1680s Jesuit Claude-Jean Allouez established a mission that ministered to the Miami and Potawatomi on the St. Joseph River several miles north of present-day South Bend. Allouez was the first of several Jesuits active in the region over the next eighty years.

An estimated 2,000 Indians survived the smallpox epidemics of 1715, 1733, and 1752[3]; the 1746 census reported that 1,350 Indians were concentrated at Vincennes and Ouiatanon (near present-day Lafayette).[4] Because the Jesuits served these trading posts/forts, they could readily evangelize the Indians.

Evangelization normally began with an explanation of how the death of Jesus Christ on the cross saved all humankind from the fires of hell. Requesting baptism signified acceptance of this simple message. To communicate more complicated beliefs, missionaries had to develop a writing system and compose dictionaries in order to translate Scripture and catechisms into local languages. Particularly troublesome were rendering the mystery of the Trinity into comprehensible words and explaining the Eucharist in the context of transubstantiation to a people familiar with ritual cannibalism.

Reaction to the Jesuits was mixed. In normal times Indians received the missionary's message politely and even showed signs of accepting the Christian message. Allouez reportedly was kept up for half the night explaining his faith. Then the Indians recounted their own beliefs, which contradicted his, and expected him to reciprocate their politeness. Yet when Indians received religious medals from the missionaries, they wore them like jewelry. Because they were familiar with ceremonials, Indians were impressed with the liturgy and administration of the sacraments. The most difficult part of Christian behavior for the Indians to accept was monogamy. Normally a husband sent an unsatisfactory wife away and married another, or a wife abandoned her husband if he mistreated her.[5]

When Indians observed the behavior of *canadiens*[6] and voyageurs (itinerant trappers/traders) who also frequented the posts, the Indians were not particularly attracted to Christianity. Like the Indians, *canadiens* were well built and physically tough, but they were vigorous, witty, vivacious, somewhat dissolute, and seldom thrifty, and they strongly disliked regulation.[7] Royal officials and missionaries noted that *canadiens* differed from the French peasant and lower urban classes from which they had come. Not subject to rigid social stratification and the remnants of feudalism, these *canadiens* experienced free frontier life and were relatively affluent.

Again like the Indians, the voyageurs were not committed to monogamy. They frequently cohabited with Indian women because European women were in short supply, and cohabitation facilitated commercial links with the tribes. If a *canadien* or voyageur married an Indian woman before a priest, that union was as fragile as if he had not married in church. Yet missionaries reported that children

St. Francis Xavier Church, Vincennes

Byron R. Lewis Historical Library, Vincennes University

born of such a union, called métis, normally considered themselves part of the Catholic community.[8]

Most eighteenth-century *canadiens* may not have been saints, but to contend that they were not interested in religion or were even irreligious would be incorrect. Jesuits regularly paddled along the Maumee and Wabash to celebrate Mass, administer the sacraments, and teach the catechism. The Jesuit Jean-Charles Guymonneau probably accompanied François-Marie Bissot, Sieur de Vincennes, when the latter founded the post named after him in 1732. The Chickasaw burned Jesuit Antoine Senat along with Sieur de Vincennes in 1736. By 1749 Jesuit Sebastien Louis Meurin opened the sacramental register of St. Francis Xavier in Vincennes, Indiana's oldest Christian congregation and the state's first Catholic parish. According to this register *canadiens,* métis, Indians, and black slaves were baptized and married there.

Two events in 1763 damaged religion on the Indiana frontier. The French government condemned Jesuits as enemies of the state and ordered them expelled from its colonies. Jesuit Julien Duvernai, pastor at Vincennes, was deported after his meager possessions were seized and sold off. When the sickly Meurin reached New Orleans, he asked to return to the Illinois Country; his request was granted because he did not appear well enough to survive the voyage back to France. This ex-Jesuit was the only priest in the Illinois Country until 1768; his bad health prevented him from ever visiting Indiana again.[9]

After two centuries the epoch of the Catholic Reformation had passed, but so had French rule in North America. The first Treaty of Paris in 1763 concluded the Seven Years' (French and Indian) War between France and Britain and transferred French holdings to Britain. The treaty guaranteed freedom of worship "as far as the laws of Great Britain permit" to the new subjects of the British crown[10]; but the residents of the Illinois Country were apprehensive, because under British law a priest could be arrested for celebrating Mass. For the first several years the British permitted no one to be ordained bishop or priest, and their local officials harassed Meurin. In 1772 their military commander ordered the *canadien* population along the Wabash deported.

The faith remained alive among *canadiens* and Indians despite these misfortunes. With no priest available to visit Vincennes in the foreseeable future, some couples traveled to the banks of the Mississippi for Meurin's blessing on their marriages. Others remained at home and married by declaring before the community "in a loud voice in the church their mutual consent."[11] The lay notary Etienne Philibert officiated at such weddings and included them among the four hundred baptisms, marriages, and funerals he recorded in the parish register over the next twenty years. The *canadiens* did not show disregard for Church norms, for these procedures were acceptable if a priest was unavailable to administer the sacraments for a long period.

After entreaties from Meurin, Philibert, and several Vincennes men, the bishop of Quebec (Indiana was under his episcopal jurisdiction) appointed the newly ordained diocesan priest Pierre Gibault to the Illinois Country. Gibault visited Vincennes for the first time in 1769:

> Upon my arrival all the people came in crowds to receive me at the shore of the Wabash river. Some threw themselves on their knees without being able to speak, others spoke only with sobs; some cried, "My father, save us, we are at the edge of hell"; others said, "God has not forsaken us yet, for it is He who sends you to us to make us repent our sins." Some said, "Oh sir, why did you not come a month ago? Then my poor wife, my dear father, my dear mother, my poor child would not have died without the sacraments."[12]

For two months Gibault remained among his fellow *canadiens*. They rebuilt the log church, and he celebrated Mass for them. At their insistence, he promised—and kept the promise—to return every two years. Gibault officiated at marriages and administered the sacraments at other Wabash settlements and even at distant Michilimackinac during the 1770s.

In 1777 Gibault and the *canadiens* faced George Rogers Clark and the American threat. The British Parliament had passed the Quebec Act in 1774, which granted Catholics religious freedom and a life

GIBAULT

Father Gibault Statue
Vincennes, Indiana

under their own laws. In local minds Americans might be like the anti-Catholic *Bostonnais* and restrict the liberties of Catholics. As British subjects, should they repulse Clark's small military force and continue to enjoy the special treatment provided in the Quebec Act?

On 5 July 1778, shortly after Clark captured Kaskaskia on the Mississippi, Gibault and a local delegation personally met Clark. Among other issues, the priest asked the Virginian directly if he could conduct religious services in church. Clark answered that he

> had nothing to do with Churches more than to defend them from Insult. That by the laws of the state his Religion had as great Previledges as any other.[13]

Gibault and the *canadiens* were pleased; two weeks later the town medical doctor and Gibault persuaded the *canadiens* at Vincennes to support the American cause.

A second Treaty of Paris in 1783 transferred the Illinois Country to the new United States of America. Frankly, the coming of the Americans affected the *canadiens* and Indians even more adversely than the coming of the British twenty years earlier. Lawless American cutthroats and interlopers (nicknamed Long Knives because of their weaponry) descended on *canadien* settlements and Indian villages. With their property open to confiscation and armed violence contributing to their insecurity, a sizable portion of Vincennes *canadiens* in 1791 abandoned their ancient homes on the Wabash for a new secure life at New Madrid, Missouri, on the Spanish side of the Mississippi.

Canadien emigration reduced the number of Catholics in Indiana. Following the expatriates was Gibault, resident priest in Vincennes since 1785. Fortunately, resident and itinerant clergy continuously served the remaining faithful in Vincennes after Gibault's departure. Among them were Benedict Joseph Flaget (1792–94), future bishop whose literacy and catechism classes prefigure Catholic education in the state, and Jean-François Rivet (1795–1804), whose efforts among the Indians received financial support from the federal government. The impoverished and frequently inebriated condition of the Indians depressed Rivet. Yet he reported that even in cases of the most degraded drunkenness the mere sight of a priest clad in the garb which distinguished his profession, inspires them with a respect and even a tender affection which we cannot but wonder at.[14]

No matter what the American impact on the *canadiens*, the American impact on the fewer than ten thousand Indians resident in the Indiana Territory was greater. Until the 1790s European descendants had coexisted with the native peoples or simply ignored them except for trade purposes. Now the Americans wanted them to be civilized; that meant they should settle down and be farmers. In the early 1800s Philadelphia Quakers sent agricultural equipment to Chief Little Turtle and the Miami.[15] Even better, Americans preferred that the Indians withdraw westward. Between 1803 and 1809 Indiana territorial governor William Henry Harrison negotiated several treaties intended to clear Indians from the land. Moreover, the low price for corn encouraged Americans to make corn whiskey and sell it to Indians, who developed a strong taste for it. Indians, corrupted physically and morally by the new drink, became anti-American because the newcomers were crowding them and their way of life.

This new situation affected Indian religion. One example is the native response to Moravian evangelization efforts. Open to evangelization and following Moravian precepts unto death in earlier decades, Indians now openly rejected the Moravians' best efforts. A second example is the support of many Indians for the Shawnee Tenskwatawa (Open Door, better known in English as the Prophet), a visionary who taught a new militant, radical, Indian revivalist religion.

Moravians, Protestant pacifists who did not conform to their state church in the present-day Czech Republic and Germany, immigrated to America in 1734. They established the settlements of Bethlehem and Nazareth in Pennsylvania and Salem in North Carolina. Struggling to evangelize Indians in Georgia, Pennsylvania, and Ohio, they were most successful among the Delaware. American revolutionaries, however, attacked neutral Moravians and their Indian converts in eastern Ohio in 1782 because they would not fight the British in support of independence.

Undaunted, Pennsylvania Moravians sent three of their number to witness Christ among the Delaware, who resided in nine villages along the west fork of the White River. Abraham Luckenbach, John Peter Kluge, and Kluge's wife, Anna Marie Ranke, arrived near present-day Anderson in 1801. Chief Tedpachsit invited his young people to go and hear the Word of God; distrust of outsiders, too much contact with American traders, and "horrid drink," however, always handicapped the mission. Only a handful of Delaware ever lived with the missionaries. Some of the sick people the missionaries nursed were baptized, but Luckenbach reported that after five years, only two healthy Indians chose to be baptized. Even trusted converts consulted shamans.[16]

The Moravian mission, however, was significant enough to attract the ire of the Prophet. A reformed alcoholic, he reported in 1805 that the Master of Life communicated to him through visions. He claimed to know all about the past and present and that he was able to drive away evil spirits. The Prophet preached that Indians should be kind to kinfolk and each other, stop drinking and being violent, and abandon promiscuity and polygamy for monogamous marriage. Fire would torture sinners, and they would never enjoy heaven.[17]

Sufficiently knowledgeable about Catholic beliefs and practices, the Prophet called the evil spirit "the Great Serpent" (recalling the incident in the Garden of Eden). Followers confessed their sins to him and were reconciled when they would "shake hands with the Prophet." During this ritual he presented them with a string of beans, somewhat reminiscent of the rosary, and told them that the beans "were made of the flesh of the Prophet." They would gently draw the string through their hands while promising to remain faithful to his teachings. Once converted, new believers were obligated to go to another village and spread the new faith.[18]

The Prophet realized how easily he could engender emotion and enthusiasm among his listeners. He insisted that the corruption and weakness of the Delaware and Shawnee before the Long Knives stemmed from their having forgotten or betrayed their spiritual traditions. Believers must follow the proper, ancestral rituals; missionaries, then, undermined Indian culture. The Prophet's followers took Chief Tedpachsit to the Moravian mission, tomahawked him, and threw him half-alive into the camp fire. They accused the Moravians' Indian interpreter of being an evil spirit, tomahawked him, and burned him too.[19] In fear for their lives, the missionaries soon abandoned Indiana.

In 1808 the Prophet and his warrior brother Tecumseh departed their White River location and moved to Prophetstown at the confluence of the Wabash and Tippecanoe Rivers just upstream from present-day Lafayette. Because of the constant inflow of American settlers, Governor Harrison then decided to acquire more land from accommodating chiefs through the Treaty of Fort Wayne in 1809. Because the combination of the Prophet's religious influence and Tecumseh's military capabilities provided the major opposition to pioneer expansion in northern Indiana, the governor had to contend with both of them. On 20 August 1810 Tecumseh met Harrison in Vincennes, upbraided him for not treating Indians as the French king had, and sarcastically linked his lack of confidence in Americans with the suffering and death of Christ.

> If you will not give up the land and do cross the boundary of your present settlement it will be very hard and produce great troubles among us. How can we have confidence in the white people when Jesus Christ came upon the earth you kill'd and nail'd him on a cross, you thought he was dead but you were mistaken.[20]

After the unsatisfactory Harrison interview, Tecumseh spent months visiting other tribes in order to persuade them to form an Indian confederacy against the Americans. While Tecumseh was absent, Harrison and a small army departed Vincennes to attack Prophetstown. In November 1811 the Americans engaged the Prophet's outnumbered warriors in the Battle of Tippecanoe. Harrison defeated the Indians, but 20 percent of his force became casualties. The Prophet had promised his warriors victory; rain and hail, he said, would dampen the Americans' gunpowder. It rained only slightly, however, and the disgraced Prophet departed for

British Canada. The defeat of the Prophet and Harrison's burning of Prophetstown showed that traditional Indian religion could consolidate native resistance to American settlement but that armed force was necessary for effective resistance.

By 1800 Americans were moving from Virginia, the Carolinas, Kentucky, and Pennsylvania into the Indiana Territory. This westward movement brought Indiana into the Protestant religious orbit of the former thirteen colonies.

The American Revolution (1775–83) had a direct effect on religion in the new United States. Before the Revolution the British king was the supreme governor of state churches in the southern colonies; Puritanism dominated New England. Between them lay the religiously tolerant Pennsylvania of the Quakers. Only two colonies, Virginia and Rhode Island, did not collect taxes to support a state church. In Maryland, a colony founded by Catholics, Catholics were disenfranchised. After the Revolution the Church of England (Episcopal Church) lost its official status from Maryland to Georgia, in New England a move to disestablish the Congregational Church occurred in three states, and in Maryland at least propertied Catholics were permitted to vote. Congregationalists and Presbyterians emerged as the two major religious bodies, but Deism was rampant. Religion did not seem to be significant in the lives of the population, for only 5 to 10 percent of adults held formal church membership.[21]

The Revolution popularized the concept of egalitarian democracy and religious freedom. Article 1 of the Northwest Ordinance of 1787 provided for religious freedom in the Illinois Country.

> No person demeaning himself in a peaceable and orderly manner shall ever be molested on account of his mode of worship or religious sentiments in the said territory.[22]

The First Amendment to the United States Constitution, ratified in 1791, was interpreted as providing state encouragement for Christianity as long as it was not incompatible with the private right of conscience and freedom of religious worship (1833).[23]

Soon after the Revolution, settlers from North Carolina, Virginia, Maryland, and Pennsylvania swept through the

Courtesy of the McLean County Historical Society

Rev. Peter Cartwright

Appalachians into the central counties of Kentucky, the most productive agricultural area in the country. Religion was surely needed
to stabilize frontier society, for depravity reputedly characterized
the pioneers. Missionaries ordinarily reported drunkenness, gam-
bling, adultery, lying, stealing, Sabbath violation, and lascivious
dancing. Methodist circuit rider Peter Cartwright described the

Kentucky of his youth as the abode of "murderers, horse thieves, highway robbers, and counterfeiters."[24] Easterners were particularly impressed with the no-holds-barred contest in the West, where quarreling men did not strike but immediately sought to gouge out eyes and bite off pieces of nose or ear.[25] On the other hand, westerners appeared God-fearing and believed in the sinful nature of humankind (including themselves). Yet they did not attend the few churches that existed.

Frontier emphasis on individual freedom and equality and the impact of personal acts exacerbated the two-centuries-old theological debate over predestination. The great sixteenth-century French/Swiss reformer John Calvin believed that God determined who would be saved by bestowing his grace and that individuals predestined to damnation could do nothing to change their fate. The seventeenth-century Dutch theologian Jacobus Arminius thought that God would save all who believed in him, but that because of individual free will, redeeming grace could be resisted because actions established conditions for salvation or damnation.[26]

Arminius's views on freedom and turning away from sin fitted the needs and environment of the pioneers and contributed to the notion of opening oneself to God's grace at a "revival." The Second Great Awakening arose in central Kentucky, the major center of religious revivalist activity west of the mountains.[27] Fiery preachers rekindled interest in religion; earnest laymen witnessed to their faith and were quickly enlisted to multiply the ranks of the ministers.

Central to frontier revivalism was effective preaching at camp meetings. Scottish Presbyterians had traditionally gathered for several days once or twice a year to listen to sermons stressing repentance and the need for forgiveness of sins in Christ before celebrating the Lord's Supper.[28] The camp meeting descended from this practice. Two Presbyterian ministers were early great revivalists. James McGready, son of Ulster immigrants, preached in Logan County, Kentucky, in June 1800. Barton W. Stone, preacher at Cane Ridge near Lexington, Kentucky, visited Logan County:

The scene to me was new, and passing strange. It baffled description. Many, very many fell down, as men slain in battle, and continued for hours together in an apparently breathless and motionless state.[29]

The revival that Stone conducted at Cane Ridge attracted an estimated twenty thousand sinners to a huge outdoor gathering. Dozens of Presbyterian, Methodist, and Baptist preachers thundered until exhaustion from a variety of vantage points (wagons to tree stumps). The revival lasted from Friday, 7 August, until Wednesday, 12 August 1801, when the food supply ran out and horses had no more grass to eat. Truly extraordinary was the religious emotion of both preachers and listeners. Jerking, rolling, barking, yelping, and swooning accompanied religious conversion. Possibly as many as three thousand were brought to the ground by the mighty power of God.[30]

The Second Great Awakening empowered the rise of evangelical Protestantism on the western frontier. Farmer-preachers and circuit riders fanned out over Kentucky. Baptist and Methodist memberships tripled within a five-year period.

Revivalism came to Indiana with settlers and preachers from south of the Ohio River. McGready himself preached in the territory before 1806 and organized churches in Washington and Clark Counties in 1816. An English traveler attended an Indiana encampment in 1819 and reported that a twelve-year-old girl leaped several times over her tallest neighbors.[31] Revivalism strengthened the practice of religion; in short order Baptists and Methodists became the largest denominations among Hoosiers.

The state's first Protestant congregation was Silver Creek Baptist Church near Charlestown, founded in 1798. A small group gathered with an elder to read, study, sing, and pray in the spirit of frontier independence and individualism. By 1802 William McCoy was regularly visiting Silver Creek Baptist Church from Kentucky. Three of his sons were also Baptist ministers in Indiana. One son, Isaac McCoy, ordained in 1810, was called to serve the small Maria Creek congregation near Vincennes. The younger McCoy dreamed of a home missions program to evangelize the Indians and thereby rejected the Calvinism of his father, who held to predestination and believed that evangelization was God's work, not man's. When Isaac McCoy began to visit churches to collect funds for the home missions, Daniel Parker of Crawford County, Illinois (northwest of Vincennes), opposed him, saying that operating missions interfered in the divine prerogative. Parker began to visit other churches too, published a pamphlet attacking the younger McCoy and his views, and became the leading antimission spokesman. Isaac McCoy and Parker divided Indiana Baptists, but McCoy persisted in his efforts despite little support in this state. He departed Maria Creek and established his first mission on Raccoon Creek north of present-day Terre Haute in 1818.[32]

In the territorial period thousands of Methodists settled in Indiana and organized a multitude of churches. Methodism originated in Britain as a force for spiritual revival in the Church of England and crossed the Atlantic just before the Revolution. Francis Asbury formalized Methodist organization in America when he assumed the title of bishop in 1785. While many Congregationalists and Presbyterians remained Calvinist, Methodists adopted a more Arminian view.[33] Asbury and the circuit riders traveled east and west, always preaching Christ to whoever would listen. Methodists established the Western Conference in Kentucky in 1796; they first preached in Indiana at Springville in Clark's Grant in 1801 and organized Old Bethel Church nearby about the same time.[34] Future bishop William McKendree preached at Charlestown in 1802, and Asbury himself visited Lawrenceburg in 1808. In his journal Asbury wrote: "In this wild there may be twenty thousand souls already. I feel for them."[35] Circuits were formed in the Whitewater valley and along the Wabash River. In 1809 Governor Harrison held a candle for William Winans so that this young Methodist preacher could read his text and sing a hymn during a night service at the fort in Vincennes.

The camp meeting was often identified with Methodism, but not all Methodists approved of its physical and emotional side. Irregularities and extravagances, they insisted, must be replaced with good order and decorum. By 1805 leaping and shouting were supplanting "the jerks." Circuit rider Cartwright, himself a spellbinding preacher, disliked the revivalist technique. His ministerial credentials were impeccable—although he was raised in Presbyterian McGready's Logan County, Kentucky, Asbury ordained him a Methodist deacon, and McKendree trained and ordained

IHS C8722

Camp meeting

him traveling elder. At an 1813 encampment in the Indiana Territory, Cartwright reported a Sunday-morning worship service where "several hundred" fell in five minutes' time and other sinners turned pale.[36] He believed that revivals were "strange and wild exercises" that could influence "weak-minded, ignorant, and superstitious persons" to go into trances, have visions, and prophesy. After consulting his Bible, he preached against jerking exercises. He sometimes "gave great offense" when he recommended fervent prayer as an effective antidote.[37] By 1820 "bodily exercises" were becoming infrequent.[38]

Indiana Presbyterianism grew primarily after the 1820s, but already in the territorial period Presbyterians were a diverse group. Traditionally they were accustomed to substantial written theology, endured long services and sermons, and strenuously kept Sunday as the Sabbath. Their ministers were expected to have formal theological education. Before 1815 the Presbyterian General Assembly commissioned eleven young theology students to travel Indiana as "horseback riders" for periods of one to four months, but their presence often resulted in cultural conflict with less-educated frontier Hoosiers. Yet Samuel Scott remained to organize Indiana Church, two miles northeast of Vincennes. Founded in 1806, it is reputedly the oldest continuous Protestant congregation in the Old

Northwest. John Dickey settled in Daviess County and William Robinson at Madison.

The Associate Presbyterians, called Seceders, were highly disciplined Scottish psalm-singers. They organized at Princeton in 1810 and formed Carmel Church outside Madison in 1812. Andrew Fulton became pastor at Carmel Church three years later.

Not all Presbyterians were put off by the noise and raw energy of revivals. In 1810 the Cumberland Presbyterians organized in Kentucky. They deemphasized predestination but stressed a strict confession of faith; they were zealous in converting sinners and advocated and conducted evangelistic camp meetings. During the territorial period, Cumberland campgrounds existed in Indiana at White Oak Springs in Pike County and Alexander Camping Ground in Dubois County.[39]

Although many recently arrived congregants were of Scotch-Irish origins, Indiana Protestantism also included German- and English-speaking members with Pennsylvania German roots. Indeed, the Second Great Awakening energized Baptists and Methodists and tested Presbyterians; however, it had little effect on immigrant religious groups during the territorial period. Among them were continental pietists like the Moravians who established the Indian mission on the White River. Those called Dunkers, because of their custom of baptizing converts by immersion three times face forward, emigrated from Pennsylvania, North Carolina, and Kentucky and settled in Clark County in 1802–3.

The United Brethren in Christ, with Reformed and Mennonite antecedents, organized in 1800 and were known for their fervid evangelism, simple piety, and stern morals. They were sometimes called Dutch (German) Methodists because they held common revivals with the larger denomination. Alsatian surgeon John George Pfrimmer arrived in Corydon from Pennsylvania in 1808. He conducted early Sunday schools in the state and organized United Brethren churches in Harrison, Floyd, and Dearborn Counties between 1812 and 1821. Pfrimmer's moral influence in the area was sufficiently great that Governor Harrison appointed him a county judge.

The Rappites were a large and significant German Protestant nonconformist group, whose leader George Rapp left Württemberg for America in 1803 to seek a place of religious freedom for his two thousand followers. In 1814 Rapp purchased thousands of acres of land along the Wabash River and founded Harmonie (present-day New Harmony) in Posey County. Rappites were known for their frugality and industry; they cleared 1,500 acres and built 150 log dwellings, a brick house for Rapp, and a large brick church. They awaited the Second Coming of Christ; meanwhile, they urged celibacy and held property in common. Internal dissent and limited business opportunities persuaded the Rappites to sell their Indiana holding and return to Pennsylvania in 1825.

The Shakers immigrated into Indiana and settled at Busro (along Busseron Creek; also called Shaker Prairie) in northwestern Knox County (1807). Similar to the Rappites, but non-German, they were celibate and pacifist, held property in common, believed in manual labor, and were good farmers and woodworkers. Looked upon as the supreme heretics in the West, they were not conventional Christians; they denied the Trinity and believed that the same Christ spirit that dwelled in Jesus of Nazareth had made a second appearance in Ann Lee, a British immigrant who founded the Shakers in America. They held that baptism was purely spiritual and advocated the gifts of healing, prophecy, and tongues. Shakers engaged in frenzied dancing and loud, joyful singing for religious purposes.

Hotly despised by their Methodist neighbors around Busro, the Shaker settlers were subjected to the fiery and effective preaching of Peter Cartwright in 1808. He sought to reclaim former Methodists, Baptists, and Cumberland Presbyterians from the snares of the Shaker "priests." (Cartwright used this inflammatory word to further discredit the Shakers.) Arriving at Busro, Cartwright launched into two three-hour sermons, calling on Shakers in his audience to return to right belief. Then he made house-to-house visits and reported that eighty-seven responded favorably.[40] After the War of 1812 Shaker numbers again declined impressively when pre-conversion children became adults and refused to submit to community discipline. The last hundred members sold their holdings and left Busro in 1827.

In its beginning stages the Second Great Awakening brought people of different denominations together, but it soon served to increase religious diversity and sharpen denominational rivalries in Indiana. Between 1810 and 1820 Methodist preachers engaged in a fierce and unpleasant controversy over infant purity and innate depravity.[41] Baptists and Methodists railed against Presbyterians for their Calvinism and called their preachers "hirelings" for accepting pay.[42] At a Whitewater Circuit gathering, Methodist preacher Robert W. Finley devoted an entire sermon to baptism rituals. Referring to Baptists' baptism, he concluded:

> I will not say that any man who baptizes by immersion is an indecent man, but I will say, he has been guilty of an indecent act.[43]

Presbyterian divisions, the Baptist "war on the Wabash" over home missions,[44] and Cartwright's confrontation with the Shakers are other examples of disagreements between and within denominations during the territorial period.

Some concluded that denominational conflict was the devil's way to weaken the cause of religion. McGready commented that "contention is one of the most subtle and effective engines of hell." No matter the controversy (predestination, final perseverance, immersion), contenders "condemn every person holding an opposite opinion" and declare that they cannot be Christians.[45] He urged all who heard his voice to adhere to their own creeds and confessions but never to make them more important than faith in Jesus Christ.[46]

Others thought Christians ought to abandon detailed statements of beliefs and stress only what the Bible sanctions. During the territorial period antiauthoritarian factions in several small congregations (usually Baptist) began this movement toward Christian unity. In the 1820s Benoni Stinson organized the General Baptists in southwestern Indiana and adjoining states in an effort to heal division caused by the home missions controversy.[47] The first congregation of the Christian Church organized in Floyd County in 1805. Seven years later four ministers served five congregations styled Christian in this state.[48] Spearheading this anticonfessional movement were Barton W. Stone and the Scottish immigrant

Alexander Campbell. By 1830 churches such as Silver Creek were dropping denominational designations from their names and joining what we know today as the Disciples of Christ, Christian Church, and Church of Christ.

Religious bodies whose core belief was not human depravity and the need for regeneration appeared to be insulated from revivalism and the effects of the Second Great Awakening, at least during the territorial period.

The Quakers emphasized the divine light of Christ within. Worship was an occasion for silent listening until a member had a prayer or experience to share. Quakers did not sing at their unstructured meetings. Their neighbors viewed them with suspicion because they were pacifists and dressed distinctively. Quakers disliked slavery on moral and economic grounds, and so they relocated from the Carolinas to Indiana because it was a free territory. Early Quakers concentrated in the Whitewater River valley as far north as Wayne County and founded First Friends Church at Richmond in 1809. Two hundred of them formed the first monthly meeting in the same year. Other Quakers settled in present-day Washington County in 1812.

The "goin's-on" at Cane Ridge were known among the Maryland Catholics who densely settled Nelson, Washington, and Marion Counties, Kentucky, after 1785. They viewed revivalism as an absurd and blaphemous fanaticism, the whole matter a sign of the weakness of Protestantism.[49] The choice of Bardstown in Nelson County as the seat of the first Catholic bishop west of the Appalachians in 1808 attested not only to a concentration of Catholic population but also to its orthodoxy. During the territorial period Pennsylvania and Kentucky Catholics were beginning to settle at Dover in Dearborn County and at Black Oak Ridge and Montgomery in Daviess County, Indiana. Although in 1814 Bishop Flaget of Bardstown was the first Catholic bishop to visit the state, no priest was assigned to reside permanently in Vincennes from 1804 to 1823.

Revivalism had little early effect on Lutherans, Unitarians, and Episcopalians. The few conservative Lutherans in Indiana had been members of the state church or residents of Pennsylvania or

North Carolina rather than Kentucky. They resided in Fayette, Union, and Harrison Counties before 1805, and Mt. Solomon Church in Harrison County and St. John in the Fayette-Union area were the first congregations founded in the state.[50] Although important in the East, the number of Unitarians and Episcopalians in the future state was negligible. Unitarians were not drawn to revivalism and were moving to a religion of enlightenment, benevolence, and rationality. They considered their views on the Trinity and Christology similar to those of "Christians" such as Stone and Campbell, but class differences were too great to encourage the groups toward union.[51] Episcopalians, not yet recovered from the blow to their membership caused by the Revolution, continued to live on the Atlantic Coast and did not organize in Indiana before 1830.

God was alive in Indiana through all the religious changes in the previous one and a half centuries. Believers in God's providence could say that even nature contributed to spiritual awareness during the territorial period. A Methodist eyewitness pointed out that shortly after the bloody Battle of Tippecanoe in 1811, from which many militiamen-settlers did not return, earthquakes emanating from the New Madrid fault hit the territory.

> The whole country became alarmed and the most vile and hardened sinners began to tremble and quake, and go to meeting, and weep and pray. . . . It seemed as if almost everybody would become religious that winter and spring.[52]

* * *

As stated earlier, Indiana has experienced several transitional periods. The first state of flux from traditional Indian beliefs through Catholicism to Protestantism (1679–1816) is not only chronologically but also historically the foundation period for Indiana religion.

The Indian and European population of eighteenth-century Indiana had appeared here almost simultaneously. Jesuit missionaries began to evangelize the Indians, but they had limited success. Maybe the legacy of Allouez and the Jesuits was not only to give Catholic roots to Indiana Christianity but also to demonstrate self-sacrifice as an expression of spiritual commitment to others.

Catholic ways influenced Indian beliefs and practices. The missionary presence gave Indians a point of reference when Indiana was transferred from France to Britain to the United States. Of course, natives were aware of ineffectiveness when the priest anointed a sick person with "bad grease" and the patient later died. Yet the religious aspect in multicultural relations reappeared when the Prophet used confession and strings of beans as part of his resistance to American expansion. Indian nostalgia continued for the "black robes." Decades later, Chief Menominee's Potawatomi were Catholic when expelled to Kansas in 1838.

Evangelization of the Indians also activated Protestants. Moravians under Luckenbach and Baptists under Isaac McCoy followed the Jesuits, but they had no greater overall success with the Indians. While Baptists established Indian missions, the question of whether the Bible sanctioned evangelization divided them for decades.

At first, religious tolerance characterized this state of flux. Catholics remained in Indiana, thanks to a British decision not to deport them and to pass the Quebec Act. Clark's statement of religious neutrality and the religious freedom article in the Northwest Ordinance at least subtracted any religious grievance against the Anglo-American newcomers.

The Catholic outmigration from Vincennes to New Madrid, caused by political and economic reasons, reduced possible tensions with Protestants during the territorial period and the early Second Great Awakening. Indiana was both sparsely populated and big enough so that both great faiths could coexist. The Catholic Church might remain "the mother of harlots," but Protestants sometimes contributed financially to Catholic church-building funds and attended notable church services to hear sermons. No confrontation comparable to Cartwright's direct attack on the Shakers marred Catholic-Protestant relations until the immigration of the Irish and Germans in the 1830s and 1840s led to the subsequent formation of the Know Nothing movement.

American settlement in the Indiana Territory sharpened religious controversy. Religious disunity within the Protestant majority heightened the tensions that fed the growth of intolerance. Some believed that contention, originating in biblical texts open to a variety of competing interpretations and resulting in different creedal statements, did not stimulate spiritual growth or facilitate personal salvation. Yet others observed that revivalism caught the attention of Hoosier frontier people and encouraged them to study the Bible and become interested in religious subjects.

Today Indiana religion is majority Protestant but strongly diversified, a characteristic already evident during the territorial period. For most believers, however, contention between Calvin and Arminius is past. In the early nineteenth century the religious counterpart of frontier freedom in thought and movement was the frequent transfer of both clergy and lay people from one church to another. The Christian Churches of Stone and Campbell were increasingly evident. "No creed but the Bible" was a generally accepted religious principle, making Protestant attitudes and services similar enough that Stone could invite parsons of other denominations to preach at Cane Ridge.

As in Kentucky, however, strong preacher personalities pushed different biblical interpretations, which led to a bewildering number of theological and doctrinal divisions. Schisms within one denomination were not uncommon and tended to endure even after the founding preachers left the scene, although the emotion around the divisive issues waned.

The Indiana Territory was able to accommodate the churched as well as unchurched, revivalists as well as antirevivalists, descendants of British colonists as well as Pennsylvania Dutch, and settlers from Virginia as well as German nonconformists such as Rappites and United Brethren. The religious intolerance that recurs in Indiana history accompanied religious diversity during the territorial period. If human beings are normally suspicious of that which is different, then periods of intolerance are the natural price we must pay for a religiously cosmopolitan Indiana.

Notes

1. James H. Kellar, *An Introduction to the Prehistory of Indiana* (Indianapolis: Indiana Historical Society, 1983), 61, and appropriate chapters in Wayne C. Temple, *Indian Villages of the Illinois Country: Historic Tribes* (Springfield: Illinois State Museum, 1987).

2. Missionaries Paul Le Jeune and Claude Allouez in Edna Kenton, ed., *The Jesuit Relations and Allied Documents* (New York: Vanguard Press, 1954), 56, 321.

3. Andrew R. L. Cayton, *Frontier Indiana* (Bloomington: Indiana University Press, 1996), 6.

4. John D. Barnhart and Dorothy L. Riker, *Indiana to 1816: The Colonial Period*, The History of Indiana, vol. 1 (Indianapolis: Indiana Historical Bureau and Indiana Historical Society, 1971), 95–96.

5. Louis Hennepin, *A Description of Louisiana* (Ann Arbor, Mich.: University Microfilms, 1966), 205 ff.

6. Historians in the Anglo-American tradition always refer to these frontier inhabitants as French to emphasize their foreign origin. Although these people (e.g., Sieur de Vincennes, Gibault) were French-speaking, they had never been to France. They were born in the older St. Lawrence River and Great Lakes settlements and were as American as Anglo-Americans. Therefore, for accuracy I will call them *canadiens*, French-speaking natives of Canada.

7. W. J. Eccles, *The Canadian Frontier, 1534–1760* (Albuquerque: University of New Mexico Press, 1983), 90–97.

8. Thomas T. McAvoy, *The Catholic Church in Indiana, 1789–1834* (New York: Columbia University Press, 1940), 29.

9. John J. Doyle, *The Catholic Church in Indiana, 1686–1814* (Indianapolis: Criterion Press, 1976), 33.

10. Fred L. Israel, ed., *Major Peace Treaties of Modern History, 1648–1967*, 5 vols. (New York: Chelsea House in association with McGraw-Hill, 1967–80), 1:309.

11. Sebastien Louis Meurin to Bishop Jean-Olivier Briand of Quebec, 23 Mar. 1767, in Doyle, *Catholic Church in Indiana*, 30. Cayton, *Frontier Indiana*, 61, considers this practice a sign of *canadien* improvisation. Meurin's letter pled with the bishop to send priests, and by citing any apparently abnormal practices strengthened his case that priests were needed there immediately. See Doyle, *Catholic Church in Indiana*, 31.

12. Pierre Gibault to Briand, probably March 1770, in Joseph P. Donnelly, *Pierre Gibault, Missionary, 1737–1802* (Chicago: Loyola University Press, 1971), 53.

13. George Rogers Clark to George Mason, 19 Nov. 1779, in *Readings in Indiana History*, eds. Gayle Thornbrough and Dorothy Riker (Indianapolis: Indiana Historical Bureau, 1956), 37.

14. Jean-François Rivet to Bishop John Carroll of Baltimore, 26 Oct. 1795, in McAvoy, *Catholic Church in Indiana*, 81.

15. Otho Winger, "A Pioneer Experiment in Agriculture" (paper presented at a meeting of the Society of Indiana Pioneers, Indianapolis, 10 Dec. 1939, 4–11), reprinted from the *North Manchester News-Journal*.

16. "Autobiography of Abraham Luckenbach," in *The Moravian Indian Mission on White River*, ed. Lawrence Henry Gipson (Indianapolis: Indiana Historical Bureau, 1938), 617–18.

17. R. David Edmunds, *Tecumseh and the Quest for Indian Leadership* (Boston: Little, Brown and Co., 1984), 79–81.

18. Ibid., 76.

19. "Diary of the Little Indian Congregation on the White River for the Year 1806," in Gipson, ed., *Moravian Indian Mission on White River*, 415, 417.

20. Logan Esarey, ed., *Governors Messages and Letters: Messages and Letters of William Henry Harrison*, Indiana Historical Collections, vol. 7 (Indianapolis: Indiana Historical Commission, 1922), 467.

21. Mark A. Noll, *A History of Christianity in the United States and Canada* (Grand Rapids, Mich.: William B. Eerdmans, 1992), 163.

22. Clarence E. Carter, ed., *The Territorial Papers of the United States*, 27 vols. (Washington, D.C.: U. S. Government Printing Office, 1934–69), 2:39–49, in Gayle Thornbrough and Dorothy Riker, comps., *Readings in Indiana History* (Indianapolis: Indiana Historical Bureau, 1956), 94.

23. United States Supreme Court Justice Joseph Story, quoted in Noll, *History of Christianity in the United States and Canada*, 147.

24. Peter Cartwright, *Autobiography of Peter Cartwright* (New York: Abington Press, 1956), 30.

25. Randy K. Mills, "The Struggle for the Soul of Frontier Baptists: The Anti-Mission Controversy in the Lower Wabash Valley," *Indiana Magazine of History* 94 (Dec. 1998): 309. Methodist circuit rider James B. Finley told a variation of this story, where bear bites hunter and hunter bites bear, in his 1853 autobiography, quoted in Bernard A. Weisberger, *They Gathered at the River: The Story of the Great Revivalists and Their Impact upon Religion in America* (Boston: Little, Brown, 1958), 20.

26. Charles A. Johnson, *The Frontier Camp Meeting: Religion's Harvest Time* (Dallas: Southern Methodist University Press, 1955), 174–76. Daniel Cohen, *The Spirit of the Lord: Revivalism in America* (New York: Four Winds Press, 1975), 31–35.

27. Historians of American religion call the general upsurge of revivalist piety resulting from the efforts of George Whitefield and Jonathan Edwards in the mid–eighteenth century the "First Great Awakening."

28. Paul K. Conkin, *Cane Ridge: America's Pentecost* (Madison: University of Wisconsin Press, 1990), 12–25.

29. John Rogers, ed., *The Biography of Eld. Barton Warren Stone, Written by Himself*, 5th ed. (Cincinnati: J. A. and U. P. James, 1847), 34. See also John B. Boles, *Religion in Antebellum Kentucky* (Lexington: University Press of Kentucky, 1976), 26. Methodist minister John McGee is given greater credit for revival than Presbyterian minister James McGready in Kenneth O. Brown, *Holy Ground: A Study of the American Camp Meeting* (New York: Garland Publishing, 1992), 16–22.

30. R. Carlyle Buley, *The Old Northwest: Pioneer Period, 1815–1840*, 2 vols. (Indianapolis: Indiana Historical Society, 1950), 2:421–22; *Cane Ridge Bicentennial Sampler* (Paris, Ky.: Cane Ridge Preservation Project, 1991), 8–9.

31. Cited in Johnson, *Frontier Camp Meeting*, 136.

32. George A. Schultz, *An Indian Canaan: Isaac McCoy and the Vision of an Indian State* (Norman: University of Oklahoma Press, 1972), 28; Mills, "Struggle for the Soul of Frontier Baptists," 311–15. The pamphlet is Daniel Parker, *The Author's Defence, by Explanation and Matters of Fact. Remarks on Church Discipline, and Reflections on the Church of Christ, with the Utility and Benefits of Association* (Vincennes, Ind.: E. Stout, 1824).

33. Weisberger, *They Gathered at the River*, 43, 62.

34. The Old Bethel building was relocated to DePauw University in Greencastle in 1953.

35. Elmer T. Clark et al., eds., *The Journal and Letters of Francis Asbury* (London: Epworth Press, 1958), 2:577.

36. Cartwright, *Autobiography of Peter Cartwright*, 87–89.

37. All quotations from ibid., 46.

38. Johnson, *Frontier Camp Meeting*, 94–98.

39. L. C. Rudolph, *Hoosier Faiths: A History of Indiana Churches and Religious Groups* (Bloomington: Indiana University Press, 1995), 119. See pages 113–30 for Rudolph's detailed discussion of early Indiana Presbyterianism. For continued Presbyterian diversity, see Robert Archer Woods, "Presbyterianism in Princeton, Indiana, from 1810 to 1930," *Indiana Magazine of History* 26 (June 1930): 94. He reported that churches representing eleven different denominations of Presbyterians existed in this strong Presbyterian town of 2,500 in the 1870s.

40. Cartwright, *Autobiography of Peter Cartwright*, 48–49.

41. Allen Wiley, "Methodism in Southeastern Indiana," *Indiana Magazine of History* 23 (June 1927): 134. This Methodist minister discussed the spread of early Methodism, describing instances and personalities involved, in several newspaper articles written in the mid-1840s. Wiley's series was reprinted over four issues of the *Indiana Magazine of History*.

42. Johnson, *Frontier Camp Meeting*, 182.

43. Wiley, "Methodism in Southeastern Indiana," 62.

44. Parker, *Author's Defence*, 5.

45. James Smith, ed., *The Posthumous Works of the Reverend and Pious James M'Gready* (Louisville, Ky.: W. W. Worsley, 1831), 1:284.

46. James Smith, ed., *The Posthumous Works of the Reverend and Pious James M'Gready* (Nashville, Tenn.: Lowry and Smith, 1833), 2:39–40.

47. Mills, "Struggle for the Soul of Frontier Baptists," 319.

48. Henry K. Shaw, *Hoosier Disciples: A Comprehensive History of the Christian Churches (Disciples of Christ) in Indiana* (n.p.: Bethany Press, 1966), 32. For a detailed account of the rise of the Christian Church until the Civil War, see H. Clay Trusty, "Formation of the Christian Church in Indiana," *Indiana Magazine of History* 6 (Mar. 1910): 17–32.

49. M. J. Spalding, *Sketches of the Early Catholic Missions of Kentucky* (Louisville, Ky.: B. J. Webb and Brother, 1844), 104. The Catholic counterpart of revivalism, the two-week "mission" of emotional sermons and fervent prayer, one week for women, one week for men, developed later. The Jesuit Francis Xavier Weninger, one of the best-known givers of missions in the nineteenth century, delivered his first mission in Oldenburg, Indiana, 8 to 18 December 1848.

50. Rudolph F. Rehmer, *Lutherans in Pioneer Indiana* (Lafayette, Ind.: Commercial Printing, 1972), 8, and "Lutheran Pioneers at the Crossroads of America," unpublished manuscript in author's possession, 7. Rehmer cited revivalism among Indiana Lutheran ministers, but both illustrations postdated statehood. J. C. F. Heyer conducted a revival in Cumberland, Maryland, in 1820, then traveled in Indiana shortly thereafter and again in 1836. Rehmer, "Lutheran Pioneers at the Crossroads of America," 10–11. Abraham Reck, Indianapolis's first Lutheran minister (1836–41), practiced "revivalistic type preaching" in competition with the Methodists. R. F. Rehmer, "Early Lutheranism in the Capital City," unpublished manuscript in the author's possession, 2. Lutheran revivalism must have been fiery sermon without the camp meeting and "the jerks."

51. Shaw, *Hoosier Disciples*, 31–32.

52. Wiley, "Methodism in Southeastern Indiana," 60.

Jefferson, Harrison, and the West:

An Essay on Territorial Slavery

by

GEORGE W. GEIB

A Fire-Bell in the Night

EW LEADERS OF THE EARLY AMERICAN REPUBLIC HAD A BETTER TURN of phrase than Thomas Jefferson. In situation after situation he had a rare ability to capture his sense of involvement, concern, or urgency in a few well-chosen words. Nowhere is that more apparent than in the crisis that erupted in 1820 over Missouri's admission to the Union as a slave state. Writing to John Holmes, a leading Maine politician, on 22 April, Jefferson observed:

> I had for a long time ceased to read newspapers, or pay any attention to public affairs, confident they were in good hands, and content to be a passenger in the bark to the shore from which I am not distant. But this momentous question, like a fire-bell in the night, awakened and filled me with terror. I considered it at once as the knell of the Union. It is hushed, indeed, for the moment. But this is a reprieve only, not a final sentence. A geographical line, coinciding with a marked principle, moral and political, once conceived and held up to the angry passions of men, will never be obliterated; and every new irritation will mark it deeper and deeper. . . . as it is, we have the wolf by the ears, and we can neither hold him, nor safely let him go.[1]

Meeting in Vincennes in the summer of 2000, at a conference called to review the territorial history of Indiana, might seem an odd time to repeat Jefferson's words. But in a surprisingly immediate way in the fall of 1804, Gov. William Henry Harrison and the three judges of the Indiana Territory helped create the situation that roused Jefferson from his retirement sixteen short years later. For a brief time Indiana and Missouri shared a common set of government officers, and decisions made by those officers in Vincennes would be felt far into the trans-Mississippi West. If we are interested in evaluating the significance of government in early Indiana, we will be well served by looking at Jefferson, Harrison, and the West.

Administering Louisiana

As early as 1801 Jefferson had instructed his ambassador to Paris, Edward Livingston, to seek the diplomatic assistance of France in obtaining some type of improved American access to the coast of the Gulf of Mexico—a coast that was then held by Spain. Livingston had been pursuing this objective with no apparent success for more than a year when he learned of the complex diplomatic arrangements that had resulted in a Spanish commitment to return the vast and ill-defined province of Louisiana to the French. Communicating this information to Jefferson, Livingston then began attempting through various intermediaries to reach the French ruler, Napoléon Bonaparte, and to discuss an American presence in the province. Concerned with the many uncertainties of the situation, Jefferson sent a second diplomat, James Monroe, to Paris with an eye to obtaining New Orleans. Almost as soon as Monroe arrived in early spring 1803, he and Livingston were startled by an unexpected offer from Napoléon to sell the entire province for a sum equal to about fifteen million dollars in gold (three-fourths for the land, one-fourth to settle American claims against France).

The two diplomats recognized the opportunity, exceeded their instructions, concluded a purchase treaty, and hurried the text to the new federal capital in Washington. Jefferson quickly presented the treaty for ratification and secured support on a largely party-line vote. It is a commonplace of political history to observe that Jefferson, historically a strict constructionist, was attacked by the Federalists, historically loose constructionists, for exceeding his powers as president.[2] It is also a commonplace to note that Jefferson's party, strong in the South and West, was pleased by the dramatic and peaceful expansion of the country and paid little attention to constitutional questions as the party approved the results.[3] Similarly, many historians have since seen the Louisiana Purchase as the greatest accomplishment of Jefferson's first administration.

We so often see classroom maps of the Louisiana Purchase that we tend to forget that its scope was not nearly as clear in 1803 as it is today. New Orleans had been the capital of Spanish administrative districts that extended along the Gulf coast into both western Florida and Texas. For a time the United States would lay claim to portions of those districts, including the Baton Rouge area annexed in 1810, the Mobile area seized in 1813, and the Arroyo Hondo area along the Red River near the Texas-Louisiana border that became a focus of the Burr affair in 1805–7. Far to the north, the ownership of the Red River would not be decided for nearly twenty years, and British (or at least Hudson Bay Company) ambitions among some of the western Indian tribes were well known. The geography of many of the western tributaries of the Mississippi was not clear, and Meriwether Lewis and William Clark's Corps of Discovery was only one of several exploring expeditions that Jefferson would send out in search of knowledge, Indian alliances, and trade.

What was more clear was that the United States had purchased a province held by France until 1763 and by Spain since then. Louisiana contained several thousand white inhabitants, commonly if inaccurately called Creoles, most of whom lived in the Mississippi valley from its mouth northward to St. Louis. Whatever else the U.S. government might do, it needed to provide a government for the Franco-Spanish inhabitants as well as for the many American settlers that all assumed would soon move to the new lands. The ensuing arrangements for the government and administration of the Louisiana Purchase are our concern.

Initially, in March 1804 Congress divided the Louisiana Purchase into two parts. To the south was the Territory of Orleans, essentially the modern state of Louisiana. It contained the bulk of the Creole population and achieved statehood within a decade. To the north, incorporating the rest of the Louisiana Purchase, was the District of Louisiana (note the use of the designation "district" rather than the more common label of "territory"). It contained a smaller Creole population, mostly French who had migrated from east of the Mississippi sometime after the 1763 Treaty of Paris. The greatest portion of these lived in villages along the Missouri and Arkansas Rivers, where they had already been joined by an equal or greater number of Americans who had begun arriving in the 1780s. The District of Louisiana would eventually be subdivided many times, contributing land to more than a dozen new states, starting with Missouri in 1821.

As it had done east of the Mississippi, Congress moved to provide a process by which these new lands could attain self-government. This meant that each new territory would move from its original status, essentially that of a colony, to become a state of the Union equal in legal status to each of the original thirteen (or seventeen, counting Vermont, Kentucky, Tennessee, and Ohio, which were added to the Union between 1791 and 1803). The process was familiar to most residents of Indiana. They had watched the creation of the Northwest Territory in 1787. They had observed the process by which it was divided in 1800 to separate Ohio from the large remaining area to the north and west, the original Indiana Territory. They had seen the southeastern part of the Northwest Territory proceed through each of the stages of government envisioned in the 1787 ordinance.[4] First that area had been ruled by a federally appointed governor and judges (with the aid of a local council). Then, as population grew past five thousand, power had been shared by an elected legislature. Finally, as population passed fifty thousand, a state constitution had been written, and Congress had admitted Ohio as the seventeenth state in 1803. The whole process had taken a mere sixteen years.

Thanks to required courses in state history, this progress toward statehood is almost as familiar to us today as it was to the early Indiana settlers. Familiarity, in turn, often causes interpreters to forget just how revolutionary the American approach to self-government was. Most European empires of that age operated upon the very different assumption that colonies not only were, but would remain, dependencies of the metropolis or mother country. The issues of British authority prior to the American Revolution come obviously to mind. But more immediate to many in the American West in 1803 were perceptions of the events on the West Indian island of Santo Domingo. There the French under Napoléon were just concluding an unsuccessful attempt to reassert their sovereignty over a slave insurrection in the breakaway sugar colony of Haiti. New Orleans was only one of several American cities that contained refugees, white and black, who carried vivid tales from that bitter conflict. Many in the United States felt that France's failure to assert control over its island colony helped explain why Napoléon made his unexpected offer to Livingston and Monroe in 1803.

Most American leaders had long been troubled by such a model of metropolitan coercion and sought an alternative that would make willing participants of the settlers who were attracted in ever increasing numbers to the West. The Northwest Ordinance, with its orderly progression to full state equality, is one obvious example. So too is the concept of an "empire of liberty" first enunciated on 25 December 1780 by Virginia governor Thomas Jefferson to George Rogers Clark. Writing in the midst of a complex imperial struggle for control north of the Ohio River, one that incorporated British ambitions, French residents, Indian allies, and Virginia/Kentucky militias, Jefferson observed:

> In the event of peace on terms which have been contemplated by some powers we shall form to the American union a barrier against the dangerous extension of the British Province of Canada and add to the Empire of liberty an extensive and fertile Country thereby converting dangerous Enemies into valuable friends.[5]

The Indiana Connection

In an unusual action, the federal government assigned the initial responsibility for the District of Louisiana to the officers of the Indiana Territory. Although the two territories remained legally distinct, the governor and judges of Indiana were to exercise administrative authority in Louisiana until replaced. For the next nine months the writ of Indiana officers effectively ran far beyond the Mississippi into the Missouri and Arkansas valleys. It is not as strange an assignment as it may at first sound. If knowledgeable territorial officials were needed quickly, Indiana offered the closest available source. The Indiana Territory then extended to the Mississippi and included many citizens of French descent. The intended capital of the new district was St. Louis, just over the river from the Illinois Country, and the settled areas of Louisiana also included a number of French speakers who were former residents of the Northwest Territory.

Among the officials charged with the earliest responsibility of bringing American institutions to the trans-Mississippi West was a central figure well known in Vincennes, Gov. William Henry Harrison.[6] Harrison was still a young man on the way up in 1804, and he had many advantages. His father, Benjamin, was a signer of the Declaration of Independence, and his father-in-law, John Cleves Symmes, was a dominant political figure in the Cincinnati area. Harrison had selected a career in the army, served under Anthony Wayne in the Fallen Timbers campaign, and later became the Northwest Territory's delegate to Congress. The 1800 Land Law, which allowed smaller acreage purchases and extended more generous credit provisions to land purchasers, is usually credited to him.

President John Adams had appointed Harrison as the first governor of the Indiana Territory, but only after determining that Jefferson would acquiesce in the appointment if elected. Basing himself at Vincennes, Harrison had already shown energy and some clear political directions in his administration.[7] In particular he was interested in extinguishing Indian title to desirable farmland and in encouraging gentry (of the type he had known in his youth in Virginia) to settle in Indiana. The former he sought to achieve through aggressive promotion of purchase treaties, the latter by permitting the use of servants (slaves among them) by larger landowners. Each left controversy in its wake.

In the case of Indian purchase treaties, Harrison followed the common U.S. practice of identifying the specific tribe with primary right to the land, such as the Delaware or the Miami. Assuming that

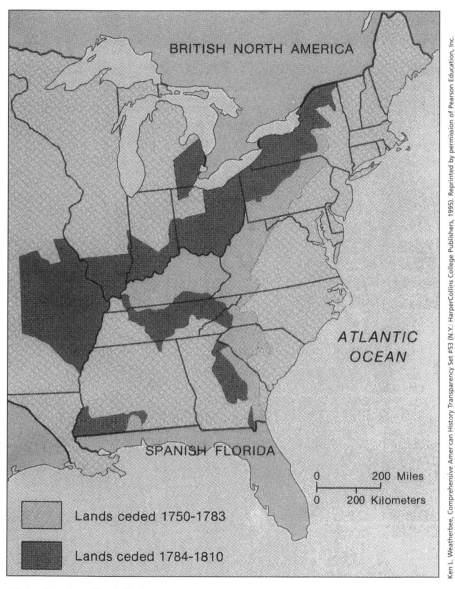

Ken L. Weatherbee, Comprehensive American History Transparency Set #53 (N.Y.: HarperCollins College Publishers, 1995). Reprinted by permission of Pearson Education, Inc.

Native American Land Cessions

other tribes, such as the Shawnee, occupied land only with the permission of the primary tribe, Harrison felt obligated to deal only with the latter. Harrison also followed the common practice of locating individuals accorded the title or status of a chief and then assuming that the signature of a representative group of chiefs constituted a valid negotiation—provided, of course, that the U.S. government offered annuities, gifts, and other accepted forms of payment. Initially this approach won him success in what became southern Indiana and southern and central Illinois. It also eventually gained him opposition from excluded chiefs and tribes, mobilized with considerable effect after 1808 by the Shawnee brothers, Tecumseh and the Prophet. But in the short run, by 1804 it had won him many friends among land-hungry American settlers and speculators.

In the case of slavery, Harrison undoubtedly reflected the social attitudes of a younger son of a Virginia gentry family. One need only visit Grouseland, the elegant gentleman's home he erected at the northern edge of Vincennes, to sense his origins and his aspirations. Living in a frontier territory where opportunities to obtain cheap and fertile land abounded, Harrison soon found ways to parlay his gubernatorial powers into extensive acreage. But living in a sparsely populated area where most poor men could also find paths to land ownership (sometimes using the Harrison Land Law of 1800 to help them), Harrison urgently needed labor. To a governor living in Vincennes where some French settlers owned slaves, and to a Virginian living near the slave state of Kentucky, black labor was an obvious possibility.

Yet a serious problem remained. Article 6 of the Northwest Ordinance was clear in prohibiting slavery, and many newly arrived settlers from the northern and middle states had little use for the institution. Eventually their opposition would help break the power of the Harrison group in Vincennes and set in motion a very different political world under such men as Jonathan Jennings. But again in the first years of his tenure as governor, Harrison enjoyed rather few checks upon his aspirations. In 1802 he had helped stage-manage a public meeting that called for a ten-year congressional moratorium on Article 6. Then, while waiting for action (which never came) on the petition, he spearheaded the enactment of a series of black codes that legitimized forms of indentured servitude (a legal contractual form of the time) and allowed slaves to be brought in practice to Indiana.

Harrison was joined in his administration by the three territorial judges appointed by the president.[8] Initially all three, William

Clark, Henry Vanderburgh, and John Griffin, had been named in 1800 by John Adams. But one of those, William Clark, an obscure Federalist from Kentucky who is often mistaken for a member of the more famous Clark family, had died in Vincennes in 1802 and been replaced by Thomas Terry Davis. Griffin, a Virginian by birth, was identified with the Detroit area and became a judge of the Michigan Territory when it separated from the Indiana Territory in 1805. Davis was a migrant from Kentucky who was identified with the Jeffersonville and Clark Grant areas until his death in 1807.

Vanderburgh was probably the most important of the three, drawing influence from both his residence and his connections in Vincennes, the territorial capital. Born in New York in 1760, he had risen to the rank of captain in the Continental Line (or regular army) during the War for Independence. After the war he had migrated west, settled in Vincennes, and married into the Racine family, a prominent local trading family. Energetic, sociable, and bilingual, Vanderburgh was a key figure who regularly moderated between the older French and newer American settlers while enjoying the confidence of both.

Vanderburgh recognized that the French and American communities were very different. The French focused heavily upon trade, particularly with the Indian tribes with which they had long been intermarrying; farming, although practiced, was a secondary activity. The Americans focused upon land settlement and speculation; many were quite willing to victimize the Indians to achieve their objectives. French society relied heavily upon custom and tradition, much of it quite similar to that of the parent communities in Quebec. American society relied heavily upon law, often treating it as both redress and entertainment. Vanderburgh, by moderating between these two very different cultures, had made himself an essential man in the Vincennes community.

Vanderburgh was particularly important in introducing Harrison to the concept of the "custom of the country," by which local practices were continued and respected in the face of proposed change. While this approach may not have appealed to the assertive American governor on some issues, it certainly suited him on the slavery question. Noting that the "custom" of the Vincennes area included slaves, perhaps over one hundred in number, Harrison saw natural allies in his own quest for a role for slavery. The alliance he forged with Vanderburgh on the issue would prove of importance in the 1804 Missouri laws.

The Louisiana Laws

Harrison formally assumed his title of Louisiana governor on 1 October 1804 and the next day left from Vincennes for St. Louis to assume his job. For the next nine months he was responsible for the governance of what later became Missouri and Arkansas. For good or for ill, he was Jefferson's choice to give the first institutional shape to the "empire of liberty" across the Mississippi. He and his Indiana territorial judges set the process in motion when they prepared and enacted the first code of laws for the new territory. On that single formative day before the governor left for St. Louis, Harrison and the three judges wrote fifteen fundamental laws for the District of Louisiana. Joined by a sixteenth dealing with civil marriage, which was added in April 1805, they are the original institutional setting for the development of the great West.[9] Those laws deserve our attention.

In outline, the new laws served to:
• establish a criminal code (including punishments)
• define and punish defalcation
• establish the sheriff's office
• regulate the appointment of constables
• establish courts of judicature
• establish the probate court
• establish justice-of-the-peace courts (for small causes)
• regulate court practices (such as writs of error)
• regulate the practice of attorneys
• regulate county rates and levies
• establish and regulate a militia
• establish the recorder's office
• define the oath of office
• regulate boatmen
• define the status of slavery
• regulate civil and religious marriages (the 1805 addition)

If many of these laws look familiar today, they certainly did to the authors in 1804. Most are simply restatements of the legal framework of the Old Northwest. Thirteen of the sixteen were based upon Northwest Territory laws, upon Indiana Territory laws, or upon some combination of the two. To cite one example of such a combination, the militia law used the language of the Indiana Territory act but imposed the age requirements of the Northwest Territory act.

Some commentators have suggested we look at the changes between Northwest Territory law and Indiana Territory law in the years from 1800 to 1804. Their argument, in outline, is that Harrison and the judges were gradually substituting practices from Virginia (or its frontier offshoot, Kentucky) for those formerly derived from Middle Atlantic or New England states. They thus argue that a more southern local system was coming into practice just as the Louisiana laws were drafted. The primary evidence for this position is found by noting the changes in the system of local justices and in the rules for attorneys. The first appears in the justice-of-the-peace system, based on Virginia and Kentucky models, which replaced an earlier system based on Pennsylvania commission models in Indiana in 1803. The second appears most clearly in the rules for attorneys, where Indiana had reduced both their required training and the fees they could charge.

The argument that a more southern system was emerging appeals to those who see the hand of Harrison, as Virginia gentleman, in the measures. It may, however, be overstated. In both Indiana and Louisiana the American population showed a higher proportion of upland southern migrants than was the case in early Ohio, and it can be argued that the changes resulted from an extension of a system familiar to the citizenry. Similarly, the matter of lawyers' behavior may owe more to the remoteness of the frontier and the lack of trained men than to any sectional attitude carried from the East.

On the whole, the laws assumed that most of the questions to be resolved were subject to administration or adjudication at a local level of government, and that level of government was the county. A word on nomenclature is in order, however. The con-

Knox County Courthouse, First Territorial Court, Vincennes

gressional enabling act, perhaps through haste or poor editing, had both created a District of Louisiana and granted power to the governor and judges to create local districts for administration. Harrison was not usually given to wit in his official correspondence. But he was moved at one later point to send an entertaining tongue-in-cheek letter to President Jefferson describing the incongruities of language that resulted from creating five districts (St. Louis, St. Charles, St. Genevieve, New Madrid, and Cape Girardeau) within the new District of Louisiana. Interpreters have generally escaped the problem by unofficially calling them subdistricts or counties.

By whatever name was used, the five districts were designed to look much like Knox County, Indiana Territory. Free white adult males, ages eighteen to fifty, were required to constitute a militia for local order and defense, providing their own arms and uniforms. Taxes were to be levied upon livestock, town homes, and other evidences of disposable wealth, but not upon land itself. A familiar variety of district (i.e., county) courts appeared, including probate, common pleas, and quarter sessions. Harsh penalties were to be inflicted for a wide range of crimes; the pillory and the whipping post continued their westward march. Only one of the original fifteen laws was really new. This was the law setting rules for boatmen, a reflection of the area's obvious dependence upon the Mississippi, Missouri, and Arkansas Rivers, as well as its close ties to such downstream cities as New Orleans. The law required boat operators to render fair service to passengers and fair treatment to employees and servants.

The "custom of the country" was not forgotten, however. As the 31 October 1803 act of Congress that permitted Jefferson to take possession of Louisiana stated, the government should work toward "maintaining and protecting the inhabitants of Louisiana in the free enjoyment of their liberty, property, and religion."[10] Capt. Amos Stoddard, the military commander who held power until Harrison's arrival, was similarly instructed that "inasmuch as the largest portion of the old inhabitants were strenuously opposed to the change of government, it would go far to conciliate them, and they would much sooner be reconciled to the new order of things, by making little, if any change in the *modus operandi* of the government, at least for a time."[11] In matters of law that meant respecting the civil law that had long prevailed under Spanish rule, as well as common local custom.

One sticking point under Harrison proved to be the issue of marriages. Under civil law, that was a function of the church, and specifically the Roman Catholic Church. Under American practice it was a civil matter in the sense that it was essentially an arrangement of property. The former was overseen by the clergy, the latter by the judges. The 1805 law that resulted basically was a compromise that attempted to recognize the American style of marriage alongside the traditional.

The other topic where law and custom obviously met was the issue of slavery in the new land. This essay has already largely established the context. American law and presidential instruction were clear upon the matter of respecting the practices, and the property, of the existing inhabitants of Louisiana. Slavery was practiced in the French and Spanish empires. Some of the French-speaking inhabitants not only held slaves but had crossed over from the Old Northwest because they feared for the safety of their property under Article 6 of the 1787 ordinance. Harrison was pursuing an opportunistic path to introduce some form of unfree labor into Indiana, and at least one of his judges was commonly supportive of the rights of French inhabitants. The president of the United States was a slaveholder. It really wasn't a hard call. With little fanfare, a slavery act that reflected much of the language of the existing Virginia statute was adopted. Jefferson's representatives had extended the institution legally into the West.[12]

If Harrison accomplished his objectives regarding slavery while still in Vincennes, he accomplished many of his objectives regarding Indiana land purchases during the brief months of his rule in St. Louis. Comparing the time and effort he spent on Indian relations to other duties tells us much about his priorities in 1804 and helps place his actions at Vincennes in perspective. Harrison was already identifiable as an aggressive and opportunistic Indian negotiator when he headed west to St. Louis in October 1804. He was in possession, moreover, of instructions from the secretary of war asking him to deal with the Sauk and Fox Indians. These two closely allied tribes occupied lands on both sides of the Mississippi starting about one hundred miles north of St. Louis. The Sauk in particular had a reputation for being troublesome. They appeared to welcome British representatives, they seemed reluctant to consider treating with the Americans, and they were hostile to the Osage. The latter probably counted for a good deal because Harrison was quick to seek advice in St. Louis from Auguste Chouteau, a prominent trader with close ties to the Osage.

Even Harrison, however, was probably surprised when the Sauk issue came to the fore within mere days of his arrival. The pattern was a familiar one on the frontier: unauthorized settlement and trade by whites, grievances over property that led to violence, and American demands for land cessions as part of the ensuing resolution of the conflict. In this case the offending whites were settlers trespassing on Sauk lands in the Cuivre River valley, the violence was a murder committed by Sauk hunters, and the negotiations were carried out by Harrison and a group of five Sauk leaders who were eager to avoid war. The resolution was a typical Harrison arrangement. One of the murderers was surrendered for trial (and later shot, allegedly while attempting to escape that trial). The Sauks agreed to become allies of the United States, to treat with the Osage, to allow American adjudication of future claims, and to accept an initial sum and a future annuity from the government. They received American recognition of their land claims but only in exchange for a huge cession—land that would form part of the future states of Missouri, Illinois, and Wisconsin. Five chiefs signed the agreement, causing tribal unhappiness that would last at least until the Black Hawk War of 1832.[13] The temptation to compare Harrison's energy on this issue to his quick treatment of the slavery issue is great.

Interpretive Contexts

The original Indiana Territory boundaries included modern Illinois and thus extended to the Mississippi River. As such the early territory stood on the far westernmost border of the young

American republic of 1800. Three short years later, however, the Louisiana Purchase dramatically altered the situation, moving America's western border out to the Rocky Mountains. Without any action by its residents or local officials, Indiana moved from the far west to the middle west, a geographical shift that—it could be suggested—anticipated a conceptual shift of great significance. At the very least, the relationship between the Indiana Territory and the issues of expansion raised by Louisiana after 1803 invite our attention. The issues of slavery discussed above invite us into a larger context of scholarly opinion and interpretation and may ultimately help us to understand better the significance of the actions of Harrison and his judges.

The Indiana Territory of 1800 stood chronologically between a past rooted in the empires of France and Britain and a future rooted in American expansion. Enough of the old still existed among both Indians and French settlers that one could draw upon their memory and experience. But enough of the new was already present—especially in Kentucky (a state since 1792), Ohio (about to become one in 1803), and even here in the new territory—that one could make some informed predictions about the near future. Surely the future held substantial in-migration, extensive agricultural settlement, growing trade, and the introduction of institutions modeled to a considerable degree upon those of the existing states of the new American union.

Historians have long used that contrast between the old and the new, between traditions and changes, to look at the frontier and at the Indiana Territory that was a part of that frontier. Those who like a traditional view will appreciate the most successful paradigm of historical interpretation ever developed: Frederick Jackson Turner's frontier thesis. Articulated in the 1890s and dominant for at least half a century, it interpreted the frontier as a process. It was a process in which savagery, defined as humanity's dependence upon nature, yielded to civilization, defined as humanity's ability to shape and rule nature. The frontier that Turner presented was a process with stages of development. It began with the Indian, an archetypal savage in the sense that nature was dominant in his world. Then the frontier moved through a series of human experiences, each characterized by a greater and greater degree of human control over the environment. Turner's world continued with early fur trappers and traders, proceeded through various extractive industries such as mining and lumbering, moved on to subsistence and then to commercial farming, and finally yielded to town and city life. Humans were not, however, passive participants in the process. As Turner portrayed them, American settlers were constantly responding in creative ways to the particular challenges of new lands and opportunities. Democracy, in his view, arose from the rough equality that existed in the face of nature on the early frontier; social order in America depended, at least in part, upon the safety valve provided by western opportunity. It was a grand framework that offered a uniquely American way to explain modern history.

Turner published relatively little in his lifetime beyond his famous thesis, and he eventually became more interested in the related question of sectionalism. But almost from its first presentation in Chicago in 1893, his frontier hypothesis enjoyed a popularity unusual among academic historians. The appeal came in part because it was a paradigm that invited exploration and study. By portraying the frontier as a series of developmental stages, and by arguing that these stages occurred repeatedly across America, Turner set in motion a host of case studies by succeeding generations of historians who tested the reliability and validity of his thesis in particular periods and settings.[14] These writers in turn were often read and enjoyed by a larger American public that liked the optimism, the nationalism, and the colorful exuberance of what they heard. If the label Progressive is intended to incorporate a belief in human progress and improvement, Turner was one of the most influential of all Progressive historians.[15]

Thomas Kuhn[16] has argued that much of modern thought is a matter of presenting and revising paradigms, and Turner's hypothesis would almost certainly fit the normal definition of a paradigm. The frontier argument sought to interpret an area of inquiry in ways that respected the available evidence, responded to contemporary concerns, and offered lines of examination that could resolve a range of related questions. Like the paradigm of the rise of the nation-state, so ably argued by Samuel Eliot Morison,[17] Turner's views became a basis for textbook instruction well into the twentieth century.

But however useful and satisfying it might have been in his own time, Turner's hypothesis eventually encountered a growing body of evidence and interpretation that called it into question. By mid–century it was a paradigm under stress. One example of a problem area was the question of the sequence of settlement on the frontier. Not all agreed, for example, that civilization came late. Many will remember Francis Paul Prucha's clever *Broadax and Bayonet: The Role of the United States Army in the Development of the Northwest, 1815–1860,*[18] in which he argued that the U.S. Army was the major civilizing agent on the northwest frontier well before most of the stages of development highlighted by Turner had even appeared there. Or consider Richard C. Wade's *Urban Frontier: The Rise of Western Cities, 1790–1830*[19] riposte, in which he showed that the cities of the trans-Appalachian West were flourishing entities that both preceded rural settlement and helped to encourage its appearance. William Cronon's *Nature's Metropolis: Chicago and the Great West,*[20] is a modern reworking of this view that civilization spawned the frontier and not vice versa.

Yet even as it was challenged, the argument changed and adapted. Beginning with Henry Nash Smith's highly influential *Virgin Land: The American West as Symbol and Myth*[21] in 1950, we began to see civilization and savagery through new cultural eyes. Now we were asked to see the frontier as a myth: a series of stories, resting upon fact without necessarily being factually true, that embodied fundamental beliefs of the people who told and heard them. Here was a land untouched by the corruption of civilization, where Americans could build a society based upon ideals of property-owning democracy. The frontier suddenly became a subjective series of participants' responses to events. It became a civic vision that, if not objectively correct, was still subjectively accurate because it captured the common cultural aspirations of an exceptional American people. Soon much of the emerging American Studies movement followed suit, drawing upon such cultural icons as the Garden of Eden and the steam engine to highlight the West of the imagination.[22]

In recent years, however, that grand theory has also fallen from favor, and one can see with some clarity the shape of its replacement. The new theory has four central elements: an emphasis upon preexisting Indian cultures, a picture of a settled landscape, an interest in accommodation and adaptation, and a darker view of the American "empire of liberty."

1. The interest in Indian cultures has made its greatest contribution by causing us to question, and often reject, two of the central features of the older paradigm: savagery and virgin land. We have good evidence today that the Woodland Indians of the Ohio valley were anything but slaves to nature. At the material level they were experienced farmers, producing a varied diet that still influences our modern foodways. At the community level they possessed a variety of well-articulated social structures. At the spiritual level they possessed a range of complex religious practices that were articulated in rich oral traditions. Far from slaves to nature, they had achieved a considerable measure of success in adapting it to their needs and aspirations. In his recent study, *Elusive Empires: Constructing Colonialism in the Ohio Valley, 1673–1800,*[23] Eric Hinderaker has shown the remarkable levels of trade that the seventeenth-century French empire achieved. By doing so he becomes one of many to document the levels of indigenous society that needed to be present to sustain the early European empires.

2. In the process, these Woodland Indians easily refute the picture of a "virgin" land. Recent demographic studies lean strongly to the view that, prior to the introduction of European diseases, the continent was perhaps as densely populated as early modern Europe. Pathfinders that we once portrayed as explorers have reemerged as tourists guided by their Indian hosts through landscapes long altered by human occupation. Sacagawea, the tour guide, replaces Lewis and Clark, the pathfinders, in this new vision. If the West was a garden, it was a garden already under cultivation when Euro-Americans got there.[24]

3. This realization has led us to reinterpret the relationship between whites and Native Americans. We no longer view it as a matter of imposing the superior ways of Europe upon savages; instead, we now picture much of the interaction as an accommodation where each group borrowed cultural aspects from the other's world and adapted them to its own. Richard White did much to direct our

attention to this situation in his work *The Middle Ground: Indians, Empires, and Republics in the Great Lakes Region, 1650–1815,* which further invited us to rethink our definitions of republicanism by looking at the republican features of tribal societies as well as those of frontier communities.[25]

A good teaching device is to offer students the example of food, discussing how the introduction of the corn and vine crops of the Indian into settler diets was at least as significant as the Indians' importation of fruit and root crops. Andrew R. L. Cayton has added an additional dimension by pointing out how some individuals and groups, such as the early French inhabitants, played a key role in facilitating this interchange of goods and ideas.[26]

Gregory H. Nobles, another student of frontier cultural encounters, adds the revealing reminder that accommodation did not always have as its end product the adoption of American technology or other cultural forms. He is quick to remind us that the most important result of the policies of Harrison and his contemporaries on the early Indiana frontier was to help call into existence an Indian resistance movement that stressed a return to native cultures. Where we used to study Tecumseh, the resistance fighter, Nobles joins those who stress the role of Tenskwatawa, the prophet of native religion and tribal tradition.[27]

4. Finally, we have been reminded that most early inhabitants did not survive the final "empire of liberty" that American settlers brought to the region in the late eighteenth and early nineteenth centuries. It causes us to pay special attention to those French residents who stayed in place when the English territorial transfer of 1763 occurred but who were less willing to stay here as the American phase began. Rather than live under American rule, many of them instead moved west across the Mississippi to the more congenial world of Spanish Louisiana.

There is a danger in the new interpretation: if taken uncritically, it sounds suspiciously like the "noble savage" arguments that have wandered around European high culture for centuries. These arguments feature hypothetical children of nature whose goodness stands in stark contrast to the dark and foreboding worlds of soldier, merchant, and priest that we inherit from our western culture. But there is no question that the new approaches have bid to be a new paradigm and are spawning studies that have reinvigorated the study of the early West.

An Indiana Perspective

Half a century ago John D. Barnhart offered an interpretation titled *Valley of Democracy: The Frontier versus the Plantation in the Ohio Valley, 1775–1818.*[28] He theorized that, over time, the power of plantation society declined in the trans-Appalachian West. His evidence was found in the state constitutions of that area, which he showed increasingly over time to represent elective principles and an absence of property restrictions upon popular participation in government. For the adult white males of the region, his evidence remains convincing. But if viewed through the eyes of African Americans, a very different perspective appears. Now a substantial portion of the great river valleys becomes home to an institution that rests upon coercion and not upon liberty. Why and how that institution survived in the new democratic West is a legitimate and intriguing question. It is one that definitely involves the Indiana Territory, where the first American laws on slavery in the District of Louisiana were written.

Central to this inquiry is the question of authorship, primarily as it calls forth the relative importance of Harrison and the three territorial judges, Davis, Griffin, and Vanderburgh, in the deliberations of 1 October 1804. Of those three judges the most interesting is clearly Vanderburgh. He had the best local connections, especially in the French community. He appears to have shown unusual skill in balancing the old French practices (the "custom of the country") with the new American law (stressing common law). His voice in council would be most likely to confirm modern historians' interpretations of accommodation.

In particular, the views of Vanderburgh might stand in contrast to the views of Harrison, who had good reasons to hearken more closely to American practices. Harrison was an associate of Jefferson, an expansionist president from Virginia. Like Jefferson, Harrison came from the Virginia plantation gentry, and like Jefferson there was much of expansion in the governor. At least as far back as his book *Notes on the State of Virginia*, Jefferson (particularly in his discussions of western rivers in Query Two)[29] looked to Virginia claims in the great West. With this went a clear interest in slave expansion on Harrison's part. Almost as soon as he arrived in Vincennes, Harrison gained a reputation for supporting some form of slavery in the territory, notably through the "servant" subterfuge—Article 6 of the Northwest Ordinance notwithstanding.

A first reading of the evidence does not give much support to the newer views of accommodation. What we see instead is primarily the Indiana structure extended west of the Mississippi River. Those hoping for dramatic innovation must—in most areas of law, local governance, and administrative regulation—find their vision in the earlier debates that created the Northwest Territory and its eventual subdivisions. On a closer reading, however, this may overstate the case by a too narrow reading of the laws in force. The congressional act that established the District of Louisiana was presumably written by men who were concerned, as Jefferson said he was, with making as little change as possible in local affairs until the population was reconciled to the American presence. Thus the March 1804 enabling act provided that local laws and customs, when not consistent with American law, remain in force until replaced by the governor and judges. In this spirit we can note that Harrison's new districts were much the same as the old Spanish subdivisions and that his appointees were often prominent local French and Spanish citizens. His new boatmen's act was primarily a call for efficient service to customers and fair treatment for crews by their captains, hardly a revolutionary demand. The most important change in local custom, the marriage act, was not added until 1805 and did not end any existing religious practice.

We could see the slavery act in the spirit of the "custom of the country" prior to 1803. Its secure presence west of the Mississippi may have been a significant inducement to migration across that river by many French settlers, especially from the Illinois bottom, in the two decades between the 1783 Treaty of Paris and the Louisiana Purchase. Thus, while Harrison's interest in slavery is not to be discounted, he could fairly argue that he was consistent with Congress and custom if he confirmed a preexisting institution. Certainly his actions attracted little comment, adverse or otherwise, at the time.

Conclusions

All this challenges us to consider some interpretive conclusions:

First, it is hard to argue too much grand theory for a set of laws adopted by four men in a single day in October 1804. Great as our admiration is for the "empire of liberty" theme, there is a sense of the routine about much of this first attempt to define the actual administration of Jefferson's great West. Even the ambition and the opportunism of Harrison are more easily argued through his later Sauk Indian Treaty than here.

Second, it is easier to argue that the issues of empire and accommodation are present here. There is clearly a tension between the new, bumptious America—with its need for criminal codes and its strong sense of decentralization—and an older French/Spanish world whose civil law and community customs may not always be consistent with that new empire.

Third, many modern interpreters who are concerned about the darker aspects of Jefferson's "empire of liberty," must stand intrigued at the ways his appointees brought American ideals and institutions to the Louisiana frontier. Sixteen years later Jefferson would call the disputes over slavery in Missouri a "fire-bell in the night." Peter Onuf, in a perceptive essay on the 1820 crisis,[30] argues that the tensions of the "empire of liberty" theme, particularly its inability to confront human slavery, are central to understanding the philosopher-president's visions. But if 1820 required a fire-bell, 1804 clearly kindled the coals of that conflagration. Whether in triumphant expansion or in accommodation to country custom, Indiana's territorial governor and judges in Vincennes made a significant contribution to the shape of the new West.

Notes

1. Merrill D. Peterson, ed., *The Portable Thomas Jefferson* (New York: Penguin Books, 1975), 567–68.

2. Marshall Smelser, *The Democratic Republic, 1801–1815* (New York: Harper Torchbooks, 1968).

3. Richard Skolnik, *1803; Jefferson's Decision; The United States Purchases Louisiana* (New York: Chelsea House, 1969), is an excellent collection of letters and other political commentary.

4. Modern rethinking of the American expansion era touches even such seemingly well-defined topics as the power and purposes of the great western ordinances. See, for example, Richard McCormick, "Ambiguous Authority: The Ordinances of the Confederation Congress, 1781–1787," *The American Journal of Legal History* 41 (Oct. 1997): 411–39.

5. Julian P. Boyd, ed., *The Papers of Thomas Jefferson* (Princeton, N.J.: Princeton University Press, 1950), 4:237–38.

6. Reginald Horsman argues persuasively that the traditional biographies of Harrison are in need of rethinking and offers an outline of a proposed reinterpretation in "William Henry Harrison: Virginia Gentleman in the Old Northwest," *Indiana Magazine of History* 96 (June 2000): 125–49.

7. The standard account of this era is John D. Barnhart and Dorothy L. Riker, *Indiana to 1816: The Colonial Period,* The History of Indiana, vol. 1 (Indianapolis: Indiana Historical Bureau and Indiana Historical Society, 1971). See especially chapters nine through eleven.

8. Territorial judges hold their authority under Article 4 of the United States Constitution, not under Article 3 as other judges do. Biographical information on early federal territorial judges is limited. Most modern works draw upon a detailed three-volume history of law in Indiana published in the state centennial year. See Leander J. Monks, Logan Esarey, and Ernest Shockley, eds., *Courts and Lawyers of Indiana* (Indianapolis: Federal Publishing Company, 1916), 2:403–7. That work's treatment of the early courts, in turn, owed much to an earlier Indiana Historical Society pamphlet by Daniel Wait Howe, *The Laws and Courts of Northwest and Indiana Territories* (Indianapolis: Bowen-Merrill Co., 1886).

9. The defining work on early Louisiana law was published in a 1906 issue of the *Missouri Historical Review.* It should be kept in mind that the territory was not officially titled Missouri until 1812. I have used that journal's modern reprint. See Isidor Loeb, "The Beginnings of Missouri Legislation," *Missouri Historical Review* 92 (Jan. 1998): 222–37.

10. Loeb, "Beginnings of Missouri Legislation," 225.

11. Ibid., 226.

12. The new edition of the Harrison papers sadly offers us few insights into the authorship of this fascinating collection of laws. A number of documents on reels one and two speak to other aspects of Harrison's role in Missouri. But on the laws themselves we have nothing directly relevant beyond the texts themselves and our knowledge of the participants and the western situation. See Douglas E. Clanin et al., eds., *The Papers of William Henry Harrison, 1800–1815,* 10 microfilm reels (Indianapolis: Indiana Historical Society, 1993–1999). See particularly reel one, 797–99 and 928–46, and reel two, 230–33. The editors have prepared a very helpful printed guide, *A Guide to the Papers of*

William Henry Harrison, 1800–1815, 2d ed. (Indianapolis: Indiana Historical Society, 1999). See especially xxx–xxxii.

13. See Anthony F. C. Wallace, *Jefferson and the Indians: The Tragic Fate of the First Americans* (Cambridge, Mass.: Belknap Press of Harvard University Press, 1999). See especially 248–51.

14. Richard W. Etulain, *Does the Frontier Experience Make America Exceptional?* (Boston: Bedford/St. Martin's, 1999), is a useful text edition that includes Turner's "The Significance of the Frontier in American History" and eight later commentaries. A standard edition is Frederick Jackson Turner, *Frontier and Section: Selected Essays*, ed. Ray Allen Billington (Englewood Cliffs, N.J.: Prentice Hall, 1961).

15. Allan G. Bogue, *Frederick Jackson Turner: Strange Roads Going Down* (Norman: University of Oklahoma Press, 1998), is the definitive modern treatment.

16. Thomas S. Kuhn, *The Structure of Scientific Revolutions*, 3d ed. (Chicago: University of Chicago Press, 1996).

17. Samuel Eliot Morison, *The Oxford History of the American People*, 3 vols. (New York: Oxford University Press, 1965).

18. Francis Paul Prucha, *Broadax and Bayonet: The Role of the United States Army in the Development of the Northwest, 1815–1860* (Madison: State Historical Society of Wisconsin, 1953).

19. Richard C. Wade, *The Urban Frontier: The Rise of Western Cities, 1790–1830* (Cambridge, Mass.: Harvard University Press, 1959).

20. William Cronon, *Nature's Metropolis: Chicago and the Great West* (New York: W. W. Norton and Co., 1991).

21. Henry Nash Smith, *Virgin Land: The American West as Symbol and Myth* (Cambridge, Mass.: Harvard University Press, 1950).

22. William H. Goetzmann and William N. Goetzmann, *The West of the Imagination* (New York: W. W. Norton and Co., 1986).

23. Eric Hinderaker, *Elusive Empires: Constructing Colonialism in the Ohio Valley, 1673–1800* (Cambridge: Cambridge University Press, 1997). The population necessary to sustain such enterprises, and its fate, has also attracted much attention. Today it is common to assume that the early native population was much above its eighteenth century levels and to attribute the decline primarily to disease theories. For those interested in this problem area, see James West Davidson and Mark Hamilton Lytle, *After the Fact: The Art of Historical Detection*, 4th ed. (Boston: McGraw-Hill, 2000), 96–121.

24. The defining work is Leo Marx, *The Machine in the Garden: Technology and the Pastoral Ideal in America* (New York: Oxford University Press, 1964).

25. Richard White, *The Middle Ground: Indians, Empires, and Republics in the Great Lakes Region, 1650–1815* (New York: Cambridge University Press, 1991).

26. Andrew R. L. Cayton, *Frontier Indiana* (Bloomington and Indianapolis: Indiana University Press, 1996). See especially 45–69.

27. Gregory H. Nobles, *American Frontiers: Cultural Encounters and Continental Conquest* (New York: HarperCollins, 1997), 116–23.

28. John D. Barnhart, *Valley of Democracy: The Frontier versus the Plantation in the Ohio Valley, 1775–1818* (Bloomington: Indiana University Press, 1953).

29. Jefferson included the Mississippi, Missouri, Illinois, and Kaskaskia Rivers, as well as the Ohio, Tennessee, and Cumberland, among his descriptions of Virginia geography. We should not be surprised: the colonial land claims, surrendered only with reluctance by Virginia in the 1780s, were of long standing. A very useful geographical perspective is found in Part Three of D. W. Meinig, *The Shaping of America: A*

Geographical Perspective on 500 Years of History, vol. 1, *Atlantic America, 1492–1800* (New Haven, Conn.: Yale University Press, 1986).

30. Peter Onuf, "Thomas Jefferson, Missouri, and the 'Empire for Liberty,'" in *Thomas Jefferson and the Changing West: From Conquest to Conservation,* ed. James P. Ronda (St. Louis: Missouri Historical Society Press, 1997), 111–54.

Great Britain and America at 1800:

Perspectives on the Frontier

by

NANCY L. RHODEN

THE WESTWARD EXPANSION OF AMERICANS INTO THE FRONTIER, including the Ohio Country and the Indiana Territory, resulted from a web of different decisions: when to leave, where to go, and whether to stay or migrate again. Yet these choices of individual migrants or family groups also owed much to larger political and diplomatic factors. Westward expansion for Americans entailed an ideological commitment to republican values, which had been defined in the American Revolution and in debate and ratification of the federal Constitution. The American victory over Britain in the Revolutionary War certainly had facilitated this expansion, but even at the war's conclusion Anglo-American relations continued to shape the development of the frontier. An examination of diplomatic relations between America and Great Britain from 1783 to 1800 allows for an evaluation of conflicting Anglo-American perspectives in the Old Northwest.[1] While Americans streamed into the frontier, anxious for landownership and eager to expand the territory of the United States, the British were unconvinced about the merits of a republican government and its potential for success. British policies, including the continued occupation of forts in the Old Northwest, reflected a fundamentally different perspective about the frontier's future. Revolutionary questions of self-determination and sovereignty (or ultimate political authority), which had been essential in the Anglo-American conflict that began in the 1760s, did not disappear at war's end but rather persisted on the frontier.

In the peace treaty that concluded the Revolutionary War in 1783, the British ceded to the Americans control of interior lands, including the region that became the Indiana Territory, despite contrary Native American claims. Twenty years earlier that land had passed from the French to the British at the end of the Seven Years' War. In both instances, European diplomats ceded territory in the western country without taking into account the perspectives of Native American tribesmen who felt that they had not been conquered. Whereas Americans envisioned this region south of the Great Lakes as a suitable area for land speculation and future agricultural development, the British government favored its usefulness to the fur trade and its links to Canada.[2] In the early 1760s American colonists likely had anticipated that the British defeat of France would facilitate colonial expansion westward, but instead Parliament enacted the Proclamation of 1763, which attempted to forbid the expansion of white settlers west of the Appalachian Mountains. As sovereign allies of the British living on land recently claimed by the British king, interior Native American tribes favored this act because they interpreted such legislation as an effort to preserve their territorial rights. Land speculators, backcountry residents, and frontiersmen bristled at the news, and hardy pioneers violated the terms by moving west anyway. Later revolutionaries, including land speculators whose profits seemed to be threatened by such policies, labeled this proclamation an early example of British treachery. European nations had long clashed about the boundaries of their respective North American empires, and in the aftermath of the Seven Years' War British colonists disagreed with imperial politicians about the frontier's destiny.[3]

From the perspective of the American frontiersman, the peace treaty that ended the Revolutionary War not only recognized the independence of the United States, but it also allowed the Americans access to those territories west of the Appalachian Mountains and secured the sovereign right of the federal government to exercise political authority there. The Paris treaty ceded to the United States the lands south of the Great Lakes, north of Florida, and east of the Mississippi River and thereby opened this land to white settlers. From the perspective of British-allied Indians during the war, this 1783 treaty marked a British betrayal of their territorial interests. The subsequent decision of the British to retain possession of frontier posts, which according to the peace treaty were supposed to be turned over to the United States, resulted from a continued desire to protect British interests among the Indians. By holding on to posts from Lake Champlain to Michilimackinac, the British seemed to suggest that they would assist Native Americans in their resistance against the United States, even though the British deliberately avoided war with the United States.[4] At the edges of American settlement the British presence persisted in the Maritimes, along the St. Lawrence River, south of the Great Lakes, and in the Mississippi valley. Just as France had formerly occupied these regions, partially in an attempt to contain British settlement along the Atlantic coastline, so the British occupied this frontier at the periphery of the American republic. Because of such competing claims, the 1783 peace, at least on the frontier, was no peace at all. The end of the Revolution unleashed years of turmoil there as individual, tribal, state, national, and international interests clashed. No permanent Anglo-American accommodation was reached before 1815.[5]

Frontier history from 1783 to 1800 is characterized by competing claims of sovereignty. For British loyalists in the West, including white and native supporters, the spirit of independence and self-government was better protected through allegiance with British forces than cooperation with the United States. Yet the American federal government, faced with serious financial difficulties in the early 1780s, urged the benefits of expanding the republican system to the West. Before the new federal Constitution was in place, the national government had no legal means of replenishing its empty treasury, except through allotments from the state governments. The sale of Indian lands in the Old Northwest provided a solution, especially after individual states gave up their claims to these western regions. Nonetheless, the federal sale of lands in the Northwest

Territory would ultimately depend upon the pacification of resident Indians, many of whom rejected the shameful peace concluded in 1783 just as vigorously as many frontiersmen proclaimed their right to acquire Indian lands as "the spoils of victory."[6] The demographic pressure of migrants moving westward proved irresistible; few Indian councils or British ministries in 1783 could have imagined its crushing force. Ultimately, as traditional and nationalistic histories of the American West reveal, the vision of white pioneers would dominate the region. This rapid flood of migrants quickly gave the Americans the numerical advantage, but in the 1780s and 1790s the Indians of the Northwest Territory and the British still hoped that they could defeat small groups of American settlers and a weak national army. That situation had changed dramatically by 1812, at which time more than a quarter of a million Americans lived in the Old Northwest. Yet on the eve of the War of 1812 British officials in London, unaware of the exact dimensions of this migratory force, still discussed the creation of a buffer state north of the Ohio River.[7]

To convince current and prospective frontiersmen that the frontier's future rested with the American republic, the Confederation Congress approved the Resolution for the Government of the Western Territory (Ordinance of 1784) to extend national authority over the West. Although sometimes depicted as impotent with respect to other policy areas, Congress acted swiftly and decisively to organize the survey and sale of western lands. The original system, drafted by Thomas Jefferson, outlined a plan by which Congress would guarantee settlers of the territories immediate self-government and republican institutions.[8] Although the Northwest Ordinance of 1787 rewrote some of Jefferson's initial plans for self-government, subsequent legislation that reduced the minimum acreage required for purchase did enable more settlers of modest wealth to become landowners. Congress had designed the terms by which the Republic could be extended. Nonetheless, the early land ordinances, including legislation from 1784 and 1785 and the Northwest Ordinance of 1787, were more theoretical than their authors might have imagined since Indian resistance remained a formidable obstacle to white settlement.

Congress, in developing its Indian policies, at first deliberately and firmly rejected British principles and understandings of native sovereignty. Indian tribes no longer were treated as equal nations but as dependents. Military defeats of the U.S. Army at the hands of Indian warriors only heightened American determination to treat Indian nations as subjects of the federal government. American commissioners would not conform to Indian protocol but rather insisted that tribal spokesmen adopt American diplomatic protocol. Offering fewer gifts than was the British custom, the Americans also expected substantial land in return. As one historian has aptly put it, "Gone were the customary belts of wampum and the elaborate Indian speeches. In their place Americans substituted blunt talk and a habit of driving each article home by pointing a finger at the assembled natives."[9] Additionally, the American Indian policy also involved a certain rewriting or misrepresentation of diplomatic history since it perpetuated the myth that all Indians had allied themselves clearly with the British in the Revolutionary War and consequently justified the dispossession of all Native Americans, regardless of their activities during the war.[10]

Continued Native American resistance in the West exposed the fiction of the American theory of conquest; Indian confederacies of the Old Northwest successfully resisted U.S. authorities well into the 1790s. In contrast to an aggressively confident posture, Henry Knox, after being appointed as secretary of war in 1785, argued that the British system of negotiation with the Indians as equals might be more effective and less disastrous than current policies of negotiating with the tribes as dependents. Knox's comments implicitly recognized the success of Indian resistance against American forces, and his suggestion that American leaders employ a British model of negotiation and purchase Indian territory influenced the more charitable tone of the Northwest Ordinance of 1787.[11] American commissioners returned to native customs, offered to pay for territories, and occasionally even returned land to its native owners, as occurred in negotiations with the Six Nations (Iroquois Confederacy) in 1794. Such practices, adopted due to necessity and borrowed from earlier British models, never secured much support among frontiersmen, but they did influence federal policy. The

Indian Intercourse Act of 1790 stated that the United States could obtain Indian lands only by treaty, although some settlers commonly pushed ahead of the surveyors and federal land office and thereby provoked Indian resistance. New practices appeared to concede the point that the United States did not automatically hold a title to all Indian land but rather the national government had the exclusive right to acquire such lands by treaty.

Although the new tone of diplomacy resulted largely from the failure of American forces to secure this territory by conquest, stereotypical images of native warriors persisted. Generally Americans blamed the Indians and their British backers for the violence on the frontier during the Revolutionary War, and horrific accounts of Indian violence and atrocities only multiplied after the war.[12] Popular captivity narratives and the striking painting *The Death of Jane McCrea* by John Vanderlyn fueled the stereotype of Indian savagery on the frontier. During the American Revolution, rebelling colonists presumed that the British had provoked Native American violence on the frontier; likewise in postrevolutionary years the assumption was that the British continued to provide crucial support for Indian resistance.

Between 1783 and 1815 the British policy regarding relations with the Americans consisted of two somewhat contradictory trends: a desire for an accommodation with former colonists, especially to restore transatlantic trade, and conversely an inclination to restrict the boundaries of the new American republic, perhaps even to encourage its demise. British occupation of frontier posts concerned American politicians, who feared that Britain wanted to regain her lost power and territory, but no such plan existed to reconquer the recently independent American colonies. Instead, the British were far more concerned about how an unstable backcountry would affect trade and whether France might try to regain a foothold in the American frontier. London statesmen favored a plan for British mediation between the Indians and the Americans, although U.S. authorities, including Alexander Hamilton, rejected any formal role, especially while Britain held the frontier posts. Likewise, American authorities never warmed to the British suggestion of a buffer state, a region closed to settlement but open to trade, which would recognize and conciliate the interests of Americans, the British, and the Indians.[13] Both plans, for mediation and a buffer state, assumed that the Indian nations possessed either sovereign territorial rights or the sovereignty necessary for third-party mediation. American politicians would accept neither premise; Hamilton and others interpreted British offers for mediation as interference from a foreign power and therefore a challenge to U.S. sovereignty.

The existing national boundaries outlined in the 1783 treaty were deceptively simple. The Old Northwest belonged to the United States on paper, but British influence in this region was far from extinguished. In fact, with the notable exception of George Rogers Clark's victories, Britain had effective control over most of the Old Northwest after Yorktown. Indian allies and agents, loyalists, land speculators, and Canadian merchants and fur traders urged the British to retain the Old Northwest posts. Mohawk leader and loyalist Joseph Brant traveled to London to make such a plea, as did other spokesmen. On the frontier British-Indian trade continued almost unabated after 1783, as a way to reward former allies for their allegiance during the war and to retain their goodwill. Largely uninfluenced by European treaties, British Indian agents and merchants continued their business, and the fur trade expanded after the American Revolution.[14] Many British Indian agents remained in the south although the British no longer could provide formal commissions and salaries, and in the north a reduced British Indian department persisted in the vicinity of Detroit, Montreal, and Niagara. An enduring British economic presence in the Indian country worried both American and Spanish politicians; practically the supply of guns and ammunition from Canada assisted interior tribes in the defense of their land claims. Because the Spanish officials did not offer guns and powder, British-Indian trade thrived.[15]

Such British activities among the Indians, Americans claimed, clearly violated the terms of the peace treaty, but immediately after the war no fixed British policy yet existed regarding the retention of frontier forts and continued economic or military assistance to Native Americans. Not until 1791–92 did the creation of a neutral

Indian barrier state as a buffer between British Canada and the United States become official policy, although the idea was articulated earlier by Frederick Haldimand, governor of Quebec.[16] As much as British and Canadian statesmen may have been interested in employing or even manipulating Indian nations as buffers, such an alliance was both uneasy and fluctuating. Long aware of the differences between Indian and European warfare, the British willingly advised and even encouraged Indian resistance against the United States after the American Revolution, but not until the War of 1812 did British and Indian soldiers officially fight together.[17]

Because the king did not formally ratify the peace treaty until April 1784 and because the preliminary treaty vaguely promised the return of frontier posts "with all convenient speed," considerable confusion existed. Many British ministers assumed they had months to withdraw from the frontier, whereas evacuation from coastal ports needed to be far more immediate. In the summer of 1783 Canadian authorities refused to hand over British forts because they accurately claimed that they had not yet received notification that the British had indeed ratified the final peace agreement. British officials, including Richard Oswald and William Petty, earl of Shelburne, had agreed to cede the Old Northwest—an agreement that led to the earl of Shelburne's removal from office since many members of Parliament felt such terms were far too generous toward the United States. Despite contradictory mapping of the border between the United States and Canada, which was not entirely resolved until 1842, in the 1780s British officials still would have expected that most of these British posts would lie south of the Canadian border.[18] Nonetheless, thirteen years would lapse before the British would evacuate the forts.

Governor Haldimand must have been pleased when he learned in the spring of 1784 that Thomas Townshend, Lord Sydney, the new home secretary, liberally interpreted the phrase "with all convenient speed" and therefore an immediate transfer would not occur. Haldimand believed in maintaining friendly relations with the Indians and retaining British forts so as to prevent the American rebels from possessing the Ohio Territory; he likely hoped eventually to recover lands previously lost by diplomats.[19] Lord Sydney's views probably had been influenced also by the fur trade, Indian alliances, and the opinions of Haldimand and other Canadian officials. In a couple of years British statesmen would argue that they retained the forts to retaliate for American nonpayment of prerevolutionary debts, although originally far more attention at Whitehall and in the British Commons was paid to claims of loyalist persecution.[20] From the British perspective it was quite plausible that eventually this republican experiment would fail. Perhaps then the United States would revert to royal control, in which case Britain should be strategically placed, in Canada and on the frontier, to protect its future interests. In the meantime, occupation of the forts might prevent Indian wars.

Occupation of the forts implied that Britain actively supported the Indians, and it also suggested that the British, like their native allies, disagreed with Americans about the relative importance of prerevolutionary treaties versus the 1783 peace agreement. Indians insisted that the western boundary of the United States was not the Mississippi but the Ohio River, as evidenced in the Treaty of Fort Stanwix in 1768. Since the 1760s the British had claimed that sovereignty over the Old Northwest resided with the British monarch and that the king's Indian subjects who lived upon this land enjoyed usufruct, or the right to use the land. Consequently the British claimed that in the 1768 treaty the natives had been compensated only for usufruct, not for the actual land title that already belonged to the crown.[21] Because Britons could readily interpret that the United States in the peace of 1783 did not acquire Indian claims of usufruct, some Canadian and British officials promised their Indian allies that the boundary set by the British and Americans could not deprive them of their land rights. As Sir John Johnson told the Six Nations in July 1783:

> You are not to believe or even think that by the line which has been described it was meant to deprive you of an extent of country of which the right of soil belongs to, & is in yourselves as sole proprietaries as far as the boundary line agreed upon, and established . . . in the year 1768 at Fort Stanwix, neither can I harbor an Idea that the United States will act

so unjustly, or impolitically as to endeavor to deprive you of any part of your Country under the pretence of having conquered it.—The King still considers you his faithful Allies, as his children, and will continue to promote your happiness by his protection, and encouragement of your usual intercourse with traders with all other benefits in his power to afford you.[22]

In this manner Johnson claimed that the British had not given away Indian land rights in settling with the Americans the western boundary of the Old Northwest. Instead, the British would continue to protect Indian claims. That the British were not evacuating the frontier posts only provided further evidence of their continued cooperation with interior tribes, whom they claimed retained at least usufruct.

John Jay, who was appointed secretary of foreign affairs by Congress in 1784, attempted to negotiate with the British concerning their occupation of frontier posts. The British claimed that these forts would not be evacuated until outstanding prewar debts had been settled. Jay also negotiated with the Spanish and was informed that the United States would have to give up free navigation of the Mississippi before the Spanish would discuss matters of territorial sovereignty and commerce. Jay's diplomatic frustrations reveal a broader problem: despite the confident claims of Americans, the destiny of the frontier was still uncertain. Huge portions of the U.S. national budget had been allocated to frontier defense, but still federal troops were unable to convince tribes of the Ohio region that American independence meant native dependence. Nor could diplomats such as Jay defend American claims of sovereignty with respect to the interior forts and navigation of the Mississippi River. Not only the Indians refused to accept the authority of the American federal government, but white frontiersmen in the Old Northwest also had substantial complaints. Clark and other leaders concluded that the East did not sufficiently appreciate the West and more specifically that it did not understand the West's crucial demand for free navigation of the Mississippi. An east-west rift was particularly evident when easterners offered to give up free navigation of the Mississippi in the Jay-Gardoqui negotiations in 1786. Given these frustrations, some westerners, including Kentucky and Tennessee residents, seriously considered joining the British rather than the U.S. Confederation. Separatist movements also sprang up in Vermont.[23]

In 1784, after a trip to the Ohio region, George Washington wrote about the competing national interests on the frontier and the potential consequences for the United States. "No well informed Mind need be told, that the flanks and rear of the United territory are possessed by other powers, and formidable ones too." He speculated that Spanish and British powers, especially with subsequent immigration, could substantially increase and thereby threaten future American interests on the frontier. "The Western Settlers—from my own observation—stand as it were on a pivet [sic]—the touch of a feather would almost incline them any way."[24] Washington's poignant words assisted him in arguing that the United States needed immediately to expand its markets westward, but they also aptly illustrate the precarious situation of frontier sovereignty after the Revolution. Our modern knowledge that eventually the Ohio Country and other western regions stretching to the Pacific would decisively be added to the American domain can obscure the contemporary picture. In the aftermath of the American Revolution, Americans, including even Washington, would have been far less confident about the future of the frontier.

By the mid-1780s Britain credited her continued occupation of frontier forts to American nonpayment of prewar debts. Legally this excuse seemed convincing, even to American secretary for foreign affairs Jay, but the posts' retention also fit with the British expectation that the United States would collapse politically. However desirable that outcome, British officials refrained from overt actions that might bring about the Republic's demise. The Mohawk leader Brant had discussions with several British politicians in the winter of 1785–86, including Lord Sydney, who would not agree to use British soldiers to defend the Ohio River as the legitimate boundary of the Indian territory. British redcoats would continue to defend forts in the Old Northwest, but they would not offer overt military aid to the Indians. British policy deliberately avoided war with the United

States, but it simultaneously considered the potential Spanish threat. If the American republic failed and westerners separated from eastern states, would the West join with Spain or Britain, and might France reemerge in the Mississippi valley? British officials, including the earl of Shelburne, who had granted the Old Northwest to the United States, still expected Britain to dominate Canada and the Mississippi. Only residents of the United States believed that the 1783 peace treaty had granted the territory permanently to the new republic. Politicians in Britain and Spain did not share that assumption.[25]

While Americans looked toward expanding republican governments in the West through a series of land ordinances in the 1780s, the British and the Spanish both independently pursued antirepublic policies deliberately intended to limit the new republic's expansion. Spain's presence in North America had been reinvigorated by the acquisition of Louisiana from the French (after the Seven Years' War), by its expansion into California and the Gulf coast, and by regaining Florida from Britain in the 1783 treaty. In West Florida, Spanish control was not absolute in the 1790s, since British trade continued. With designs on territory south of the Ohio, Spain managed to control both sides of the lower Mississippi and earlier in 1784 had closed the river to American shipping.[26] With only limited success in attracting immigrants to Louisiana and Florida, the Spanish had relied on the presence of Indian nations to serve as a pro-Spanish barrier to American settlement. Likewise, the British hoped to contain American expansion and simultaneously offer an alternative to the new American republic. The 1791 Canada Act, which created Upper Canada (now Ontario), granted residents limited self-government under a monarchical system. British troops in American frontier posts such as Detroit were intended to protect Canada, as well as Britain's interests in North America, by creating a buffer to American expansion.

Disagreements in the 1790s about U.S. foreign relations, specifically whether relations with either Britain or France were preferable, also impacted frontier development. In their early support of the French Revolution, Americans affirmed their faith in republican government, but by 1793 the bloody excesses of the Reign of

Terror, the execution of the French king, and the outbreak of war between France and Great Britain divided Americans. Washington urged neutrality. So did American merchants who claimed neutrality and attempted to trade with both parties. Federal politicians who also agreed publicly with Washington's neutral position, including members of his cabinet, disagreed about the intended outcome. Whereas Hamilton promoted strong relations with Great Britain, Jefferson, who favored France, argued that American sovereignty would best be demonstrated with more international independence. Instead of looking east for European models, Jefferson advised that western expansion provided not only an alternative vision of America's destiny but also a means of safeguarding the fledgling Republic.[27]

Independent western farmers, Jefferson thought, were not only vital to the economy but the key to the Republic's political success. Perhaps such an independent spirit caused some of these American frontiersmen to challenge the authority of their own federal government. Rival claims of sovereignty involved not only British, Spanish, French, and Native American assertions about traditional rights or newly acquired boundaries and jurisdictions; some disagreements about sovereignty on the frontier also pitted Americans against the claims of their national government. The threat of international intrigue persisted, but western residents were concerned not only about Spanish restrictions on American navigation of the Mississippi and the British presence in the northern fur trade; their concerns over local autonomy also erupted in rebellion against federal authority. The Whiskey Rebellion was a result of western discontent with Hamilton's federal excise on whiskey, and Washington's reaction, in sending thousands of troops to western Pennsylvania, demonstrated that the federal government was committed to protecting the western boundary and to asserting the supremacy of the national government over the local or regional community. Observant Spanish and British officials noted that given such discontent, western settlements might prefer union with Canada or Florida rather than domination by a distant eastern government. English and Spanish agents secretly worked toward that end.

Contrary views about republicanism clashed on the frontier in the 1790s. Britain's retention of frontier posts, the rapid expansion of American settlers westward, and continued Indian defense of traditional territorial rights practically guaranteed the eruption of local violence, but differing international attitudes about republicanism also fueled the conflict. British politicians, through their collective experiences both in the American and French Revolutions, had come to see republicanism as a threat to society. Such attitudes influenced western policies because British statesmen mused that if the French or American presence on the frontier could be minimized, so too might radical republicanism be contained. The frontier forts remained important not only as an asset to the fur trade but also as an impediment to the spread of republicanism in Canada. The threat of radical republicanism loomed especially large, according to Lt. Gov. John Graves Simcoe of Upper Canada and other British statesmen, even on the frontier. Edmond Charles Genêt, French minister to the United States, in raising troops against Spanish Florida and Spanish Louisiana in 1793, seemed to announce the potential of a renewed French presence in the West. The Anglo-Spanish declaration of war against France later that year effectively prevented France's reemergence in North America. Instead, British officials suggested that Britain become more involved in the Mississippi valley so as to assist Spain in the protection of the Floridas and Louisiana. In return, Britain might be granted West Florida and free navigation of the Mississippi. In such a manner, British interests in the Old Northwest could be preserved and Canada's security protected. After all, many British and Canadian officials feared that if the American army defeated the Indians, troops would continue to march north and by attacking Canadian possessions attempt to drive Britain from North America.[28]

The Americans assembled a large army in 1791 under Gen. Arthur St. Clair. No doubt they hoped that, in winning a campaign against the Indians, American forces would gain control of those regions formally ceded by Britain and, consequently, British-allied Indians would abandon both their British advisers and their defense of the Ohio River boundary. Instead, St. Clair's defeat, the largest

Indian victory ever against the American army, energized the followers of the Shawnee Blue Jacket and facilitated the expansion of
an Indian confederacy. Meanwhile, British politicians, including
especially Simcoe, believed that by retaining both the forts and
Indian allies, Canada's security could be protected from the threat
of republicanism. Such a buffer state would preserve the Old
Northwest for Indians, loyalists, and other opponents of republican
government. Additionally, a British buffer state, if geographically
situated to include portages between the Great Lakes and the
Mississippi River, could assist in another important British goal:
obtaining free navigation of the Mississippi. The United States
agreed that Britain should be permitted free navigation of this
important river, and yet American officials focused on securing
Spanish permission for the use of New Orleans and the lower
Mississippi River, neither of which seemed crucial to British-
Canadian interests.[29] British and American opinions about both the
future of the Old Northwest and navigation of the Mississippi clearly
diverged, for U.S. officials were not prepared to concede any territory for such a buffer state, and they considered the appropriate
river boundary to be the Mississippi, not the Ohio.

A series of intertwined domestic and international crises of the
early 1790s portended increasing turmoil between the United
States and Britain. Britain had blockaded France and failed to recognize American claims as a neutral trader. Instead, the British navy
continued to impress American sailors and confiscated the cargoes
of more than 250 American ships in 1793 and early 1794; war with
Britain seemed increasingly likely. In addition to the problems on
the high seas, Washington feared that a perceived weakness in the
federal presence in the West could encourage British or Spanish
intervention. American politicians believed that they had found
serious evidence of British interference already, including a speech
that appeared to endorse Indian violence. Early in 1794 Sir Guy
Carleton, Lord Dorchester, invited to Quebec an Indian delegation.
His widely circulated address delivered on 10 February angered
Americans who felt it was an attempt to excite the Indians to arms.
Lord Dorchester argued that because the United States had violated
the 1783 treaty, the Canadian boundary need not be observed;

instead, he affirmed the Ohio boundary as set by the Treaty of Fort Stanwix and declared the illegality of American settlement on the frontier.[30]

Although it did not materialize, Americans particularly feared that a reinvigorated Indian confederacy might emerge with combined Anglo-Spanish support. The American general Anthony Wayne believed that Britain and its Indian allies aimed to limit the expansion of the American republic to the Ohio River. While some British officials, including Simcoe, might have agreed to retreat from that Ohio boundary if a buffer state could be established, northwestern and southern Indians were less willing to compromise about the Ohio boundary. Simcoe, who previously believed that the Indians might be effectively turned against the Americans, had to contend with the impressive strength and independent character of native resistance. Their hardy determination to end American expansion, as well as the flood of settlers, meant that Simcoe's plan for a barrier state had little hope of success. As Britain's allies, Spanish politicians discussed whether they should encourage southern Indians to join a pro-British confederation. Yet if Britain improved her position in North America, Spain might be pressured to cede Louisiana and the Floridas. Still, the Spanish and British appeared to have much in common. Their involvement in European hostilities suggested that a shared hatred of republicanism, whether on the frontier or on the continent, naturally urged them to combine together against France and the United States. British officials, who worried increasingly about the security of Fort Detroit, rebuilding Fort Miamis, and promoting Indian unity, hoped that they could benefit from the domestic turmoil within the United States. Frontier opposition to the whiskey tax and other Federalist policies meant that western regions might prefer a British connection.[31]

In early 1794 an Anglo-American war seemed probable, if not inevitable, but by the summer British policy turned toward reconciliation. Lord Dorchester's speech, the rebuilding of Fort Miamis, and British-Spanish collaboration concerning an Indian confederation might be seen as precursors to an Anglo-American war, but by summer French military victories urged British policy makers to concentrate on the European arena. To improve relations between the United States and Great Britain, Washington sent Jay to London in April 1794. Britain's main reason for settling long-standing disagreements with the United States was its need to concentrate on its war against France. A declaration of war against the United States could prevent Americans from shipping food to France, but British officials were reluctant to add another enemy, especially when that foe appeared to be rejecting French-style Jacobinism. The American republic was not embracing radical republicanism, and Federalist officeholders had demanded Genêt's recall. Consequently, Whitehall sent instructions to politicians in Canada to refrain from any actions that might upset the diplomatic proceedings. Only if diplomacy failed would the British join with Spanish and Indian allies to attempt a revision of the balance of power in the frontier. Instead, an American victory over northern Indians influenced the peace process.[32]

This American victory, at the Battle of Fallen Timbers in August 1794, subdued the Miami Confederacy under Little Turtle and thereby secured vast portions of the Old Northwest for white American settlers. During battle the British had not offered the military assistance that their Indian allies expected. Nor were retreating warriors allowed into Fort Miamis, probably so as not to provoke an American attack on the fort. Despite previous British provisioning of Indian allies, Britain's failure to intervene militarily at Fallen Timbers created serious suspicions of British abandonment. Yet Canadian officials had been urged not to intervene, since British diplomats were attempting to negotiate a reconciliation with the United States. To pursue that goal, British officials had dropped plans concerning the annexation of Pennsylvania, Kentucky, and Vermont. A British interest in peace combined with American military success in the West encouraged the negotiation of Jay's Treaty later that year. Meanwhile, hope subsided for a strong Indian confederacy.[33]

Both Jay's Treaty and the Treaty of Greenville answered many of the Anglo-American arguments concerning frontier sovereignty that had raged since the Revolutionary War. Jay's Treaty, chiefly an international commercial agreement that recognized Britain and

America as favored trading partners, influenced frontier development. The British promised to withdraw from American soil by 1796, and in that year they left Detroit, the fort that had been so central to earlier policies as a buffer zone protecting Canadian and British interests. Through the evacuation of frontier posts, Britain appeared superficially to recognize American claims of sovereignty in the West, although such matters would flare up again in the War of 1812. Northwestern Indians who met in August 1795 with Wayne to sign the Treaty of Greenville had to recognize that, as one historical expert has suggested, "The Treaty of Fort Stanwix was dead."[34] Dead was the hope that the Ohio River could be defended as the westernmost border of the United States. Ironically, the federal government recognized the sovereignty of these Indians for the purpose of concluding a binding treaty through which much of present-day Ohio was ceded to the United States. Indian hopes for a confederation dissolved. Along with the evacuation of frontier posts, the Treaty of Greenville supported long-standing American federal government claims that the future of western regions lay with the Republic.

While American politicians could readily agree that the Ohio region should become part of the U.S. domain, more opposition surrounded Jay's Treaty. The Senate ratified the treaty in June 1795 by a bare two-thirds majority, despite serious opposition by southerners, westerners, and pro-France advocates. In bitter treaty debate, Republicans claimed this treaty reduced the United States to an economic satellite of Britain. They feared that the ultimate success of the Republic and the future of American independence might be compromised through such an agreement. Still, from the perspective of 1795 the balance of power on the frontier clearly had turned to favor the United States. Britain was evacuating frontier forts, Indian alliances had fragmented, and Spanish-American relations were shifting.

Spain also had interests in improving American relations. The Spanish had been defeated in their war with republican France, and in 1795 Thomas Pinckney, an American envoy, negotiated the treaty that bears his name. By its terms Spain abandoned its claims to territory south of the Ohio River, set a boundary with the United States at the thirty-first parallel, and opened the Mississippi to American shipping. Congressmen from the West and South were far more pleased with the terms of this treaty than those of Jay's Treaty, but both Jay's Treaty and Pinckney's Treaty were important American victories. In each agreement Americans had attempted and to some extent succeeded in asserting their sovereignty over western lands. Perhaps fear of French republicanism brought Britain and the United States closer together in the last few years of the 1790s; although disagreements over trade, impressment, and shipping persisted, Britons and Americans shared one frontier goal: to keep France from reasserting its interests on the American frontier. Spain had made peace with the new conservative French government, the Directory, in 1795 and almost had given Louisiana and the Floridas to France. From the perspective of British statesmen, Spain's new alliance threatened to spread Jacobinism in America. If France attempted to recover its North American empire, British commerce would certainly suffer. Consequently, British officials reconsidered their policies in North America and the possible merits of cooperating with the United States.

The narrow Federalist victory in the 1796 American presidential election must have reassured British politicians who worried that the United States might ally itself more firmly with France had Jefferson won the election rather than John Adams. Still, Jefferson's Republicans had significant influence; not only was Jefferson vice president, but Republicans in the House of Representatives almost defeated Jay's Treaty by refusing to grant the funds for its implementation. American Federalists and the British ministry seemed natural allies. Unlike the Republicans, many Federalists were lukewarm about western expansion, and many British officials were anxious to take the Floridas and Louisiana. The predominant reason for improved Anglo-American cooperation in 1797–98 was a common fear of France and the international forces of republicanism.[35] Popular anti-French sentiment increased in America; France had opposed Jay's Treaty as a violation of the Franco-American alliance established in 1778 and retaliated by seizing American merchant ships in 1797. A diplomatic incident, the XYZ Affair, and the threat of a naval quasi-war with France in 1798 did little to calm Franco-American relations. Instead, U.S. disagreements with France automatically resulted in improved relations with Britain. To keep France off the North American continent and to limit the effects of republican extremism, the British ministry in 1797–98 worked with the Federalist administration. Although Federalists had not been known for promoting western expansion, they could accept that adding the Floridas and Louisiana to the American domain might be preferable to allowing them to fall into French hands. Hamilton, who urged cooperation with Britain, reasoned that Britain could be content if these territories became American possessions, for that would mean France had not recovered its North American empire. British officials were far less sure that the Floridas and Louisiana should become part of the United States.

British statesmen, who had not concluded a formal agreement with the United States in 1797 or 1798, discovered in 1799 that the United States did not declare war on France as expected. Likely Whitehall could not determine precisely which groups held power in the American federal system: the Federalists divided over John Adams's policies, including his decision to send commissioners to Paris, and the Republicans' strength was improving on the eve of their 1800 presidential victory. In such circumstances British officials found it problematic to link themselves too closely with the pro-Hamilton Federalists, pro-Adams Federalists, or the Republicans. British-American cooperation had been founded largely upon fear of a common enemy, France, and consequently it soured, or at least cooled substantially, when the United States did not become involved in a full-blown war with France. Meanwhile, the British navy stepped up its impressment of American sailors and its seizure of U.S. ships.[36] British policy had focused consistently on its goal of preventing France from regaining an important role in North America; by so doing, both Canada and the frontier could be kept safe from radical republicanism. Cooperation with the United States had appeared to favor that anti-French goal in 1797 and 1798, but later in 1799 this informal alliance dissolved. After the Federalist era, the British presence in the frontier would again threaten the authority of the U.S. government and its vision of the frontier's future.

By 1800 Americans had experienced almost two decades of postrevolutionary conflict with Britain and other foreign powers concerning American sovereignty—its claims as a neutral trader, its claims of citizenship when faced with impressment, and its territorial claims in the West. Such arguments continued well into the early 1800s as America defended its independence and its territories again in the War of 1812, but in 1800 at the creation of the Indiana Territory, concerns about the future of the Republic continued. The frontier situation was far from stable. The 1783 peace treaty had provided no immediate frontier peace but rather unleashed further conflict—among diverse peoples and nations, about revolutionary questions of self-determination and sovereignty. More recent diplomatic negotiations in the 1790s had secured American rights to navigate the Mississippi and had persuaded the British to vacate forts in the Old Northwest, and so American federal authority in the West seemed more certain. Still, the British threat did not entirely vanish in the frontier: at the end of the 1790s British officials began to revert to previous frontier policies, and the British presence would reassert itself most vigorously by 1812. Nevertheless, Americans by 1800 may have felt increasingly confident, or at least optimistic, that their claims of sovereignty in the West could be recognized internationally.

Notes

1. For general studies of postrevolutionary–British-American diplomacy, see especially, J. Leitch Wright, Jr., *Britain and the American Frontier, 1783–1815* (Athens: University of Georgia Press, 1975); Charles R. Ritcheson, *Aftermath of Revolution: British Policy toward the United States, 1783–1795* (1969; reprint, New York: W. W. Norton and Co., 1971); Bradford Perkins, *The Creation of a Republican Empire, 1776–1865*, The Cambridge History of American Foreign Relations, vol. 1 (New York: Cambridge University Press, 1993); Lawrence S. Kaplan, *Entangling Alliances with None: American Foreign Policy in the Age of Jefferson* (Kent, Ohio: Kent State University Press, 1987); and Alfred L. Burt, *The United States, Great Britain, and British North America from the Revolution to the Establishment of Peace after the War of 1812* (New Haven, Conn.: Yale University Press, 1940).

2. Reginald Horsman, "The Collapse of the Ohio River Barrier: Conflict and Negotiation in the Old Northwest, 1763–1787," in *Pathways to the Old Northwest: An*

Observance of the Bicentennial of the Northwest Ordinance (Indianapolis: Indiana Historical Society, 1988), 33.

3. For a useful discussion of the links between imperial and western history, see Jay Gitlin, "On the Boundaries of Empire: Connecting the West to Its Imperial Past," in *Under an Open Sky: Rethinking America's Western Past*, eds. William Cronon, George Miles, and Jay Gitlin (New York: W. W. Norton, 1992), 71–89.

4. Colin G. Calloway, *The American Revolution in Indian Country: Crisis and Diversity in Native American Communities* (Cambridge: Cambridge University Press, 1995), 272–77.

5. Ibid., 283; Wright, *Britain and the American Frontier*, ix.

6. Calloway, *American Revolution in Indian Country*, 281. On postwar Indian policies, see Reginald Horsman, *Expansion and American Indian Policy, 1783–1815* (East Lansing: Michigan State University Press, 1967), chapters 1 and 2.

7. Horsman, "Collapse of the Ohio River Barrier," 43–44; Wiley Sword, *President Washington's Indian War: The Struggle for the Old Northwest* (Norman: University of Oklahoma Press, 1985), 79–83.

8. For an especially succinct account, see Peter S. Onuf, "The West: Territory, States, and Confederation," in *The Blackwell Encyclopedia of the American Revolution*, eds. Jack P. Greene and J. R. Pole (Cambridge, Mass.: Blackwell Reference, 1991), 346–55.

9. James H. Merrell, "Declarations of Independence: Indian-White Relations in the New Nation," in *The American Revolution: Its Character and Limits*, ed. Jack P. Greene (New York: New York University Press, 1987), 201.

10. Calloway, *American Revolution in Indian Country*, 285; Horsman, *Expansion and American Indian Policy*, 3–15.

11. Horsman, *Expansion and American Indian Policy*, 32–34.

12. Horsman, "Collapse of the Ohio River Barrier," 36–37; Ritcheson, *Aftermath of Revolution*, 166.

13. Wright, *Britain and the American Frontier*, ix, x; Ritcheson, *Aftermath of Revolution*, 151, 159–60, 244–56.

14. Colin G. Calloway, *Crown and Calumet: British-Indian Relations, 1783–1815* (Norman: University of Oklahoma Press, 1987), 131–88, especially 131–36.

15. Wright, *Britain and the American Frontier*, 5, 13, 26, 30–31, 37–38; Sword, *President Washington's Indian War*, 7–21; Reginald Horsman, *The Frontier in the Formative Years, 1783–1815* (New York: Holt, Rinehart and Winston, 1970), 47.

16. Robert F. Berkhofer, Jr., "Barrier to Settlement: British Indian Policy in the Old Northwest, 1783–1794," in *The Frontier in American Development: Essays in Honor of Paul Wallace Gates*, ed. David M. Ellis (Ithaca, N.Y.: Cornell University Press, 1969), 254–55.

17. Sword, *President Washington's Indian War*, 231; Calloway, *Crown and Calumet*, 193–239, especially 193–200.

18. Wright, *Britain and the American Frontier*, 15–20; Jonathan R. Dull, "Foreign Relations, after 1783," in Greene and Pole, eds., *Blackwell Encyclopedia of the American Revolution*, 375–76.

19. Berkhofer, "Barrier to Settlement," 249–76, especially 250.

20. Ritcheson, *Aftermath of Revolution*, 49–69; Wright, *Britain and the American Frontier*, 22, 24–25.

21. Ritcheson, *Aftermath of Revolution*, 246–47; Wright, *Britain and the American Frontier*, 38–40.

22. Berkhofer, "Barrier to Settlement," 253.

23. Wright, *Britain and the American Frontier*, 34, 42–43; Dull, "Foreign Relations," 377.

24. George Washington, 4 Oct. 1784, *The Diaries of George Washington*, vol. 4, *1784–June 1786*, eds. Donald Jackson and Dorothy Twohig (Charlottesville: University Press of Virginia, 1978), 66.

25. Wright, *Britain and the American Frontier*, 37, 41–46.

26. Horsman, *Frontier in the Formative Years*, 14–16.

27. For a solid general treatment of diplomacy in the 1790s, see Perkins, *Creation of a Republican Empire*, 81–110.

28. Wright, *Britain and the American Frontier*, ix–x, 67, 82–84.

29. Sword, *President Washington's Indian War*, 191, 195–200; Wright, *Britain and the American Frontier*, 68–74.

30. Wright, *Britain and the American Frontier*, 87–89.

31. Ibid., 77, 81, 90–95.

32. Ibid., 95–97.

33. Berkhofer, "Barrier to Settlement," 275; Reginald Horsman, "The British Indian Department and the Resistance to General Anthony Wayne, 1793–1795," *Mississippi Valley Historical Review* 49 (1962): 269–90.

34. Wright, *Britain and the American Frontier*, 98.

35. Ibid., 107–8, 116.

36. Ibid., 118–20.

Adventures in Historical Editing:

The William Henry Harrison Papers Project[1]

by

DOUGLAS E. CLANIN

W HEN I WAS ATTEMPTING TO COME UP WITH A TITLE FOR THIS presentation, I thought about calling it "What a Long, Strange Trip It's Been," but out of deference to the memory of Jerry Garcia and to the survivors of the Grateful Dead band, along with their lawyers, I decided to use the bland title "Adventures in Historical Editing." At the outset, however, I want to observe that from the beginning it *has* been a long, strange trip for those of us who worked on the William Henry Harrison Papers project at the Indiana Historical Society. From the project's inception in the late 1970s and early 1980s, it evolved in ways that no one associated with it could or did anticipate. For example, we never thought it would take us more than fifteen years to complete the project. Also, we never anticipated that our publishing format would be microfilm, and we had never heard of CD-ROM technology, which presents us with another potential way to disseminate our document transcripts to the public.

For more than seven decades Professor Logan Esarey's two-volume edition of the papers of William Henry Harrison from 1800 to 1815 was the standard printed source for Harrison's correspondence. In 1999 the Indiana Historical Society's ten-reel microfilm edition of transcripts became the standard edition of Harrison's papers for this period.

In this paper I will give some historical background on the provenance of the Harrison papers, present a brief history of the Harrison project, and make some remarks that summarize Harrison's life and career. In the process of going over the trials and tribulations that faced us, I hope you will gain a greater appreciation of the labors and achievements of all documentary editors. Also, I hope you will develop a greater understanding of who William Henry Harrison was.

First, I will present historical background about the Harrison papers, which I have summarized from the guide to our microfilm edition.[2] On 15 December 1830, at the second meeting of the Indiana Historical Society, William Henry Harrison, future ninth president of the United States, former governor of the Indiana Territory, and hero of the Battle of Tippecanoe and the War of 1812, was chosen one of eight honorary members of the Society.[3] On 17 January 1833, during a Harrison speaking engagement in Indianapolis, John Hay Farnham, the Society's first corresponding secretary, announced that Harrison "had presented to the Historical Society of this State, to be deposited in its archives the original correspondence of the Territorial Executive with the Government of the U. States, and that of the individual states, together with other interesting and valuable papers relating to the Territorial History of Indiana."[4] We were unable to locate any record in the Society's archives or in the Harrison papers that asserts that Harrison's generous gift was ever delivered to our organization.

Although Harrison apparently intended to donate the bulk of his papers to the Indiana Historical Society, it became clear to us that he retained control of many, if not most, of his documents after Secretary Farnham made his announcement in 1833. President Harrison died in office on 4 April 1841, only one month after his inauguration. Anna Harrison, his widow, and other family members retained control of his correspondence for almost eighty years after his death. As proof for the correctness of this statement, I want to quote from a widely printed news item that describes the destruction of the old Harrison homestead in North Bend, near Cincinnati, Ohio, on the night of 24–25 July 1858. In this report is the following observation: "The public has sustained a great loss in the destruction of a mass of valuable correspondence and papers. . . . These papers were stored in one of the garrets, and only a basketful or two [were] saved."[5]

Despite the assertion in the Cincinnati newspaper report that at least some of Harrison's papers had been saved, for many years it was generally believed, even by members of the Harrison family, that little, if anything, had survived. Even Benjamin Harrison, one of William Henry Harrison's grandsons, thought that most of Harrison's documents had been consumed in the 1858 fire.[6] Benjamin Harrison's belief was perpetuated in the preface that Esarey prepared for his 1922 edition of Harrison's papers. Esarey wrote, in part, as follows: "In offering this collection of Harrison papers the editor is entirely conscious of its meagerness. No doubt the best collection of historical material for the time and place covered was destroyed when the home of General Harrison at North Bend burned July 25, 1858."[7] Despite Esarey's pessimistic conclusion, he did manage to publish in his edition approximately 650 Harrison documents, located primarily in the United States War Department files, which are now housed in the National Archives as part of Record Group 107.

Despite the statements about the destruction of most of Harrison's papers, some of them did survive the fire and the ravages of time. In September 1919 the Library of Congress received a large box of Harrison's papers among a larger collection of the papers of his grandson Benjamin Harrison. This donation of William Henry Harrison papers formed the core of what became the Library of Congress collection. It is likely that this collection is composed primarily of documents that had been rescued from the 1858 fire.[8] Unfortunately for Esarey, none of the documents donated by the Harrison family to the Library of Congress was made available to him, and, consequently, none of them appears in his edition.

From the early 1930s until the present the Indiana Historical Society has purchased hundreds of Harrison documents, particularly those written while he was Indiana territorial governor

IHS C5941

Maj. Gen. William Henry Harrison

(1800–1812) and a general during the War of 1812. Currently the Society's collection contains approximately one thousand manuscripts that Harrison wrote during his lifetime (1773–1841) plus numerous rare illustrations, broadsides, pamphlets, and books on Old Tippecanoe.

The late Gayle Thornbrough and the late Dorothy Riker, remarkable documentary editors, worked at the Society for many years and utilized both Esarey's printed edition of the Harrison papers and the Society's impressive collection of Harrison documents to prepare several printed works that cover Indiana's territorial history, including a revised edition of the executive journal of the Indiana Territory[9] and the definitive edition of the journals of the Indiana territorial legislature.[10] As Thornbrough and Riker searched the Esarey edition and compared his printed versions of various Harrison documents with manuscript copies in the Society's collection, they discovered a number of errors in the printed edition. Thornbrough and Riker correctly judged the Esarey edition to be an inadequate and unreliable source, and they soon contemplated a revised edition of the Harrison papers.

In Esarey's defense we should note that because of his teaching duties at Indiana University–Bloomington, he had little free time to work on the Harrison papers and certainly did not have many opportunities to visit all of the repositories that contained Harrison documents. In addition, Esarey probably had limited secretarial assistance and a modest travel budget. Unlike modern editors, he had no access to four important editorial tools: the copy machine, the word processor, microfilm, and published finding aids and indexes. Thus, by 1922 standards, Esarey's compilation was probably as good as one could expect.

As their editorial duties permitted, Thornbrough and Riker continued to plan for a revised edition of the Harrison papers. They decided to maintain basically the same date range for the project as Esarey had in his edition, 1800 to 1815. They felt that this period in Harrison's life would be of most interest to members of the Indiana Historical Society and that it would encompass the majority of documents in the Society's collection of Harrison papers. Despite the number of documents in that collection and in the Library of Congress, they still felt that all the documents could be reproduced in a two-volume letterpress edition.

Nevertheless, in August 1981, when I made a preliminary search of the Lyman C. Draper collection at the State Historical Society of Wisconsin in Madison, my first in-person research trip on behalf of the Harrison project, I realized that we would require many more than two volumes for our revised letterpress edition since none of the large number of Harrison manuscripts I found in the Draper collection were in Esarey's edition. Although Thornbrough and Riker were not able to anticipate the large number of documents we found, it is largely because of their vision and their masterful editorial work that we were able to launch and complete the Harrison project, and it is for these reasons that our edition is dedicated to these two Hoosier editorial giants.

After I was hired in 1980 following the retirement of Riker, I devised a search strategy to help ensure that our revised Harrison edition would be as complete as possible, regardless of the number of volumes in it. In 1981 Susan H. Truax was hired as a full-time editorial assistant to take care of some of the editing chores, such as typing initial document transcripts, in anticipation of the preparation of the projected two-volume letterpress edition. After a few years we joined the computer revolution and began to produce computer-generated transcripts. Truax also contacted eleven hundred repositories in the United States, Canada, and Great Britain. We sent each institution or society a questionnaire asking if it had any Harrison correspondence in the 1800–1815 period covered by our documentary edition. Almost 90 percent of the repositories completed the questionnaire, and they sent us copies of more than 250 Harrison documents.

After analyzing the results of the questionnaire and after consulting various manuscript guides, particularly the *National Union Catalog of Manuscript Collections* (published under the auspices of the Library of Congress), Truax and I decided to concentrate our in-person searches to a handful of the eleven hundred repositories previously mentioned. From 1983 to 1988 we visited, at least once, thirty-two repositories in eight states and the District of Columbia. Ninety-four repositories and individuals from twenty-three states, the District of Columbia, Canada, and England provided us with material on Harrison and his times from more than 525 separate collections. We also collected printed items from periodical literature; state and local histories; Ohio, Kentucky, and Indiana newspapers of the period; and several hundred auction catalogs. Altogether we gathered 5,856 printed and manuscript pieces. We excluded duplicate or different versions of the same document and reproduced in full or in abstract form 3,965 documents, including enclosures, in our edition, more than six times as many documents as are in Esarey's compilation.

In 1984 Thornbrough retired as the Society's executive secretary and head of the Publications Division. Her successor, Dr. Peter T. Harstad, executive director from 1984 to 2001 and acting director of the Publications Division from 1984 to 1987, decided, based on the large number of document copies we had collected and were continuing to collect and on the advice of an outside consultant and other documentary editors, that we would have to scrap the proposed two-volume letterpress edition in favor of a microfilm edition of transcripts. After this format change was made, Harstad directed me to devote all of my work activities toward the completion of the Harrison project.

The microfilm format gave us much flexibility by allowing us to transcribe in whole or in part numerous routine or less-important documents, ones that would have to be abstracted in a letterpress edition. Microfilm also has an advantage over a format such as CD-ROM because if proper materials are used, it is a stable medium with a shelf life comparable to books printed on acid-free paper. There are two principal disadvantages to microfilm, however. First and foremost, a microfilm user has to have access to a microfilm reader. Second, because we were unable to prepare a full index to the Harrison papers, the user has to examine the table of contents and decide if a particular document might have content of interest or relevance. On the other hand, a CD-ROM edition would be searchable by name and by topic. Whereas microfilm readers are generally available only in large libraries, a CD-ROM edition would be accessible on most home, library, and school computers.

As complex and large as it was, the Harrison project required not only my full-time work efforts but also the labor of many other people. We could not have prepared this comprehensive edition without the active, sustained support of the administration and board of trustees of the Indiana Historical Society. My editorial assistants and I also received the assistance of many other Society staff members and countless others who assisted us from outside our organization.

Because of space limitations, I will not be able to detail or mention the aid we received from people from within and outside the Society, but I urge you to read the acknowledgments section in the printed guide to our microfilm edition for these details.

Over the years several people have asked me to relate anecdotes about my time on the road as I attempted to locate Harrison documents via plane, auto, and bus. I have the space to relate only a few amusing, and not so amusing, stories. In all the years I worked on the Harrison project, I think my most embarrassing experience occurred during my last visit to the Library of Congress (LC). My final day at the LC was a Saturday, and on that particular day I rushed to copy a massive number of pages from a series of documents I had tagged earlier that week. By the time I was ready to leave the James Madison Building, I had more than two hundred pages of photocopies. The library assistant at the reading room desk checked my stack of copies, and two security guards also examined the photocopies. The following day, after I arrived back in my hometown of Anderson, I discovered to my horror that I had inadvertently brought back with the photocopies an original indenture (or deed) written and signed by Harrison's father-in-law, John Cleves Symmes. The document was probably worth $3,000. After I drove to the Indiana Historical Society on Monday, I promptly called the manuscripts curator at the LC and asked him how I should return the "borrowed" document. He instructed me to pack it well, insure it for $5,000, and send it back via registered mail. In a couple of days the unique Symmes document reached the LC in good order. I was certainly relieved when I found out that it was back in its proper location.

A few days after that, however, a gentleman who identified himself as the head of security for the LC called and asked me to tell him exactly how I managed to thwart their security procedures and to take the original Symmes document out of the Madison Building. My heart sank for a moment because I was certain that I had violated some federal law and that I was in serious legal trouble. Fortunately, the LC's head of security was simply trying to determine what steps he and his staff would have to take in order to prevent or attempt to prevent a repeat of this occurrence. At the end of our conversation he thanked me for being so frank with him and for promptly returning the American people's document. To say I was relieved to hear his final comments is putting it mildly!

Some people have asked me to rate the best overall institution I visited during my Harrison project research trips. I know that comedians, journalists, and tourists have subjected Cleveland and the people of Cleveland to years of verbal abuse. Nevertheless, I feel the best overall repository I visited was the Western Reserve Historical Society, which is located on the east side of Cleveland in a cultural complex near Case Western University. In my opinion this historical society has struck a proper balance between its museum and library elements. Members of other state and local historical societies could learn much by touring the Western Reserve Historical Society and talking to the friendly staff. Even though I visited this historical institution in early winter, I had a very pleasant stay there. Also, during my visit I discovered an important collection of Harrison documents in the Gen. Simon Perkins Papers. Most of the documents I found in the Perkins papers had not been cataloged or previously published.

In this public forum I won't identify the following places, but two repositories located in the Midwest frustrated my efforts to expedite my searches of their relevant holdings. The first institution had a very friendly, helpful staff, but over the years each manuscripts curator who had worked there had created his or her own card-cataloging system. As a result the researcher there was forced to examine four or more card catalogs in order to find relevant collections. I found it very time-consuming to examine each card catalog, and the entire experience left me with doubts about how well I had searched the institution's holdings.

The second repository, which is located in a neighboring state, has a huge collection of documents in the 1800–1815 period. Unfortunately, the library staff in this repository insisted that each researcher take only one manuscript folder at a time to his or her desk. While conducting research there, I was almost always directed to the back of the reading room, and consequently I spent a considerable amount of time walking between my table and the front desk.

While visiting a small but important local historical society in a neighboring state, I had a most unusual experience. This society owns an impressive collection of early-nineteenth-century documents, but as of my last visit there, the directors of that organization did not have the money to adequately take care of or catalog these documents. To be blunt, their priceless collection was, and possibly continues to be, housed in an old mansion that one can only describe as being a firetrap. During the times I visited this mansion, the downstairs rooms were air conditioned, but the upstairs vault where I conducted some of my research felt like an oven. There was no copy machine on the premises, but volunteer staff members I met were so trusting and cooperative that they allowed me to take a briefcase full of manuscripts, possibly worth $50,000, to the public library, which was located down the street from the historical society. I copied the borrowed material while the mansion was shut down during the volunteers' lunch hour. As soon as I returned to my office, I contacted the reference librarian of that state's historical society and urged him to send a microfilming crew to that local historical society to copy all the manuscripts and printed materials that were housed in that old mansion. It is my hope that the collection was microfilmed shortly after my visit, but I never checked back with the state historical society to see if someone actually followed up on my recommendation.

My purpose in relating some of these Harrison project "war stories" is to illustrate how the staff, search aids, and research facilities in a specific institution can make or break a scholar's research trip. If the staff of a repository is competent and friendly, if adequate finding aids are available to researchers, and if liberal search rules are applied, a visit to a particular repository can be an altogether profitable and pleasant experience. If the reverse is the case, however, a research trip can become very time-consuming, frustrating, and costly.

On 10 May 1999 I took part in a C-SPAN program devoted to the life and career of William Henry Harrison. This program was part of a series on the presidents of the United States that C-SPAN broadcast on several occasions. During the program, host (and

C-SPAN founder) Brian Lamb threw me something of a verbal curveball when he asked me what I liked *least* about Harrison. Thinking quickly, I replied that I felt Harrison was too thin skinned, too sensitive to criticism. While I think this is a correct observation about his behavior on more than one occasion, my offhand remark was more a reflection on the fifteen-plus years I spent conducting editorial work on Harrison's letters and documents rather than an objective analysis. My relationship with Harrison was almost like a marriage, and as is the case in most marriages, quirks and personality traits can often lead to irritation, not to understanding. In this case, Harrison's repeated defense of his conduct became an irritant, a tiresome exercise to me as I dealt with letter after letter on the same theme. On reflection, I see that Harrison's response to criticism was an all-too-human quality that I and many others living today share with him. Also, I want to add that at least he did not respond to criticism with violence. Rather, he used newspaper essays that were written by his friends (and possibly also by himself) or legal action, such as when he launched a slander suit against one of his principal critics, William McIntosh, and won the case. That is, Harrison responded to criticism in a legal way, whereas some of his contemporaries, such as Andrew Jackson, Henry Clay, Aaron Burr, and Alexander Hamilton, fought duels over similar "affairs of honor."

In the months since C-SPAN's Harrison program first aired, shortly before we released the last seven microfilm reels of the Harrison papers, I began to think more about our role as editors and what we learned about Harrison's life and career as we worked on the project for more than fifteen years. For us the principal goal was to transcribe accurately the surviving Harrison documents for those fifteen years of his life, rather than interpret that life in part or in whole. For the editors of every documentary project, this is how it should be.

Richard Leffler, senior associate editor of the *Documentary History of the Ratification of the Constitution,* expressed this point most eloquently in his 1995 presidential address at the Association for Documentary Editing's annual convention: "We do not in our [modern documentary] editions write interpretive history. Our duty is to present the record, the documents, with a disinterested devotion solely to the document. We search for these documents in order to create an historical record. To us the document is not a piece of evidence, not a tool, a means with which to interpret history, at least not by us in the edition. To an historical editor, a document is an end—and let me be a romantic here—a document is truth itself. It has a value because it reveals a truth. As we bring it to the attention of the scholarly world, we facilitate the writing of interpretive history. As Stanley Idzerda has said, 'No document. No history.'"[11]

As an illustration of our "devotion" to the documents we located and attempted to transcribe accurately, we spent countless hours struggling to decipher difficult handwriting. The problem was particularly acute when we tried to figure out some of the signatures on various petitions. We knew these names would be of great importance to political and social historians as well as to genealogists, so we made every effort to transcribe them accurately. Sometimes we relied on pure luck as well as "devotion" to a document in order to transcribe it. Several years ago, while I was a member of the staff of the Documentary History of the Ratification of the Constitution project at the University of Wisconsin–Madison, we were attempting to proofread a key document that we wanted to print in the Pennsylvania volume. In this particular document the original transcriber had interpreted a key phrase as "jaguars opposed to the Constitution." This phrase made no sense to us. Finally, a project staff member who hadn't been involved in the proofreading process glanced at the word and said, "The word is 'quakers,' not 'jaguars.'" All of the proofreaders, including yours truly, let out a collective groan, but at least we had figured out what this eighteenth-century writer had actually written. No reader of this important letter will ever again stumble over the word "quakers." In this case, luck and an independent eye had saved the day and once again demonstrated our "devotion" to the documents.

Those of us who worked on the Harrison papers microfilm edition hope that scholars and other interested individuals will use these ten reels of transcribed documents to write new books and articles on Harrison's life and times. If they do, then the thousands of hours and the thousands of dollars we at the Indiana Historical Society and elsewhere have invested in this documentary enterprise will have been worthwhile. This investment is already beginning to pay off. Recently, Reginald Horsman, distinguished professor emeritus of history at the University of Wisconsin–Milwaukee, wrote an excellent, balanced essay about Harrison's life and times for the *Indiana Magazine of History* and expressed an interest in preparing a full modern biography on the life of the ninth president.[12]

Before I conclude this paper, I want to state that all future Harrison biographers need to go beyond the documentary record we transcribed in order to gain a fuller understanding of Harrison and what made him tick. The late professor Robert G. Gunderson, who worked on a Harrison biography for many years, once told me during a tour of our offices and an examination of our files that the most revealing documents about Harrison's life were not those that would appear in the microfilm edition, but rather documents we also collected (described in our official reports as "non-Harrison documents") that third parties wrote about Old Tippecanoe. George Washington came to Gunderson's mind when he told me that Harrison, like Washington, revealed little about his inner self in his writings.

In Harrison's case, part of the problem is that, whether by accident or design, none of the letters that Harrison and his wife wrote each other during the time period covered by our edition survives. However, even in the family letters that do survive, such as those written by Harrison to his nephew and son-in-law John Cleves Short, he revealed few details about family life in the Harrison circle. In fact, I can recall only one letter Harrison wrote in which he expressed himself in an emotional manner about his wife and children. In a letter to old army friend Gen. Thomas H. Cushing on 24 April 1813, he stated that he had left Cincinnati on the first of that month and that he was in the city "but a few days & had not Seen my family for Seven months during the greater part of which they had laboured under aflictions which Are perhaps without a parrallel— No less than 3 of my Children have lost for ever as I beleive the Sight of an Eye—The efforts to [releive?] them Could only promise Success under my personal Care my wife as you know having a Very delicate Constitution & at present almost Sinking under the weight of Care which the almost Universal Sickness of her large family imposes."[13] Again, I want to reiterate that in the surviving letters we reproduced in our microfilm edition, Harrison seldom expressed himself in such a feeling manner. Thus it will be essential for future biographers and writers about Harrison and his times to examine also the surviving writings of Harrison's friends and foes to flesh out his story.

Although my main task over the years was to gather and assemble a documentary edition of Harrison's papers from 1800 to 1815, with little thought devoted to Harrison's complete life and career, I did prepare one paper in 1986 in which I surveyed the strengths and weaknesses Harrison exhibited during his governorship of the Indiana Territory from 1800 to 1812.[14] In concluding this paper I would like to borrow and expand on the remarks I made then, but I will only survey the period of Harrison's life that is covered in our edition.

William Henry Harrison, Indiana's first territorial governor, was not a brilliant, original thinker or the originator of new programs, but he was very good at implementing national policies at the regional level. This is probably best illustrated by Harrison's ability to make treaties with some of the Native American leaders in the area of the Old Northwest, the most enduring legacy of his governorship, for good or for ill. Although he has been often criticized for his methods in obtaining these treaties, Harrison did get the results that Presidents Thomas Jefferson and James Madison wanted from the Native Americans: assimilation into white society or removal. This was a stark choice for the native populace, and in most cases the Native Americans were forced farther west.

For faithfully carrying out such national policies, Democratic-Republican presidents Jefferson and Madison rewarded Harrison with repeated reappointments as territorial governor, which was a remarkable feat for a man who had first been appointed to office by Federalist president John Adams. In implementing the policies of Jefferson and Madison, it probably helped Harrison (and it certainly didn't hurt) that he, too, was a native of Virginia and his father had signed the Declaration of Independence.

Harrison was less successful on the local political level, however, particularly after Indiana advanced to the second stage of government in 1805. Like Northwest Territory governor Arthur St. Clair before him, Harrison failed to adapt to changing political realities, such as those represented by political rival Jonathan Jennings and his followers, even if Harrison did realize what transformations were occurring in the territory. For example, Harrison's proslavery stand became increasingly the minority position in the Indiana Territory, but he still persisted in his support for the "peculiar institution." His stand on slavery does not demonstrate that Harrison was an evil man, only that he was at heart a conservative man (albeit a leader who could also be a pragmatic conservative from time to time) who clung to the institutions from his aristocratic Virginia past. He shared this point of view with many of his contemporaries across the South and rest of the country.

Harrison attempted to wield power through the patronage system that the territorial governor controlled, a system that was prone to abuse by all who held the office. All in all, however, I think that Harrison was a competent, basically honest administrator who managed his governorship as well as, if not better, than the rest of the territorial governors of the period.

In business affairs Harrison was less successful. He, his father-in-law John Cleves Symmes, his brother-in-law Peyton Short, and their friends were involved in a number of enterprises, especially in land speculation. Harrison and his family and friends were greatly overextended in their land purchases. The surviving documentary record demonstrates that they were guilty of poor, even reckless, record keeping, and many of their land parcels were seized and sold at sheriffs' sales because they failed to pay taxes on them. Also, Harrison and his family and friends had difficulty in collecting rent from tenants, in establishing property boundaries, and in keeping squatters off their lands. Despite his largely negative experiences in land speculating, Harrison persisted in buying land throughout the period covered by our microfilm edition.

When I examine Harrison's military service, I see a very mixed bag. He is most noted for the Battle of Tippecanoe, fought on 7 November 1811, where he commanded federal troops and state militia units against the Shawnee Prophet, brother of Tecumseh, and his Native American followers. Although Harrison's troops held the field of battle at the end of this sharp engagement, they probably suffered as many, if not more, casualties as the Native Americans. Shortly after this clash, Harrison and his troops relinquished the field of battle and retreated back to Vincennes. On numerous occasions from that day until the end of his life, Harrison was forced to defend his conduct during the Battle of Tippecanoe.

During the War of 1812 Harrison served as commander of the United States Northwest Army from 1812 to 1814. Again his military service record shows mixed results. He won a great victory at the Thames River, Upper Canada (now Ontario) on 5 October 1813, which resulted in the defeat of the British forces and, more important, in the death of Tecumseh, but Harrison's success was made possible by the brilliant victory on 10 September 1813 of United States naval forces commanded by Commodore Oliver Hazard Perry over the British fleet on Lake Erie.

Much of the time, Harrison's military operations were marked with great caution, a characteristic that has been noted by many writers. In letter after letter, Harrison complained about the lack of supplies and transportation, the weather and terrain problems, the unruly nature and lack of training of his troops, especially those in state and territorial militia units, and the failure of other military commanders to cooperate with him. Future writers on Harrison and his times need to be more aware of all these issues and use Harrison's letters and the observations of his contemporaries on the scene of his campaigns in order to reassess his military career. It was easy for many of Harrison's contemporary critics to complain about his lack of progress in fighting a military campaign in the Northwest, particularly because these critics were safely lodged in large eastern towns, far removed from the painful reality of War of 1812 combat in the Northwest. Modern critics need to move beyond the standard description of Harrison's wartime service, which was often established by his eastern critics, and examine a whole range of documents in order to prepare a more accurate picture of what really happened to Harrison and his troops in the Northwest during the War of 1812.

In conclusion, I want to say that it has been an honor and a privilege for me to work at the Indiana Historical Society on the Papers of William Henry Harrison. To everyone inside and outside the Society who helped to make this experience largely a positive one for me, thank you for your assistance and thanks for the memories.

Notes

1. I have based this paper on my earlier report on the Harrison project that was published under the title "A Phoenix Rising from the Ashes: The William Henry Harrison Papers Project," *Documentary Editing* 10 (June 1988): 6–10. I presented earlier and shorter versions of this paper on 4 May 1996 at the Indiana Historical Society's spring history conference at Spring Mill State Park near Mitchell, Indiana, and on 29 June 2000 at the Society's "*Traces* on the Road" program at the Knox County Public Library, Vincennes.

2. Douglas E. Clanin et al., eds., *A Guide to the Papers of William Henry Harrison, 1800–1815*, 2d ed. (Indianapolis: Indiana Historical Society, 1999).

3. Lana Ruegamer, *A History of the Indiana Historical Society, 1830–1980* (Indianapolis: Indiana Historical Society, 1980), 32, 33.

4. *Indianapolis Indiana Journal*, 23 Jan. 1833.

5. *Lawrenceburg* (Ind.) *Democratic Register*, 30 July 1858, from the *Cincinnati Gazette*, 26 July 1858.

6. Benjamin Harrison to unknown recipient, 3 Mar. 1883, quoted in Paul C. Richards Autographs, *The Beacon Bulletin*, catalogue no. 17, issue no. 9 (Brookline, Mass., n.d.): 16, item no. 548; Benjamin Harrison to Rev. Burke A. Hinsdale, 9 July 1896 (copy, Tibbott transcript, Benjamin Harrison Papers, Library of Congress, quoted in *Index to the William Henry Harrison Papers* (Washington, D.C.: Library of Congress, 1960), v.

7. Logan Esarey, ed., *Governors Messages and Letters*, Indiana Historical Collections, vol. 7 (Indianapolis: Indiana Historical Commission, 1922), 3.

8. *Index to the William Henry Harrison Papers*, v.

9. William Wesley Woollen, Daniel Wait Howe, and Jacob Piatt Dunn, eds., *Executive Journal of Indiana Territory, 1800–1816*, rev. ed. (Indianapolis: Indiana Historical Society, 1985).

10. Gayle Thornbrough and Dorothy L. Riker, eds., *Journals of the General Assembly of Indiana Territory, 1805–1815*, Indiana Historical Collections, vol. 32 (Indianapolis: Indiana Historical Bureau, 1950).

11. Richard Leffler, "Documentary Editing: Some Essential Elements," *Documentary Editing* 18 (Mar. 1996): 2.

12. Reginald Horsman, "William Henry Harrison: Virginia Gentleman in the Old Northwest," *Indiana Magazine of History* 96 (June 2000): 125–49.

13. Douglas E. Clanin et al., eds., *The Papers of William Henry Harrison, 1800–1815,* 10 microfilm reels (Indianapolis: Indiana Historical Society, 1993–99), 8:106–7.

14. Douglas E. Clanin, "Governor William Henry Harrison's Administration of the Indiana Territory, 1800–1812" (paper presented at the annual meeting of the Society of Historians of the Early Republic, University of Tennessee–Knoxville, 25 July 1986).

William Henry Harrison and the Indian Treaty Land Cessions

by

M. TERESA BAER

Introduction: Considering Harrison, the Man and His Legacy

WHEN I STARTED WORK ON THE HARRISON PAPERS PROJECT, I knew little about Harrison or the Indian tribes in the American Midwest and even less about the Indian treaties. But the papers drew me in. Reading letter after letter, government document after government document, I developed a familiarity with the young Harrison, and I began to better understand Vincennes during the changing of the guard from its French and Indian era to its early American era. Many voices were speaking—in the town, among the military, from the territorial government, and from the government back East. Settlers, Native Americans, and money-grabbing merchants all clamored at Harrison. Everybody wanted a piece of the pie. Everybody was excited about the possibilities. The melancholy and angry Indians who desperately wanted for the white tide to stop were the only ones looking back. Everybody else was looking with starry eyes and oftentimes drooling mouths toward personal prosperity and independent living in the near future.

While working with Harrison's papers I sometimes asked myself what I would have done if I had been an educated young gentleman and soldier from Virginia. How would I have approached the duties I had accepted while trying to live up to the legacy of my aristocratic family? How would I have attended the diversity of interests, nurtured my ambitions to be somebody, and retained my dignity and honor, which were foremost concerns in that day? When I looked at Harrison this way—and compared his daily and yearly decisions to those I make to survive in the professional world today—I found myself emphathizing with his thinking and justifying his compromises. Even though I hated that he had taken millions of acres of land from Native Americans—for whom I feel much compassion and sadness now—I could understand why he did it—to keep his place in society. I could understand how he could allow himself to do it—he believed that it was inevitable that the Indians would lose their land. And I could understand how he tried to be fair to the Indians—by steering them into an alternative lifestyle that would sustain them because their native way of life no longer could.

By reading Harrison's papers I realized that people in history are just people who happened to live in the past. Their world was as complicated as ours, and their needs and desires paralleled our own. What we can know from Harrison's papers is that he was an ordinary human being with somewhat more than ordinary ambitions due to his background. He served his country through an extraordinary period and did so competently for the most part. Through political upheavals and changing social constructions he held on to a prestigious and yet rancorous job by adapting to circumstances. In the process he acquired a huge chunk of the present-day Midwest for his fledgling nation, and he dispossessed thousands of Indians of their homeland forever.

Hero or Villain? Harrison and the Indian Land Treaties

Between 1803 and 1809 William Henry Harrison purchased fifty million acres of Native American land for less than two cents per acre. He reported these figures to War Department chief clerk George Graham in November 1815 in response to a congressional request that he submit the accounts from his tenure as the Indiana Territory's superintendent of Indian Affairs. His estimate was a fair assessment of what it cost the United States to purchase most of Illinois, approximately the southern third of Indiana, and small por-

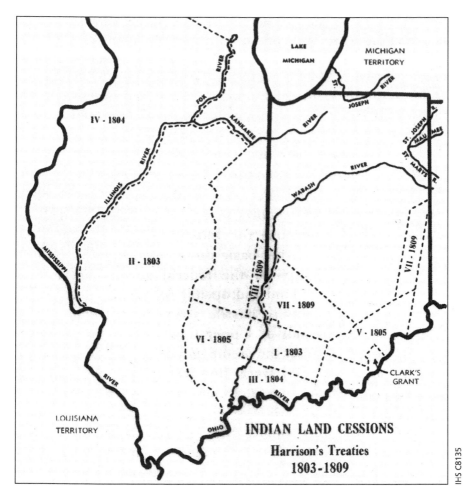

Map by John McCord showing the various land-cession treaties Harrison negotiated from 1803 to 1809

tions of Wisconsin and Missouri via treaties with several Indian tribes. Indeed, under the terms of the 1809 Treaty of Fort Wayne, Harrison's last and most expensive land-cession treaty, the United States would have had to pay the proscribed annual annuities to several tribes for more than twenty years in order to pay two cents for each of the nearly three million acres it purchased.[1]

Harrison's land acquisitions quickly opened for settlement what became the Midwest. Settlers, land speculators, and many federal government officials welcomed this accomplishment. Most Native

Americans and their supporters regretted it, however. Thus, Harrison garnered both praise and bitter criticism for his land-cession treaties. Was Harrison a hero for winning a wealth of prime farmland, ancient forests, and mighty rivers upon which immigrants could become landowners, artisans, and American citizens—or was he a villain who tricked unsuspecting bands of American Indians into relinquishing vast regions for a mere pittance?

Recent historians have found that judging Harrison's motives, methods, and accomplishments is more complicated than deciding whether his deeds were right or wrong.[2] As an ambitious fledgling statesman, Harrison put himself in a position to be appointed governor of the Indiana Territory and chief negotiator with the Indian tribes northwest of the Ohio River. Once in power, he assumed responsibility for the welfare of all the residents and interested parties on the northwestern American frontier. He had to protect and defend the interests of the U.S. government, American settlers, French residents, and numerous disparate Indian tribes, not to mention dealing with traders, speculators, and British and Spanish agents. Furthermore, he had to perform his duties in such a manner that he retained his commissions as governor and principal Indian agent. Examining Harrison at the beginning of his political career, it is clear that his mission was difficult and that the several facets of his job provided multiple opportunities for internal contradiction. In order to complete successfully the assignments he accepted in 1800, Harrison had to alter his approach and attitude toward each group. Some might call this duplicitous or worse; others would say that the candidate for this position needed to be shrewd, flexible, and ever on guard for opportunities to protect and to further the goals of his many constituents.

The microfilm edition of *The Papers of William Henry Harrison, 1800–1815*, completed in July 1999 by the Indiana Historical Society, contains transcriptions of thousands of documents from the territorial period that were written to, by, or about Harrison. These documents confirm that Harrison realized the multifaceted nature of his mission and strove to fulfill it with as much honor and integrity as possible under the circumstances. His statement to Graham in 1815 indicates that he believed he had met the federal government's goals regarding Indian land. His letters, speeches, and reports show that he thought he performed his duties in a practical, economic manner while treating the Native Americans as fairly as he could.[3] Correspondence and official accounts sent to Harrison from the federal government and from a network of political, military, civilian, and Indian agents reveal the clamoring interests that he strove to appease.

Harrison's number one priority was to satisfy the federal administration that appointed him governor and Indian commissioner. Until 4 March 1809, that meant pleasing President Thomas Jefferson, who took office at the beginning of the settlers' push northwest across the Ohio River. One of Jefferson's most important actions was to establish a national policy toward the Indian tribes that resided in U.S.-claimed territories. The president's policy, spelled out to territorial governors in correspondence from him and from Secretary of War Henry Dearborn, offered Native Americans two choices: become farmers like the settlers or move west beyond the Mississippi River.[4] Harrison's papers highlight the conflicting passions that were inherent in these missives. They demonstrate that Jefferson, Dearborn, and Harrison committed themselves to aiding Native Americans if they agreed to settle on generous acreage and become farmers. During treaty negotiations, Harrison granted annual payments, called annuities, to tribes that agreed to these terms and that were willing to sell large land tracts recognized as theirs. The government paid the annuities to the tribes in several ways, including money, weapons, livestock, tools, farm equipment, and in payment to agriculturalists who taught them the newest methods of farming and animal husbandry. Each year the chiefs who accepted the annuities on behalf of their people could stipulate to some extent how they wished the payments to be divided. United States authorities monitored the payments to ensure the tribes received the intended benefit of the annuities—to prevent them, for example, from using the largesse to purchase prohibited items such as liquor.

Another standard part of these treaty bargains was the promise by the natives to live as U.S. citizens by refraining from either warring or allying with other Indian tribes or European countries and by following federal and territorial laws. In return, the United States

THE INDIANA TERRITORY 1800–2000

vowed to protect the tribes under treaty and to treat them equal to U.S. citizens. The record reveals that Harrison fought to induce the territorial government and its early citizenry to treat the Native Americans fairly. In his message to the territorial assembly on 4 November 1806, for example, he beseeched the members to create "any regulation" that "would promise more impartiality in the execution of the laws."[5] Unfortunately, his efforts often failed. A few Indians and whites murdered, plundered, and vandalized throughout the frontier. In case after case, chiefs captured and surrendered to American authorities persons from their tribes who were then found guilty of their crimes, while at the same time white offenders were either acquitted or escaped permanently from jail with the help of their neighbors. Harrison reported two such incidents to Jefferson at the end of 1801. A chief named Captain Allen surrendered two members of his tribe in October that year even though whites had killed his son the year before. His son's murderers escaped successfully from jail; one of the two Native Americans stood trial and was executed while the other saved his life by testifying in the case.[6]

Jefferson's policy stipulated that all territorial tribes must agree to a treaty before it could be valid. Jefferson also wanted Indian commissioners to acquire as much land as possible as quickly as possible. Thus, another top priority for Harrison was to persuade diverse groups of Indians to sign treaties with him. During mass gatherings of Indians, Harrison expounded on the benevolence of the "great father" in Washington, D.C. In smaller settings he offered personal friendship and concrete assurances of his esteem toward the Indians. He presented gifts, settled disputes between tribes, and found individual ways of drawing dissatisfied leaders into group negotiations. He utilized Indian agents and friendly chiefs as spokesmen when they could better accomplish his goals. He resorted to a show of strength only when necessary, such as when dealing with the Shawnee leaders Tecumseh and his brother, the Prophet, who attempted to gather numerous eastern and southern tribes into a confederation against the United States in the years prior to the War of 1812.[7] At these times Harrison likened the potential American force to blades of grass or grains of sand,

One of Harrison's most onerous duties as governor of the Indiana Territory was keeping peace between the Native Americans and settlers. As these two drawings by Will Vawter depict, both sides committed atrocities.

so numerous that all Indian warriors fighting together could not stop them.[8]

Those Native American leaders who reacted positively to Harrison conveyed a sense of trust in him and a belief, to varying degrees, in his interpretation of their recent past. Harrison wove parts of this history into his speeches during councils and treaty negotiations.[9] Since then, generations of historians have added to this interpretation of Indian history. It describes how the Indians had thrived by hunting in the abundance of the American wilderness but warns that their lifestyles began to change when the French came. The French and later the British fur trade bade Indians to kill as many animals as could be harvested rather than just those needed for sustenance. Americans who migrated to the newly formed Northwest Territory in the last two decades of the eighteenth century exacerbated this overhunting. Before another quarter of a century had passed, they had seriously depleted much of the large game in the area. The American bison was all but extinct.[10]

As large game was dying off, Indians were moving from intertribal self-sufficiency to becoming trading partners with whites. From 1680 to 1760 the Miami, for example, purchased a surprising array of European goods, from hoes and awls to bed lace, shoe buckles, bells, and tea. The list grew exponentially before 1800.[11] Meanwhile, several migrations began. British settlers displaced Native Americans along North America's east coast. Many Indians moved west. During the eighteenth century these migrations led to intertribal warfare and European wars fought on North American soil. At the same time, disease decimated Indian populations. By the dawn of the American republic, white encroachment threatened the weakened population of Native Americans in the Northwest Territory. The pressures upon the small, uprooted tribes caused indigence, frustration, and increasing hostilities among the Indians and between them and whites.[12]

Following Jefferson's lead, Harrison argued tirelessly to the Indian chiefs that they could no longer continue their native ways of life, that in order to survive they must adapt using the example of the American farmers who were themselves turning away from subsistence farming to commercial agriculture. Looking around at

IHS C8117

As an aide to General "Mad" Anthony Wayne, Harrison (holding his hat, standing to the right of Wayne), then a lieutenant, signed the Treaty of Greenville on 3 August 1795.

their poverty-stricken families and at the anger and drunkenness of many of their young men, some tribal leaders agreed with Harrison's assessment. These chiefs negotiated with Harrison and signed away vast acreage in return for peace, protection, and living assistance. Treaty negotiation minutes, council notes, and correspondence about the Indians disclose some of the reasons these chiefs sold their land and what they wanted in return for it. In a 26 February 1802 letter to Dearborn, Harrison explained some of the concerns mentioned by chiefs prior to negotiating an 1802 treaty for a 1.6 million-acre tract of land surrounding Vincennes. This was an area that had been agreed upon but not surveyed at the time of the Treaty of Greenville in 1795.[13] Harrison stated that the Piankashaw "expressed great uneasiness that a boundary line had not been ascertained." Because of the growing number of white settlers in their midst, the Indians were growing fearful that the

"Americans meant to take from them all their country."[14] At a council held on 15 September 1802, Ground Hog, an Eel River Miami Indian, indicated why legal boundaries were important to the Indians, saying that they wished to be "at a distance" from whites. He also offered two additional reasons why his people would negotiate with Harrison—for friendship (peace) and U.S. protection from settlers, other native tribes, and Europeans.[15]

Many of the land-cession treaties contained an article stating that "the said Tribe" desired to procure the means to improve itself "in the Arts of civilized Life" in order to provide "a more certain and effectual Support for their Women and Children." The August 1803 treaty with the Kaskaskia by which the United States purchased between seven and eight million acres in central Illinois included such an article.[16] The Kaskaskia, a tiny remnant of a once-powerful confederation, desperately wanted three things: to become farmers, to retain enough acreage on which to thrive, and to be protected from the neighboring tribes.[17] The treaty provided all of this and more. Chief Jean Baptiste Ducoigne received a new house with a fenced yard, and some of the money from the annual annuity paid for a church building and a Catholic priest to teach the Indians how to read and write.[18]

With federal permission, Harrison often granted favors—such as the building of Ducoigne's house—in order to push treaties to conclusion. In the August 1804 treaty with the Delaware and Piankashaw, Harrison compensated U.S. citizens for horses the Delaware had stolen from them, thus relieving the Delaware from paying for the loss with the tribe's annuity, which was customary. This concession was well worth the money, for with this treaty the Delaware and Piankashaw signed away approximately 1.5 million acres in the southwestern corner of the Indiana Territory for less than one-third cent per acre.[19]

Later that year Harrison completed a treaty with the Sauk and Fox tribes, who lived west of the Kaskaskia. The Sauk had long wanted an alliance with the United States. At the September 1802 council, Kaskaskia chief Ducoigne had told Harrison, "Your brothers the sauks wish a merchant to be sent among them—the Spanish ask them too high for their goods—they kill abundance [*sic*] of game but get nothing for it. . . . Send a merchant among them so that they may have plenty of cheap goods."[20] The Sauk request for a trader dovetailed with Jefferson's policy. He reasoned that as Indians started farms, they would become indebted to U.S. government traders for farm implements. Once in debt, they would be willing to sell huge amounts of surplus land in order to pay the traders, leaving just enough land to sustain themselves comfortably.[21] The Sauk, who were not planning on becoming farmers, also "wished to be in peace and in alliance" with the Americans "as the other indians are."[22] Thus the Sauk, and a closely associated group, the Fox, signed a treaty on 3 November 1804 in St. Louis. In return for an alliance with the United States, $2,234.50 in hand, a permanent annual annuity of $1,000, the settlement of their debt to the local trader, and a pardon for a tribal member who had killed a white man, the Sauk and Fox exchanged nearly fifteen million acres in what is now northwestern Illinois, southern Wisconsin, and western Missouri.[23]

As Harrison signed successive treaties with Indians, their chiefs grew anxious to garner as much support for their individual tribes as the neighboring tribes were receiving and to ensure that the United States would recognize their rights to land in the region. The Miami chiefs were especially concerned because they and the Potawatomi perceived that the land the Delaware had sold in their 1804 treaty belonged to the Miami nation. They wanted Harrison to pay annuities and goods to them in exchange for their assent to the 1804 treaty. Harrison refused, stating that if they wanted more money and supplies, they must sell more land to the United States. After much negotiating, the two sides agreed on the Treaty of Grouseland in August 1805. With this treaty, Harrison bought some two million acres surrounding Clark's Grant in the southern part of the Indiana Territory. He paid substantially more than he had in previous treaties—slightly more than one cent per acre to the Miami, Delaware, and Potawatami who signed the document. In addition, one of the articles specified that all the Miami tribes in the territory, including the Wea and Eel River, owned all the land in common. None of them could sell land without all of them agreeing to it.[24]

In a separate treaty in December 1805, Harrison acquired the Piankashaw tract in what is now southeastern Illinois. By this treaty, the Piankashaw retained forever two square miles of land and received $1,000 in hand and $300 in yearly annuities.[25] On 1 January 1806 Harrison asked Dearborn for an extra concession as well—to send an armorer to the Piankashaw to maintain their American-made weapons. Armorers were evidently in some demand by natives, for Harrison told Dearborn, "The neighbouring Tribes would be highly pleased with such an indulgence for which they have made frequent applications."[26]

By 1806 many Native Americans were alarmed at the number of new settlers and at the amounts of land that had been sold to the United States. The Shawnee leaders Tecumseh and the Prophet were confederating disgruntled tribes throughout eastern North America. Furthermore, rumblings of a possible war with Great Britain heightened tensions between the natives and the Americans as British agents and traders worked to attain the Indians' loyalty. Under these circumstances, Harrison effected only one more land-cession treaty, but not until 1809. From 1805 to 1809 he watched and listened carefully to ascertain what would motivate the Indian tribes to sell land despite their general misgivings toward relinquishing more territory. In a 27 January 1808 letter to Dearborn, he wrote that the Delaware—invited to do so by that part of their nation residing in what is now southeastern Missouri—were determined to move west of the Mississippi River. Jefferson endorsed the letter and noted at the bottom, "I think we should not only approve of their emigration, but give them what aid we can for their journey and new establishment."[27] One month later Harrison stated to Dearborn that U.S. Indian agent William Wells reported that the Potawatami were in "great Want."[28]

The Delaware desire to move and the Potawatami poverty played into the 1809 Treaty of Fort Wayne. The treaty journal from September 1809, however, noted that the Miami "had determined on no account ever to part from another foot of their lands."[29] Miami chief Little Turtle explained that "great complaints were made by the Indians on account of the compensation [formerly] allowed."[30] From this remark, Harrison gathered that the amount of

IHS B12

Miami Chief Little Turtle led the confederation of Native Americans that won a great victory over the United States at Fort Recovery in Ohio in 1791.

compensation was the true sticking point. The Miami chiefs supported his logic on 24 September stating that "it was time to put a stop to the encroachments of the whites who were eternally purchasing their lands for less than the real value of them."[31] One of the chiefs, the Owl, specified that they were willing to sell some land "for the price that it sells for amonghst [*sic*] yourselves."[32]

The Miami also insisted that Harrison detail their legal rights to land in any new treaties they might make with him. They complained bitterly of legal injustices to their people and of financial swindling by traders. In separate negotiations the following month, the Wea chiefs "most earnestly entreated" Harrison to stop the sale of whiskey to the Indians because it kept them from using their annuities to become farmers, as the chiefs and Jefferson had planned, and it caused their young warriors to be disobedient and disrespectful to their elders.[33] Harrison had his hands full to come to an agreement this time. Approximately fourteen hundred Indians attended the negotiations because several tribal groups claimed rights to the land, and Harrison's negotiated purchase price would have to be divided among them. At the end, Harrison and the various tribes signed three separate documents—the main treaty on 30 September with the Miami, Delaware, Potawatami, and Kickapoo; a separate article the same day with the Miami and Eel River; and a separate treaty with the Wea at the end of October. The latter group agreed to move to the upper Wabash with the main body of the Miami nation so that Harrison could purchase their land. As stated above, the cessions of 1809 amounted to nearly three million acres for less than two cents per acre. Specific land ownership was spelled out for the Miami and Delaware. One article stated that if one tribe stole from another tribe, it would compensate the victim tribe with money from its annuities.[34]

The Treaty of Fort Wayne angered Indians from all tribal groups, including the hundreds who were allied with Tecumseh and the Prophet. They believed the Americans had swindled them out of their lands and that no more land should ever be sold.[35] Speaking on behalf of these disaffected Indians in council with Harrison at Grouseland in August 1810, Tecumseh narrated an alternative interpretation of recent Native American history. He told the story of French fur trappers and traders who lived among them in peace, never asking to buy their lands, but rather perpetually offering them gifts and assistance in return for living among them peacefully. The British, he said, were like the French at first, but then they had put the tomahawk into Indian hands and bade them fight against the French and the Americans. The British "never troubled us for our lands," he said, "but they have done worse by inducing us to go to war." Continuing, he told of British stinginess, saying that they "gave us but a small piece of Pork every day."

Tecumseh recapped the stories of murders that Americans had committed upon Native Americans despite the United States's "promises of friendship" and "security." Then he spoke directly about the Indian land policy. "You have taken our lands from us," he accused. "You want by your distinctions of Indian tribes in allotting to each a particular tract of land to make them [go] to War with each other." He complained, "You are continually driving the red people . . . into the great Lake." Moreover, he charged, "Since the land was sold to you . . . no traders come among us." But apparently the traders brought only evil, for Tecumseh declared, "By your giving goods to the Kickapoos you kill'd many[;] they were seized with the Small pox by which many died."[36]

War followed closely on the heels of Tecumseh's speech, first the Battle of Tippecanoe in 1811 by which Harrison tried to dispel the Prophet's power in the Indiana Territory, then the War of 1812 in which Tecumseh died during a clash with Harrison's troops at the Battle of the Thames in 1813. At war's end, Harrison made two more treaties with the northwestern Indian tribes—at Greenville, Ohio, in 1814 to make peace between the United States and willing tribes and at Spring Wells, Michigan Territory, in 1815 to end the war between the United States and hostile tribes. The latter treaty also returned the Native Americans to their status before the war and reinstated all the land-cession treaties that Harrison had made prior to 1810.[37]

By the end of the War of 1812, the Indian tribes in Indiana and surrounding territories reluctantly put aside the belief they had in Tecumseh's interpretation of their history. The war had shown them that regardless of how they interpreted their past, the present

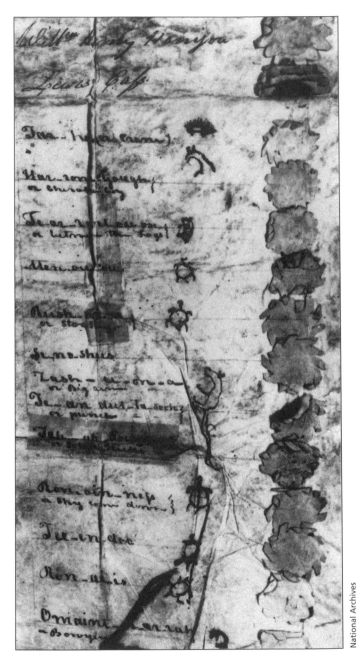

National Archives

The pictograph marks that several Wyandot Indian chiefs made next to their names and the signatures of Harrison and Gen. Lewis Cass, United States commissioners, as displayed on the treaty signed at Greenville on 22 July 1814.

was much as Harrison and Jefferson had tried to persuade them. They were but small, disparate groups surrounded on all sides by a flood of whites who were no longer encroaching but now surging across the Appalachian Mountains and the Ohio River with dreams of owning their own small parcels of land and living independent lives. If the Indians did not cooperate and assimilate, they would face either annihilation or removal. Harrison had offered them a way to stay and create decent lives for themselves. He had offered them assistance in learning agriculture and husbandry, in becoming literate, in learning to deal with the white man's economic system. He, like Jefferson, had wanted them to become like the "yeoman" farmers of Jefferson's dream—independent, responsible U.S. citizens. Still, most Native Americans found the wealth and sanctity of their past more compelling than the hope of comfortable lives lived similar to the aliens around them. Thus the United States eventually forced most of them to move beyond the Mississippi.[38]

So was Harrison a hero or a villain for his Indian land treaties? The answer depends upon one's interpretation of history. Many Native Americans and their supporters will continue to curse him for willingly acting as the instrument of American expansionism. At the same time, midwestern residents may thank the man who fought tenaciously to acquire their homeland and retain it for future generations. In his own sometimes arrogant estimation, William Henry Harrison was an able administrator, a just arbiter, a friend to settler and Indian alike, and a loyal, hardworking frontier servant of the United States. Harrison's papers reveal that he was the competent leader he thought himself—and a hero and a villain, too.

Notes

1. The author determined the number of acres that Harrison purchased from Native Americans and the amount he paid for them using monetary figures and land descriptions from the Treaty of Fort Wayne, calculating the acreage using current maps of the Midwest, and dividing the acreage by the amount the federal government would pay in annuities during a twenty-year period. Harrison could not know when the government would cease paying for lands or exactly how much it would finally pay for the lands. Using the twenty-year period approximated Harrison's own estimation of what he paid for the lands and is a reasonable time frame to use for gauging the cost of the lands. For the treaties that constitute the Treaty of Fort Wayne, see Treaty with the Delawares, et al., a Separate Article Signed with the Miami and Eel Rivers, and Associated Documents, 30 Sept. 1809, in Douglas E. Clanin et al., eds., *The Papers of William Henry Harrison, 1800–1815*, 10 microfilm reels (Indianapolis: Indiana Historical Society, 1993–99), 3:531–36; Separate Article Signed with the Miami and Eel Rivers, 30 Sept. 1809, ibid., 3:537–39; Convention with the Wea and Associated Documents, [26 Oct. 1809–1 May 1810], ibid., 3:601–2, 617, 621; William Henry Harrison to William Eustis, 15 Nov. 1809, ibid., 3:648–52; and Treaty with the Kickapoo and Associated Documents, [9 Dec. 1809–1 May 1810], ibid., 3:676–78, 690–97. For Harrison's estimate of the cost of the land he won through treaties, see Harrison to George Graham, 25 Nov. 1815, ibid., 10:713–21.

2. For examples of recent literature about William Henry Harrison during the Indiana territorial period, see John D. Barnhart and Dorothy L. Riker, *Indiana to 1816: The Colonial Period*, The History of Indiana, vol. 1 (Indianapolis: Indiana Historical Bureau and Indiana Historical Society, 1971), 314–411; Andrew R. L. Cayton, *Frontier Indiana* (Bloomington: Indiana University Press, 1996), 167–235; Andrew R. L. Cayton and Peter S. Onuf, "The Origins of Politics in the Old Northwest," in *The Midwest and the Nation: Rethinking the History of an American Region* (Bloomington: Indiana University Press, 1990), 65–67; James H. Madison, *The Indiana Way: A State History* (Bloomington and Indianapolis: Indiana University Press and Indiana Historical Society, 1986), 36–54; Allan R. Millet, "Caesar and the Conquest of the Northwest Territory: The Harrison Campaign, 1811," *Timeline* 14 (July–Aug. 1997): 2–19 and "Caesar and the Conquest of the Northwest Territory: The Second Harrison Campaign, 1813," *Timeline* 14 (Sept.–Oct. 1997): 2–21. Cayton's and Madison's views about Harrison in their papers delivered at the territorial bicentennial conference (and published herein) are particularly interesting in light of their earlier works. Their most recent papers highlight the deepening and broadening of historical perspective about Harrison, the early American Indian land policy, and the nature of the frontier experience in Indiana. The Harrison papers microfilm edition furthers this understanding.

3. See, for example, Message to the Indiana Territorial General Assembly, 27 Sept. 1808, Clanin et al., eds., *Papers of William Henry Harrison*, 4:252–53.

4. See especially Thomas Jefferson to Harrison, 27 Feb. 1803, ibid., 1:519. For an up-to-date analysis of Jefferson's Indian policy, see Peter S. Onuf, "'We Shall All Be Americans': Thomas Jefferson and the Indians," *Indiana Magazine of History* 95 (June 1999): 103–41, and Anthony F. C. Wallace, *Jefferson and the Indians* (Cambridge, Mass.: The Belknap Press of Harvard University Press, 1999).

5. Message to the Indiana Territorial General Assembly, 4 Nov. 1806, Clanin et al., eds., *Papers of William Henry Harrison*, 2:657.

6. Harrison to Jefferson [extract], [ca. Oct. 1801], ibid., 1:193.

7. Two excellent sources regarding Tecumseh and his quest for tribal unification are R. David Edmunds, *Tecumseh and the Quest for Indian Leadership* (Boston: Little, Brown, 1984), and John Sugden, *Tecumseh: A Life* (New York: Henry Holt and Co., 1997). See also Cayton, *Frontier Indiana*, 196–225.

8. Harrison to Els-Kwau-Ta-Waw (the Prophet), 24 June 1808, Clanin et al., eds., *Papers of William Henry Harrison*, 3:176.

9. See, for example, Harrison, Speech at an Indian Council, [12 Sept. 1802], ibid., 1:373, and Harrison, Journal of the Treaty Negotiations with the Delawares, et al., 28–30 Sept. 1809, ibid., 3:517–30.

10. Stewart Rafert, *The Miami Indians of Indiana: A Persistent People, 1654–1994* (Indianapolis: Indiana Historical Society, 1996), 65; Cayton, *Frontier Indiana*, 199.

11. Rafert, *Miami Indians of Indiana*, 34, 38–39.

12. Elizabeth Glenn and Stewart Rafert, "Native Americans," in *Peopling Indiana: The Ethnic Experience*, eds. Robert M. Taylor, Jr. and Connie A. McBirney (Indianapolis: Indiana Historical Society, 1996), 392–418. See also Cayton, *Frontier Indiana*, 196–225.

13. Barnhart and Riker, *Indiana to 1816*, pp. 327–29.

14. Harrison to [Henry Dearborn], 26 Feb. 1802, Clanin et al., eds., *Papers of William Henry Harrison*, 1:271–72.

15. Notes of Speeches at an Indian Council, 15 Sept. 1802, ibid., 1:388–91.

16. Treaty with the Kaskaskia and Associated Documents, [13 Aug.–23 Dec. 1803], ibid., 1:632. See also Barnhart and Riker, *Indiana to 1816*, p. 339, and Freeman Cleaves, *Old Tippecanoe: William Henry Harrison and His Time* (New York: Charles Scribner's Sons, 1939), 40–41.

17. Chief Jean Baptiste Ducoigne, Notes of Speeches at an Indian Council, 15 Sept. 1802, Clanin et al., eds., *Papers of William Henry Harrison*, 1:392; Harrison to [Dearborn] [extract], 24 May 1804, ibid., 1:801.

18. Treaty with the Kaskaskia and Associated Documents, [13 Aug.–23 Dec. 1803], ibid., 1:632–37.

19. Treaty with the Piankashaw and Associated Documents, [27 Aug. 1804–3 Mar. 1805], ibid., 1:881–85. See also Barnhart and Riker, *Indiana to 1816*, pp. 339–40.

20. Notes of Speeches at an Indian Council, 15 Sept. 1802, Clanin et al., eds., *Papers of William Henry Harrison*, 1:392.

21. Jefferson to Harrison, 27 Feb. 1803, ibid., 1:519. See also Onuf, "'We Shall All Be Americans,'" 103–41.

22. Sauk chief to Harrison, in Notes of Speeches at an Indian Council, 15 Sept. 1802, Clanin et al., eds., *Papers of William Henry Harrison*, 1:393.

23. Treaty with the Sauk and Foxes and Associated Documents, [3 Nov. 1804–1 Jan. 1806], ibid., 2:3–12, 23–29. See also Cleaves, *Old Tippecanoe*, 44.

24. Harrison to Dearborn, 10 July 1805, with enclosure: Minutes of a Council with the Delawares, et al., 21 June 1805, Clanin et al., eds., *Papers of William Henry Harrison*, 2:245–54; Treaty with the Delawares, et al., and Associated Documents, [21 Aug. 1805–8 Jan. 1807], ibid., 2:287–93, 300; and Harrison to Dearborn, 26 Aug. 1805, ibid., 2:323. See also Barnhart and Riker, *Indiana to 1816*, p. 340, and Cleaves, *Old Tippecanoe*, 48–49.

25. Treaty with the Piankashaw and Associated Documents, [30 Dec. 1805–23 May 1807], Clanin et al., eds., *Papers of William Henry Harrison*, 2:446–48, 455, 459–62. See also Cleaves, *Old Tippecanoe*, 50.

26. Harrison to Dearborn, 1 Jan. 1806, Clanin et al., eds., *Papers of William Henry Harrison*, 2:472.

27. Harrison to Dearborn, 27 Jan. 1808, ibid., 3:103.

28. Harrison to Dearborn, 18 Feb. 1808, ibid., 3:113–14.

29. Journal of the Treaty Negotiations with the Delawares, et al., 20 Sept. 1809, ibid., 3:496.

30. Journal of the Treaty Negotiations with the Delawares, et al., 23 Sept. 1809, ibid., 3:502–3.

31. Journal of the Treaty Negotiations with the Delawares, et al., 24 Sept. 1809, ibid., 3:504.

32. Journal of the Treaty Negotiations with the Delawares, et al., 29 Sept. 1809, ibid., 3:521.

33. Journal of the Treaty Negotiations with the Wea, 24–29 Oct. 1809, ibid., 3:597–600, 621.

34. For treaties that constitute the Treaty of Fort Wayne, see note one above. See also Barnhart and Riker, *Indiana to 1816*, pp. 375–81, and Cleaves, *Old Tippecanoe*, 67–68.

35. See especially Barnhart and Riker, *Indiana to 1816*, pp. 375–81.

36. Speeches of Tecumseh, 20–21 Aug. 1810, Clanin et al., eds., *Papers of William Henry Harrison*, 4:156–67.

37. For the 1814 Treaty of Greenville, see Treaty with the Wyandots, et al., and Associated Documents, [22 July 1814–23 Feb. 1815], ibid., 10:348–58, and Harrison and Lewis Cass to John Armstrong, 23 July 1814, ibid., 10:371–73. For the 1815 Treaty of Spring Wells, see Treaty with the Wyandots, et al., [8 Sept.–26 Dec. 1815], ibid., 10:662–71, and Harrison and John Graham to William H. Crawford, 9 Sept. 1815, ibid., 10:680–85.

38. Documents in reel ten of the microfilm edition of Harrison's papers portray some of the feelings of Native Americans in the Old Northwest at the end of the War of 1812 and Harrison's attitude as a federal Indian agent. See especially Journal of the Treaty Negotiations with the Wyandots, et al., 10, 12, 21 July 1814, Clanin et al., eds., *Papers of William Henry Harrison*, 10:283–90, 294–300, 341–45; Harrison and Cass to Armstrong, 17 July 1814, ibid., 10:326–37; Journal of the Treaty Negotiations with the Wyandots, et al., 22 Aug., 4, 5, 8 Sept. 1815, ibid., 10:587–90, 644–50, 651–59, 677–79; and Harrison and John Graham to Crawford, 9 Sept. 1815, ibid., 10:680–85. See also Rafert, *Miami Indians of Indiana*, 77–115, and Glenn and Rafert, "Native Americans," 392–418.

Index

Adams, John, 7, 50, 62, 104, 107, 143, 144, 162
African Americans, 41–42, 63–68, 119
Alexander Camping Ground (Dubois County), 89
Allouez, Claude-Jean, 74, 93
American Association for State and Local History (AASLH), 35
American Revolution, 83, 93, 103, 125, 126, 127, 129, 130, 131, 135, 138
Anderson, 81
Arkansas, 22, 108
Arkansas River, 102, 111
Arminius, Jacobus, 85, 95
Arroyo Hondo (Texas-Louisiana border), 101
Asbury, Francis, 87
Associate Presbyterians. *See* Seceders
The Association for Documentary Editing, 159

Badollet, John, 19
Baer, M. Teresa, 18, 25
Baptists, 89, 90; and revivals, 86; division among, 87, 91; and evangelization of Indians, 94
Bardstown (Ky.), 92
Barnett, Mark, 11
Barnhart, John D., 23, 40, 41, 63, 119
Baton Rouge (La.), 101
Battle Ground, 13
Bissot, François-Marie, Sieur de Vincennes, 6, 76
Black Hawk War (1832), 113
Black Oak Ridge (Daviess County), 92
Blue Jacket, 139
Brant, Joseph, 131, 135
Brewer, John, 52

Broadax and Bayonet: The Role of the United States Army in the Development of the Northwest, 1815–1860, p. 116
Buffalo Trace, 15
Buley, R. Carlyle, 33
Burr, Aaron, 101, 159
Busro (Knox County), 90
Busseron Creek (Knox County), 15, 19, 90

California, 136
Calvin, John, 85, 95
Calvinism, 91
Campbell, Alexander, 92, 93, 95
Canada, 131, 132, 133, 136, 137, 138, 144
Canada Act (1791), 136
Canadiens, 75, 76, 80; population removed from along the Wabash, 76; and Catholic faith, 77; and relations with Americans, 79
Cane Ridge (Ky.), 85, 86, 92, 95
Cape Girardeau (Louisiana District), 111
Captain Allen (Indian chief), 172
Carleton, Guy, 139, 140
Carmel Church (Madison), 89
Carter, Harvey Lewis, 60
Cartwright, Peter, 84–85, 87, 88, 90, 91, 94; (illus.), 84
Case Western University (Cleveland), 157
Catholic Church: reduction of Catholic population in Indiana, 21, 79, 94; and Catholic Reformation, 72, 73, 76; missionaries, 73, 74, 76, 79; treatment of priests by British, 76; faith remains strong among *canadiens* and Indians, 77; Catholics granted religious freedom in

America, 77, 79; disenfranchisement of Catholics, 83; and view of revivalism, 92; and marriages in Louisiana District, 112
Catholic Reformation, 72, 73, 76
Catholicism, 20, 93
Cauthorn, Henry S., 39
Cavelier, René-Robert, Sieur de La Salle, 21, 71, 72
Cayton, Andrew R. L., 19, 118
Charlestown, 86, 87
Chicago Tribune, 34
Chickasaw Indians, 76
Chouteau, Auguste, 113
Christian Church, 91
Church of England, 83, 87
Clanin, Douglas E., 18, 24
Clark, George Rogers, 19, 37, 39, 63, 77, 79, 94, 103, 131, 134
Clark, William, 101, 117
Clark, William (territorial judge), 7, 106-7
Clark County, 86, 89
Clark's Grant, 6, 87, 177
Clay, Henry, 159
Cleveland, 157
The Colonial History of Vincennes: Under the French, British and American Governments, 37-38
Columbus, Christopher, 73
Confederation Congress: extends national authority over the West, 128; Indian policies, 129
Congregational Church, 83
Congregationalists, 83, 87
Connecticut, 50
Corps of Discovery, 101
Corydon, 8, 11, 89
Creoles, 101, 102
Cronon, William, 116
C-SPAN, 158, 159
Cumberland Gap, 15
Cumberland Presbyterians, 89, 90
Cushing, Thomas H., 161

Daviess County, 89, 92
Davis, Thomas Terry, 107, 119

Day, Richard, 18
Dearborn, Henry, 171, 175, 178
Dearborn County, 89
The Death of Jane McCrea, 130
Decker, Luke, 41
Delaware Indians, 57, 59, 60, 72, 104, 176, 177, 178, 180; and Moravians, 81
Detroit, 13, 131, 136, 142
Dickey, John, 89
Disciples of Christ, 92
District of Louisiana, 7, 22, 102, 103; laws of, 108-9, 111; slavery in, 111; division of, 111, 120
Divita, James J., 20, 21
Documentary History of the Ratification of the Constitution, 159
Documentary History of the Ratification of the Constitution project, 160
Dover (Dearborn County), 92
Dowd, Gregory Evans, 61
Draper, Lyman C., collection, 153, 154
Ducoigne, Jean Baptiste, 176
Dunkers, 89
Dunn, Jacob Piatt, Jr., 41, 42, 63, 65, 66
Dutch (German) Methodists, 89
Duvernai, Julien, 76

The Earth Shall Weep: The History of Native America, 57
Eckert, Allan, 60
Edmunds, R. David, 60, 62
Eel River, 72
Eel River Miami Indians, 177, 180
1800 Land Law. *See* Harrison Land Law of 1800
Ekberg, Carl J., 39, 40
Elusive Empires: Constructing Colonialism in the Ohio Valley, 1673-1800, p. 117
"Empire of liberty," 117, 118, 121
Episcopalians, 92, 93
Esarey, Logan, 24, 59, 60, 61, 63, 149, 151, 153
Ewing, Nathaniel, 19

Fallen Timbers, battle of (1794), 6, 104, 141

Farnham, John Hay, 150
Fayette County, 93
Federalists, 101, 137, 140, 141, 143, 144
Finkelman, Paul, 64, 65
Finley, Robert W., 91
First Friends Church (Richmond), 92
Flaget, Benedict Joseph, 79, 92
Florida, 101, 127, 136, 137, 140, 143, 144
Floyd County, 89, 91
Fort Detroit, 140. *See also* Detroit
Fort Harrison, 13
Fort Knox II, 13
Fort Miamis, 140, 141
Fort Recovery, 50
Fort Sackville, 37
Fort Wayne, 7
"Fortress of Freedom" (Vincennes), 34
Fox Indians, 7, 113, 176, 177
France, 103, 130; settlements, 38–41, 104; early explorers, 71; North American holdings, 71, 72, 76, 100, 127, 143; and slavery, 106, 112; cedes land to Britain, 126; and impact on frontier development, 136, 137; British blockade of, 139; war with Britain, 141; disagreements with the United States, 144
Franciscan Recollects, 74
French Revolution, 136–37
French Roots in the Illinois Country: The Mississippi Frontier in Colonial Times, 39
Fruehauf Trailer Company, 31
Fulton, Andrew, 89
Funke, Kathy, 3

Garcia, Jerry, 149
Geib, George W., 21, 23
General Baptists, 91
Genêt, Edmond Charles, 138, 141
George Rogers Clark Memorial, 18, 30, 41, 43
George Rogers Clark National Historical Park, 2
Georgia, 83

Gibault, Pierre, 77, 79; (illus.), 78
Gibson, John, 7
Graham, George, 168, 170
Grateful Dead, 149
Great Awakening, 72
Great Britain, 23; tribes aligned with against Americans, 13; and North American holdings, 72; gains French holdings, 76; and relationship with United States, 125–45; cedes land at end of American Revolution, 126; supports Native American resistance, 127, 130, 131, 132, 133, 178; retains possession of frontier posts, 127, 131, 132, 134, 135; and support of buffer state, 128, 130, 131, 132, 139; and Native American sovereignty, 129; threat to American interests on frontier, 135; and impressments of American sailors, 139, 144; and collaboration with Spain, 140; abandons Indians at Fallen Timbers, 141; allies in war with France, 141; evacuates posts, 142, 145
Great Lakes, 127, 139
Greenville (Ohio), 13
Griffin, John, 7, 107, 119
Ground Hog (Eel River Miami), 176
Grouseland (William Henry Harrison's Vincennes home), 7, 13, 18, 41, 43, 58, 106, 180
Grouseland Treaty Line (1805), 36
Gunderson, Robert G., 161
Guymonneau, Jean-Charles, 76

Haiti, 22, 103
Haldimand, Frederick, 132, 133
Hamilton, Alexander, 130, 131, 137, 144, 159
Hamilton, Henry, 37, 38
Harmonie, 15, 90. *See also* New Harmony
Harmonists, 15
Harper, Ellen, 3
Harrison, Anna, 150, 161
Harrison, Benjamin (president), 151
Harrison, Benjamin, 104

Harrison, William Henry, 2, 13, 15, 20, 21, 22, 24, 51, 52, 54, 57, 59, 62–63, 87, 89, 100, 104, 119, 121, 158, 159, 161, 162, 167; service in Congress and United States Senate, 6, 7, 12; territorial governor of Indiana, 7, 8, 50, 163, 170; negotiations and treaties with Indians, 7, 12, 25, 80, 82, 104–6, 112–13, 174, 175, 176, 178, 180, 181, 183; elected to the Ohio senate, 12; resigns from army, 13; takes Detroit from the British, 13; owns slaves, 41, 64; meets with Tecumseh, 58, 82; and Battle of Tippecanoe, 82–83; and slavery, 104, 106, 107, 108, 112, 120, 163; governor of Louisiana District, 108, 111–12, 114; and laws for District of Louisiana, 109, 120; Indian policies, 118; intention to donate bulk of his papers to the IHS, 150; papers destroyed in fire, 151; and land speculation, 163; military service, 164, 165; land acquisitions from Indians, 167–83; and fair treatment of Indians, 172; and annuity payments to the Indians, 177; (illus.), 152, 175
Harrison, William Henry, Papers project, 149–65, 167, 168
Harrison County, 8, 89, 93
Harrison family, 151
Harrison Land Law of 1800, pp. 104, 106
Harstad, Peter T., 2, 155
Hawkins, Hubert H., 3
Hendricks, William, 11–12
Hinderaker, Eric, 61, 117
Historic Southern Indiana (HSI), 1, 2
Historical Sketches of Old Vincennes: Founded in 1732, p. 37
A History of Indiana from Its Exploration to 1850, p. 59
Holmes, John, 99
Homestead Act (1862), 3
Hoosier Casualty Company, 31
Hoosier Heritage Caravan, 31, 34, 37, 42, 43

Hoosier Historical Institutes, 33
Horsman, Reginald, 60, 161
Hudson Bay Company, 101

Idzerda, Stanley, 160
Ignatius of Loyola, 73
Illinois, 1, 8, 113, 168, 176, 178
Illinois Country, 40, 74, 76, 77, 104; transferred to the United States, 79
Illinois Territory, 8, 14
Immigrants, 89
Indenture Act (1805), 14
Indian Intercourse Act of 1790, p. 130
Indiana, 8; admitted to the Union, 12; and revivalism, 86
Indiana: A Redemption from Slavery, 65
Indiana Bell, 34
Indiana Constitution (1816), 16, 31, 65; (1851), 66
Indiana Gazette, 14
Indiana General Assembly, 10; petitions Congress for statehood, 11; House of Representatives, 11, 17
The Indiana Historian: A Magazine Exploring Indiana History, 3
Indiana Historical Bureau, 2, 30–31, 33, 34
Indiana Historical Society, 1, 2, 24, 31, 33, 149, 150, 155, 156, 161, 165, 170; purchases Harrison documents, 151; Harrison collection, 152, 153
Indiana Junior Chamber of Commerce, 31
Indiana Legislative Council, 10
Indiana Magazine of History, 161
Indiana Manufacturers Association, 31
Indiana Motor Truck Association, 31
Indiana Society of Chicago, 33, 35
Indiana Society of Washington, D.C., 33
Indiana Supreme Court, 14
Indiana Territory, 1, 2, 7, 8, 10, 16, 40, 50, 56, 102, 103, 145, 170, 176, 177; white settlers to, 15, 83, 125; French inhabitants, 38–41; and religious diversity in, 71–95; Native American population of, 80; and camp

meetings, 88; religious controversy in, 95; size of, 104; and slavery, 104, 106, 107–8, 119, 163; division of, 107; laws of, 109, 111; boundaries of, 113–14; Native American claims to, 126

Indiana Territory Sesquicentennial Commission, 30, 31, 32, 35

Indiana University–Bloomington, 153

Indianapolis Star, 34

Indiana's Road to Statehood: A Documentary Record, 3

International Harvester, 31

Jackson, Andrew, 159

Jacobinism, 141, 143

Jay, John, 134, 135, 141

Jay's Treaty (1794), 24, 50, 141–42, 143

Jefferson, Thomas, 20, 21, 22, 51, 52, 54, 62, 99, 100, 101, 103, 104, 108, 111, 119, 120, 121, 128, 137, 143, 162, 171, 172, 174, 178, 183

Jefferson Academy (Vincennes), 14

Jennings, Jonathan, 40, 41, 106, 163; first Indiana state governor, 11; elected to Congress, 14

Jennings County, 36

Jesuits. *See* Society of Jesus

Johnson, John, 133, 134

Johnston, General Washington, 66

Jolliet, Louis, 74

Journals of the General Assembly of Indiana Territory, 1805–1815, p. 34

Kaskaskia, 53, 79

Kaskaskia Indians, 176

Kekionga, 53, 57, 60

Kentucky, 89, 92, 93, 95, 106, 141

Kentucky Gazette, 54

Kickapoo Indians, 180, 181

Kluge, John Peter, 81

Know Nothing movement, 94

Knox, Henry, 6, 129

Knox County, 6, 19, 90, 111

Kuhn, Thomas, 115

Lake Champlain, 127

Lake Erie, 164

Lake Michigan, 72, 74

Lamb, Brian, 159

Law, John, 37, 38, 41

Lawrenceburg, 87

Lee, Ann, 90

Leffler, Richard, 159

Lenni Lanape Indians, 72

Lewis, Meriwether, 101, 117

Lexington (Ky.), 85

Library of Congress (Washington, D.C.), 33, 151, 153, 156

Little Turtle, 57, 60, 80, 141, 178; (illus.), 179

Livingston, Edward, 100, 103

Lockridge, Ross F., Sr., 33, 39

Logan County (Ky.), 85, 87

London (Ontario), 13

Lord Dorchester. *See* Carleton, Guy

Lord Sydney. *See* Townshend, Thomas

Louisiana, 22, 23, 100, 104, 136, 140, 143, 144

Louisiana District: and slavery, 111, 112, 119; laws of, 112

Louisiana Purchase, 22, 101, 102, 114, 120

Luckenbach, Abraham, 81, 94

Lutherans, 92

McCoy, Isaac, 86, 87, 94

McCoy, William, 86

McGready, James, 85, 87, 91

McKendree, William, 87

McNutt, Paul, 35

Madison, 89

Madison, James, 11, 16, 162; signs resolution admitting Indiana to the Union, 12

Madison, James H., 2, 18

Marchal, Antoine, 11

Maria Creek, 19, 87

Marietta (Ohio), 6

Marion County (Ky.), 92

Maritimes, 127

Marquette, Jacques, 74

Maryland, 83, 92

Maumee River, 72, 76

Menke, William, 3
Menominee, 94
Methodists, 87, 89, 90; and revivals and camp meetings, 86, 87–88; and circuit riders, 91
Meurin, Sebastien Louis, 76, 77
Miami Confederacy, 141
Miami Indians, 59, 60, 72, 74, 104, 174, 177, 178, 180
Michigan, 1
Michigan Territory, 8, 107, 181
Michilimackinac, 77, 127
The Middle Ground: Indians, Empires, and Republics in the Great Lakes Region, 1650–1815, p. 118
Minnesota, 1, 8
Mississippi, 134
Mississippi River, 22, 71, 101, 111, 113, 133, 136, 139, 145
Missouri, 21, 22, 99, 100, 108, 113, 169, 178
Missouri River, 102, 111
Mobile (Ala.), 101
Monroe, James, 100, 103
Montgomery, 92
Montreal, 71, 131
Moravians: and evangelization of Indians, 80, 81, 89, 94; mission camp attacked by the Prophet's followers, 82
Morison, Samuel Eliot, 116
Mound Builders, 72
Mt. Solomon Church (Harrison County), 93

Napoléon, 22, 100, 103
National Union Catalog Manuscript Collections, 154
Native Americans, 36–38, 51–52, 117, 167, 168; and missionaries, 73, 74, 75, 76, 79, 81, 86, 89, 93, 94; and spiritual beliefs, 73, 74, 80; population, 74, 80; and liquor, 74, 80, 180; and Catholic faith, 77; and treaties with Harrison, 104–6; claims to land ignored, 126; British assist, 113, 127, 131, 132, 133, 139, 178;

and resistance to western expansion, 128, 129, 130; and boundaries to the United States, 133, 134, 135, 137; and defeat of American army, 138–39; British abandon at Fallen Timbers, 141; land cessions, 162, 167–83; treatment of, 171, 172, 181; lifestyles change, 174; and debts, 177; alarmed by number of new settlers, 178; confederations, 178
Nature's Metropolis: Chicago and the Great West, 116
Nelson County (Ky.), 92
New Deal, 35
New England: and Puritanism, 83
New France, 72; Jesuits arrive in, 73–74
New Harmony, 90
New Madrid (Mo.), 79, 111
New Orleans (steamboat), 15
New Orleans, 71, 76, 100, 101, 103, 111
Niagara, 131
Nobles, Gregory H., 118
North Bend (Ohio), 13, 151
Northwest Ordinance of 1787, pp. 3, 4, 6, 14, 17, 41, 51, 56, 65, 94, 102, 103, 128, 129; (Article 1), 83; (Article 6), 13, 14, 22, 64, 106, 120
Northwest Territory, 1, 7, 8, 10, 50, 102, 104, 120, 163, 174; government, 6; laws of, 109; sale of lands in, 127–28. *See also* Old Northwest
Notes on the State of Virginia, 120

Ohio, 1, 7, 102; becomes state, 50
Ohio Country, 125
Ohio River, 133, 136, 139
Old Bethel Church (Springville), 87
Old Northwest, 15, 125, 127, 139, 145, 162; ownership of, 131; British claim sovereignty over, 133; boundary of, 134; and British interests in, 138; portions of open for settlers, 141. *See also* Northwest Territory
The Old Northwest: Pioneer Period, 1815–1840, pp. 33–34
Onuf, Peter, 121
Open Door. *See* Tenskwatawa

Ordinance of 1785, pp. 3, 7, 17, 128
Osage Indians, 113
Oswald, Richard, 132
Ouiantanon, 74
Owl, the (Miami chief), 180

The Papers of William Henry Harrison, 1800–1815, p. 170
Paris, 100
Parke, Benjamin, 10
Parker, Daniel, 86–87
Peckham, Howard, 30–31, 33, 34, 35
Pennsylvania, 137, 141; religious tolerance in, 83
Perkins, Simon, papers, 157
Perry, Oliver Hazard, 164
Petty, William, 132, 136
Pfrimmer, John George, 89
Philibert, Etienne, 77
Phillips, Dale, 3
Piankashaw Indians, 19, 72, 175, 176, 178
Pinckney, Thomas, 142
Pinckney's Treaty, 24, 142, 143
Pittsburgh, 15
Pontiac, 12
Posey, Thomas, 41
Posey County, 15, 90
Potawatomi Indians, 59, 72, 74, 177, 178, 180; expelled to Kansas, 94
Predestination, 85
Presbyterian General Assembly, 88
Presbyterians, 85, 87, 89, 91; and revivals, 86; growth of, 88–89
Princeton, 89
Proclamation of 1763, p. 126
Procter, Henry, 13
Prophet, the. *See* Tenskwatawa
Prophetstown, 13, 82
Protestantism, 20, 21, 73, 93; Great Awakening, 72; and western expansion, 83; Second Great Awakening, 85, 86, 89, 90–91, 92; and diversity of beliefs, 85, 87; and frontier revivalism, 85–86; conflicts among, 91, 95
Prucha, Francis Paul, 116

Pulitzer Prize, 33
Puritans, 83

Quakers. *See* Society of Friends
Quebec, 139
Quebec Act (1774), 77, 94

Racine family, 107
Ranke, Anna Marie, 81
Rapp, George, 15, 89–90
Rappites, 89–90, 95
Religion: effects of western expansion on, 83; as stabilizing influence on frontier, 84; and camp meetings, 87–88 (illus.), 88; and immigrants, 89
Republicans, 142, 143, 144
Resolution for the Government of the Western Territory (Ordinance of 1784), 128
Revivalism, 85–86, 92
Reynolds, Jane, 3
Rhode Island, 83
Rhoden, Nancy L., 23
Richmond, 92
Riker, Dorothy, 24, 36, 152, 153, 154
Rivet, Jean-François, 79
Robinson, William, 89
Roosevelt, Franklin, 35
Roosevelt, Nicholas, 15

Sacagawea, 117
St. Charles (Louisiana District), 111
St. Clair, Arthur, 6, 138, 163; governor of Northwest Territory, 49, 50
St. Francis Xavier parish (Vincennes), 14
St. Genevieve (Louisiana District), 111
St. John, 93
St. Joseph River, 74
St. Lawrence River, 71, 127
St. Louis, 7, 101, 104, 108, 111, 112, 113, 177
Santo Domingo (West Indies), 103
Sauk Indians, 7, 22, 113, 121, 176, 177
Schricker, Henry F., 30, 31, 33, 34, 35
Scott, Samuel, 88

Seceders, 89

Second Great Awakening, 21, 85, 86, 89, 90–91, 92

Senat, Antoine, 76

Seven Years' War, 76, 126, 136

Shake, Curtis G., 30, 31, 33

Shaker Prairie (Knox County), 90

Shakers, 90, 91, 94; organize community on Busseron Creek, 15

Shawnee Indians, 57, 59, 60, 72, 105, 106

Sheehan, Bernard W., 37

Shelburne, earl of. *See* Petty, William

Shell Oil, 31

Shoemaker, Raymond L., 2

Short, John Cleves, 161

Short, Peyton, 163

Silver Creek, 92

Silver Creek Baptist Church (Charlestown), 86

Simcoe, John Graves, 137, 140

Six Nations (Iroquois Confederacy), 129, 133

Slavery, 104, 111, 114, 120, 163; and Quakers, 92

Smallpox epidemics: and Native Americans, 74, 181

Smith, Elihu Hubbard, 53

Smith, Henry Nash, 116

Smith, Hubbard Madison, 37

Society of Friends, 66, 80, 83, 92

Society of Jesus, 73, 74, 76; and missions to Indians, 93, 94

South Bend, 72, 74

Spain, 134; and territory in North America, 100, 101, 136, 140; and slavery, 112; threat to American interests on frontier, 135; and interests in improving American relations, 142

Spanish Florida, 138

Spanish Louisiana, 118, 138

The Spectator, 53

Springville, 87

State Historical Society of Wisconsin, 153

Steele, Richard, 53

Stevenson, Adlai, 33

Stinson, Benoni, 91

Stoddard, Amos, 111

Stone, Barton W., 85, 86, 91, 95

Stout, Elihu, 14

Suffrage Act of 1808, p. 10

Sugden, John, 60

Symmes, John Cleves, 104, 156, 163

Taylor, Robert M., Jr., 2

Taylor, Zachary, 13

Tecumseh, 12, 13, 20, 56, 57, 58, 59, 60, 62, 63, 106, 118, 164, 172, 178, 180, 181; killed, 13; meets with William Henry Harrison, 58, 82

Tedpachsit, 81, 82

Tenskwatawa (Open Door; the Prophet), 12, 13, 20, 56, 57, 58, 60, 94, 106, 118, 164, 172, 178, 180, 181; and Indian religion, 80, 81; followers attack Moravian camp, 82; and Battle of Tippecanoe, 82–83

Terre Haute, 13, 87

Territorial Days of Indiana, 1800–1816, p. 33

Territory of Orleans, 101–2

Texas, 101

Thames, battle of (near present-day London, Ontario), 13, 164, 181

Thames River (Canada), 164

Thornbrough, Gayle, 24, 152, 153, 154, 155

Tippecanoe, battle of, 11, 13, 20, 93, 150, 164, 181

Tippecanoe County, 13

Tippecanoe River, 82

Toledo (Ohio), 6

Townshend, Thomas, 132, 133, 135

Treaty of Fort Stanwix (1768), 133, 140, 142

Treaty of Fort Wayne (1809), 12, 13, 82, 169, 178, 180

Treaty of Greenville (1795), 6, 24, 32, 49, 57, 141, 142, 175

Treaty of Greenville (1814), 13, 181

Treaty of Grouseland, 177

Treaty of Paris (1763), 76, 102

Treaty of Paris (1783), 50, 79, 120, 126, 127, 131, 132, 133, 145
Treaty of Spring Wells (near Detroit) (1815), 13, 181
Troy, 15
Truax, Susan H., 154
Truman, Harry, 33
Turner, Frederick Jackson: frontier thesis, 23, 114–15, 116

Union County, 93
Unitarians, 92, 93
United Brethren in Christ, 89, 95
United States: and relationship with Great Britain, 125–45; shift in policies toward Native American sovereignty, 129, 130; domestic turmoil in, 135, 137, 140; western expansion, 136, 137, 140; and British impressments of sailors, 139, 144; sets boundary with Spain, 142–43; disagreements with France, 144; annuities and promises to Indians, 171–72, 176, 181
United States Army, 129, 130, 138–39
United States Congress, 102, 104
United States Constitution, 3, 83
United States War Department, 8, 168
United States War Department files (RG 107), 151
University of Southern Indiana (USI), 1
University of Wisconsin–Madison, 160
University of Wisconsin–Milwaukee, 161
Upper Canada (now Ontario), 136, 137, 164
Urban Frontier: The Rise of Western Cities, 1790–1830, p. 116

Valley of Democracy: The Frontier versus the Plantation in the Ohio Valley, 1775–1818, pp. 40, 119
Vanderburgh, Henry, 7, 22, 107, 119
Vanderlyn, John, 130
Vermont, 135, 141
Vigo, Francis, 11, 19

Vincennes, 1, 6, 53, 57, 77, 87, 92, 100, 104, 106, 108, 112, 164, 167, 175; first territorial capital, 7; and tribal population of, 74
Vincennes Chamber of Commerce, 41
Vincennes Historical and Antiquarian Society, 14
Vincennes Historical Society, 38
Vincennes–Knox County Convention and Visitors Bureau, 3
Vincennes Society for the Encouragement of Agriculture and the Useful Arts, 14
Vincennes State Historic Sites, 2, 3, 11
Vincennes Tract, 6
Vincennes University, 14
Virgin Land: The American West as Symbol and Myth, 116
Virginia, 50, 83

Wabash-Maumee portage, 6
Wabash River, 15, 21, 72, 76, 82, 90
Wade, Richard C., 116
Wallace, Anthony F. C., 52
War of 1812, pp. 11, 13, 72, 90, 132, 142, 145, 150, 164, 165, 172, 181
Washington, George, 135, 137, 139, 141, 161
Washington County, 86, 92
Washington County (Ky.), 92
Wayne, Anthony, 31, 104, 140, 142; (illus.), 175
Wayne County, 92
Wea Indians, 72, 177, 180
Wells, William, 178
Western Conference (Methodists), 87
Western Reserve Historical Society (Cleveland), 157
Western Sun, 14, 43
Wheeling (W. Va.), 15
Whiskey Rebellion, 137
White, Richard, 37, 61, 62, 63, 117
White Oak Springs (Pike County), 89
White River, 72, 81
Wilson, James, 57
Winans, William, 87
Wisconsin, 1, 8, 72, 113, 169

Woodland Indians, 117
Württemberg (Germany), 89

XYZ Affair, 143–44

Yorktown (Va.), 131